ENVIRONMENT IN HISTORICAL PERSPECTIVE

Essays in Honour of

Prof. Panchanand Mishra

ENVIRONMENT IN HISTORICAL PERSPECTIVE

Essays in Honour of

Prof. Panchanand Mishra

Edited by

RAMAN SINHA

ANAMIKA PUBLISHERS & DISTRIBUTORS (P) LTD.
4697/3, 21A, Ansari Road, Daryaganj,
New Delhi 110002
Phone: 23281655

First Published 2007

ISBN 81-7975-190-2

PRINTED IN INDIA

Published by Anamika Publishers & Distributors (P) Ltd.
4697/3, 21A, Ansari Road, Daryaganj, New Delhi 110002.
Typset by Aadil Printographics, Delhi 110092 and
Printed at Nagri Printers, Delhi.

CONTENTS

PART III

ACKNOWLEDGEMENTS

The continuity and change in the Indian society has been a study of unabated interest. Because the Indian civilization is thousands of years old with enormous diversity and, peculiarly enough, is a continuity which is its most unique feature. In the beginning of their existence human beings were hunters and food gatherers for their livelihood. But with the advent of civilised existence they settled down near the rivers and became agriculturists and traders. However, the early settlers could not change their habits and they moved away to forests and mountains and preserved their identity. They lived in natural surroundings and the forests, mountains and torrents supplied them enough food for their survival. There was a pious relationship between nature and man and both of them profited from such a relationship. In such surroundings people of India were happier, prosperous and healthier. The history of human survival stands as a good example of the interdependence, co-operative living, and close association which exists among the forces of human and non-human nature. History relates that the wisdom of Vedas, and the Hindu religious and moral doctrines, emerged at a later date in the co-existence between man and his environment.

Hindu philosophers believed that *Sristi*—process of creation, uses the five basic elements to determine the physical characteristics of all creatures. These five elements are known as sky, water, fire, air and earth. Environment includes water, air and land and the inter-relationship which exists among water, air and land, and human beings, other living creatures, plants, micro-organism and property. Environment means those natural things that surround us and are the essentials to sustain human life, such as the earth's atmosphere, healthy air and drinkable water, together with the non-essential that help to make life sustainable, such as wild animals or wild places or human living space.

But with the technological advancement and British colonisation of India the maximum utilisation of natural resources and their exploitation completely devastated the Indian economy and people became poorer and physically weaker and also victims of frequent natural calamities like famines and fatal dieases, such as cholera and plague. The importance of ecology for economic prosperity is being completely lost sight of. After independence India stood up to achieve economic development in order to become self-dependent. Industrialisation became the main source of gaining the goal of economic development. The industrialisation has thus started growing rapidly and has consequently brought about the problem of urbanisation. Thus, the natural environment has been adversely affected.

TSUNAMI (Sunday, 26th December, 2004 and Monday 17th July, 2006) has exposed the short-sightedness of policies that disregarded the importance of natural environmental safeguards. In 1991, the Hon'ble Supreme Court of India realised that individuals were not living *environmentally sustainable* life-styles. After thirteen years in 2004 the Hon'ble Supreme Court re-asserted that environmental education be made a mandatory, independent subject in all schools and colleges and that it must be an "action-oriented" subject.

The United Nations has declared *2005 to 2015* as the "Decade of Education for Sustainable Development." Because, on a long-term basis, the socio-economic health of a nation depends on and is directly proportional to the health of its environment. So, India, and also the world are slowly acknowledging the close link between economy and environment and recognising that "*Sustainability*" is the most essential part of educational curriculum.

However, a majority of English medium (+2) schools only need to be empowered with data on environmental problems which will sensitise them to Nature. Therefore "Environmental Education" is equated with the popularly known subject of "Environmental Science" or "Environmental Studies".

A few pioneering institutions across the country have taken the initiative to impart "Environmental Education" in a truly holistic manner with a focus on History. In the model curriculum circulated by the U.G.C. in 2001, there is a clear indication that environmental history has to be taught at both undergraduate and Post-graduate levels. Jadavpur University and Calcutta University have already introduced ENVIRONMENTAL HISTORY or ENVIRONMENTAL STUDIES related courses at the undergraduate level. Semester courses on Environmental History also feature in the current syllabi of Jawaharlal Nehru University, New Delhi, Banaras Hindu University, Banaras. There is Post-Graduate Courses in Viswabharti, Shantinekatan. So many a University introduces this course.

Environment in Historical Perspective, a volume of articles, may be of great help for a study of environment and ecology in the historical perspective. This volume has been prepared in honour of Prof. (Dr.) Panchanand Mishra. Prof. Mishra is a founder head of Post-Graduate Department of History, Bhagalpur University, Bhagalpur (Bihar), now it is Tilkamanjhi Bhagalpur University. He is an expert in American History as well as British Constitutional History. He is also well versed in Indian History. Despite deteriorating health and growing age he successfully runs Vikramshila Research Institute. Under the banner of this institute Prof. Mishra organised a number of I.C.H.R. Sponsored National Seminars and special lectures. He publishes bi-annually *Vikramshila Journal of Social Sciences* since 2004. He is a well known figure not only in the history circle but also in other disciplines all over the country and abroad. He is the inspiration of academicians, teachers and students. Prof. Panchanand Mishra is the friend, philosopher and guide to any one who comes in his contact.

I express my indebtedness and gratitude to Prof. (Mrs.) Shamim Afza Qumar Towheed, Prof. Ratneshwar Mishra, Prof. Ajay Kumar Jha, Sri. Jagdishwar Jha, and Dr. Rakesh Kumar who furnished the life sketch of Prof. Mishra. I owe a special debt of gratitude to Prof. Manazir Ashique Harganvi and Prof. Benoy Kumar Mahata who translated from Urdu and Bengali into Hindi.

My utmost gratitude goes to Prof. J.S. Datta Munshi, Prof. Chittabrata Palit. Prof. Debashis Guha, Prof. S.M. Mishra, Prof. Surendra Jha, Dr. (Mrs.) Pratima Ganguli, Dr. Mritunjay Kumar, Dr. V.N. Dinesh, Sri. Bhavesh Chandra Pandey, Dr. Ranjan Kumar Sinha and Dr. S.P. Roy who contributed scholarly papers on different aspects of environmental history. Dr. Rajan Kumar Gupta, Dr. Shiv Shankar Mishra, Dr. Vijay Kumar Sinha, Dr. Ashok Kumar Sinha and Dr. Birendra Pandey co-operated with me with meaningful papers. I express my gratitude to the contributors to this volume, without whose co-operation this project could not have been executed at all.

I express my sinceremost indebtedness to the members of the Editorial Board comprising Prof. Abhay Prakash, Prof. Benoy Kumar Mahata, Prof. Manazir Ashique Harganvi, Dr. Ranjan Kumar Sinha, Dr. Pawan Kumar Singh, Mr. Ravindra Kumar Srivastava, Mr. Basil Micheal Quadros and Dr. Girish Chandra Pandey, who took great pains to go through the papers minutely and gave valuable suggestions.

I am thankful to my wife Alpana Sinha who helped me arrange the papers and constantly extended moral support. I am also thankful to the young computer operator Mr. Nadeem who typed patiently.

Last but not the least, I desire to thank the Anamika Publishers & Distributors (P) Ltd. of New Delhi, for undertaking the task of publishing this volume.

March 2007 Raman Sinha

LIST OF CONTRIBUTORS

1. Dr. Raman Sinha, Lecturer, Dept. of History, S.S.V. College, Kahalgaon, Dist., Bhagalpur, Bihar.
2. Dr. (Mrs.) Shamim Afza Qumar, Retd. Professor of Urdu, Tilka Manjhi Bhagalpur University, Bhagalpur, Bihar.
3. Dr. Ratneshwar Mishra, Retd. Professor & Head, Dept. of History, L.N.M. University, Darbhanga, Bihar. Resi.: B-12, Professors Colony, Sheopuri, Patna-23.
4. Dr. Ajay Kumar Jha, Professor, Dept. of History, Tilka Manjhi Bhagalpur University, Bhagalpur, Bihar
5. Sri, Jagdishwar Jha, Retd. Principal, Saharsa College, Saharsa, Bihar.
6. Dr. Rakesh Kumar, Lecturer, Dept. of Mathematics, Govt. Teacher's Training College, Bhagalpur, Bihar.
7. Dr. J.S. Dutta Munshi, Retd. Professor & Head, Dept. of Zoology and INSA Senior Scientist, Tilka Manjhi Bhagalpur University, Bhagalpur, Bihar. Resi.: P-124 A, Usha Park, Garia, Kolkata-700054.
8. Dr. Chittabrata Palit, Visiting Prof. Jadavpur University, Kolkata. Resi.: 222, Jodhpur Park, Kolkata-700068.
9. Dr. Debashis Guha, Professor, Dept. of Philosophy, Ranchi University, Ranchi-834008, Jharkhand.
10. Sri S.M. Mishra, Member, Indian Council of Historical Research (ICHR), 35, Ferozeshah Road, New Delhi-110001.
11. Dr. Surendra Jha, Head, Dept. of History, Sido-Kahno Murmu University, Dumka, Jharkhand.
12. Dr. (Mrs.) Pratima Ganguli, Reader, Dept. of Philosophy, Tilka Manjhi Bhagalpur University, Bhagalpur, Bihar.

13. Dr. Mritunjay Kumar, Lecturer, Dept. of Philosophy Tilka Manjhi Bhagalpur University, Bhagalpur, Bihar.
14. Dr. V.N. Dinesh, Reader, Dept. of History, Sido-Kahno Murmu University, Dumka, Jharkhand.
15. Sri, Bhavesh Chandra Pandey, Head, Dept. of English S.K.R. College, Barbigha, Dist. Sheikhpura, Tilka Manjhi Bhagalpur University, Bhagalpur, Bihar.
16. Dr. Ranjan Kumar Sinha, Principal Investigator, ISRO, RESPOND Project Centre for Regional Studies Tilka Manjhi Bhagalpur University, Bhagalpur, Bihar.
17. Dr. S.P. Roy, Head,Dept. of Zoology Tilka Manijhi Bhagalpur University, Bhagalpur, Bihar.
18. Dr. Benoy Kumar Mahata, Retd. Head, University Dept. of Bengali, Tilka Manjhi Bhagalpur University, Bhagalpur, Bihar.
19. Dr. Rajan Kumar Gupta, Sr. Lecturer, Dept. of Botany, Govt. P.G. College, Rishikesh, Uttrankhand.
20. Dr. Shiv Shanker Mishra, Sr. Lecturer, Dept. of Sanskrit, Govt. P.G. College, Rishikesh, Uttrankhand.
21. Dr. Vijay Kumar Sinha, Reader, Dept. of Philosophy, Magadh University, Gaya, Bihar.
22. Dr. Ashok Kumar Sinha, Lecturer, Dept. of History, G.B. College, Naugachia, Dist. Bhagalpur, Bihar.
23. Dr. Virendra Pandey, Head, Dept. of Pali, S.K.R. College, Barbigha, Dist.: Sheikhpura, Tilka Manjhi Bhagalpur University, Bhagalpur, Bihar.

BOARD OF EDITORS

PART I

1. शैक्षणिक गतिविधियों में उम्र को दर-किनार करने वाले : प्रो. पंचानंद मिश्र

रमन सिन्हा

शैक्षणिक गतिविधियों के लिए नौकरी से अवकाश एवं उम्र कोई मायने नहीं रखता, इसके प्रमाण हैं प्रो. पंचानंद मिश्र। भागलपुर विश्वविद्यालय के स्नातकोत्तर इतिहास विभाग के विभागाध्यक्ष पद से 1991 में अवकाश ग्रहण करने के बाद भी एकाकी जीवन को न अपनाकर अपने आपको शैक्षणिक गतिविधियों में संलग्न कर लिया। 1992 में विक्रमशिला रिसर्च इंस्टीट्यूट की स्थापना कर अपनी ज्ञान-पिपासा शांत करने लगे तो दूसरों को ज्ञान देने की आदत बरकरार रखे हैं। यहां तक कि उम्र के आठवें दशक के अंतिम चरण में भी अपने इंस्टीट्यूट के माध्यम से नेशनल सेमिनार, विशेष व्याख्यान तथा वर्ष में दो जर्नल निकालकर अन्य लोगों के प्रेरणास्रोत आज भी बने हुए हैं। भारी शरीर को दिमागी गतिविधियों के कारण अपने आपको संतुलित रखने का मूल-मंत्र बनाकर खुद की रोशनी से कइयों का अंधेरा मिटाने का सफल प्रयास आज भी बरकरार है।

क्षिति, जल, पावक, गगन, समीरा।
पंच तत्व रचित यह अधम शरीरा।।

पृथ्वी, जल, वायु, आकाश तथा अग्नि इन पंच तत्त्वों के सम्मिश्रण अर्थात् प्रकृति एवं पर्यावरण का नायाब नमूना है मानव। कभी मानव प्रकृति पर निर्भर था। आज उच्च शिक्षा पाकर शिक्षित मनुष्यों ने प्रकृति पर नियंत्रण करने का असफल प्रयास किया जिससे पर्यावरण संतुलन बिगड़ने लगा। लेकिन प्रो. मिश्र ने प्रकृति तथा पर्यावरण से सामंजस्य बैठाते हुए विपरीत परिस्थितियों में भी अपने को संतुलित रखा है। यही उनकी सफलता का राज है।

शाक्यद्वीप ब्राह्मण सरस्वती देवी एवं महादेव मिश्र के सुपुत्र पंचानंद का जन्म 15 दिसंबर 1929 ई. को भागलपुर में हुआ था। इनकी प्रारंभिक शिक्षा भागलपुर के जिला स्कूल में हुई। वर्ष 1944 में इन्होंने मैट्रिक की परीक्षा क्रिश्चियन मिशन हाई स्कूल, पटना से प्रथम श्रेणी में पास की। स्कूली दिनों से ही वे मेधावी थे तभी तो स्कूल में ही अंग्रेजी एवं संस्कृत भाषा में लिखे गए लेख पर उन्हें पुरस्कार प्राप्त हुआ था।

भागलपुर के ही टी.एन.जे. (तेज नारायण जुबली) कॉलेज से वर्ष 1948 में बी.ए. करने के बाद वे उच्चतर पढ़ाई हेतु पटना गए। टी.एन.जे. कॉलेज का वर्तमान नाम टी.एन.बी. (तेज नारायण बनैली) कॉलेज है। पटना से ही 1950 ई. में एम.ए. डिग्री हासिल की।

पंचा बाबू ने कॉलेज शिक्षक के रूप में नौकरी की शुरुआत आर.के. कॉलेज, मधुबनी से 1951 में की तथा अध्ययन-अध्यापन का पड़ाव बना भागलपुर। मधुबनी के बाद तत्कालीन टी.एन.जे. कॉलेज में इतिहास के प्राध्यापक के रूप में अपना योगदान 1953 ई. में दिया। उन्होंने अपना शोधकार्य (Ph.D.) प्रो. एम.पी. शर्मा, सागर यूनिवर्सिटी के राजनीतिशास्त्र के प्रोफेसर के निर्देशन में 'मेकिंग ऑफ दी इंडियन कांस्टीट्यूशन' विषय पर 1964 ई. में पूरा किया।

उस समय भागलपुर के सभी कॉलेज बिहार विश्वविद्यालय, मुजफ्फरपुर के अधीन थे। 12 जुलाई, 1960 को भागलपुर विश्वविद्यालय का निर्माण हुआ। 1963 में भागलपुर विश्वविद्यालय ने स्नातकोत्तर इतिहास विभाग बनाया तो पंचानंद मिश्र उस विभाग के संस्थापक विभागाध्यक्ष बनाए गए। दो शिक्षक क्रमशः पंचानंद मिश्र, श्री गोविंद मिश्र द्वारा इतिहास विभाग की शुरुआत की गई।

प्रो. पंचानंद मिश्र के नेतृत्व में भागलपुर का इतिहास विभाग मात्र भारत में ही नहीं वरन् विश्व के इतिहास जगत में एक स्थान रखता था। छोटे से ऐतिहासिक कमरे (टीन का बना कमरा) में 1967 से 1969 तक भागलपुर विश्वविद्यालय के कुलपति रहे प्रो. विश्वेश्वर प्रसाद के अलावा प्रसिद्ध इतिहासकार डी.सी. सरकार, जे.एन. सरकार ने विजिटिंग प्रोफेसर बनकर भागलपुर के इतिहास विभाग का सम्मान बढ़ाया था। प्रो. मिश्र के नेतृत्व (स्थानीय सचिव) में 1968 में 'इंडियन हिस्ट्री कांग्रेस' का 30वां वार्षिक सम्मेलन सफलतापूर्वक भागलपुर में हुआ था। प्रो. पंचानंद मिश्र के संबंधों के कारण विभाग के वार्षिक कार्यक्रमों में प्रसिद्ध इतिहासकार डॉ. के.के. दत्ता, डॉ. ए.सी. बनर्जी तथा डॉ. एम.एन. दास ने शिरकत की थी।

इतिहास विभाग ने यूनाइटेड स्टेट्स एजुकेशन फाउंडेशन इन इंडिया के सहयोग से 1965 ई. में अमेरिका के इतिहास पर एक कार्यशाला का सफल आयोजन किया था।

प्रो. मिश्र के संबंधों की देन थी कि अमेरिकी संस्था ने प्रोफेसर एन. फ्रेंक तथा ब्रूस एम. स्टेव (1965-1966) को विजिटिंग प्रोफेसर के रूप में इतिहास विभाग भेजा था।

स्नातकोत्तर विभाग को एक संपूर्ण इतिहास विभाग के रूप में विकसित करने का सपना लेकर प्रो. मिश्र ने एक संग्रहालयाध्यक्ष का पद तथा एक फोटोग्राफर का पद सृजन विश्वविद्यालय तथा सरकार से करवाया।

इसी कड़ी में प्रसिद्ध इतिहासकार, भागलपुर विश्वविद्यालय के कुलपति रहे प्रो. विश्वेश्वर प्रसाद स्मृति व्याख्यानमाला की शुरुआत की। इस सीरीज का पहला व्याख्यान 7 फरवरी, 1989 को जर्मनी के प्रो. दित्मेर रोथमंड ने अपना लेक्चर 'दी इंडियन पीजेंट इन दी ग्रेट डिप्रेशन, 1929-1939' विषय पर दिया। इस प्रथम व्याख्यानमाला का उद्‌घाटन बिहार तथा भारत के प्रसिद्ध इतिहासकार प्रो. रामशरण शर्मा ने कर भागलपुर के इतिहास विभाग को गौरवान्वित किया था।

अगली उपलब्धि स्नातकोत्तर इतिहास विभाग तथा रीजनल स्टडीज सेंटर के संयुक्त तत्वावधान में इंडियन कॉउंसिल ऑफ हिस्टोरिकल रिसर्च, नई दिल्ली प्रायोजित *पीजेंट एज एन इंस्ट्रूमेंट ऑफ सोशल चेंज इन बिहार,* पर 20 अप्रैल, 1991 को एक दिवसीय व्याख्यानमाला आयोजित किया गया था।

प्रो. विश्वेश्वर प्रसाद स्मृति व्याख्यानमाला के द्वितीय क्रम में वर्ष 1991 के दिसंबर माह में प्रो. रामशरण शर्मा ने *सम वेस्टर्न व्यूज ऑन दी स्टेट एंड इकॉनामी इन अरली इंडिया* विषय पर अपनी विद्वतापूर्ण व्याख्यान दिया। प्रो. सी.पी.एन. सिन्हा के विभागाध्यक्ष काल में स्मृति व्याख्यानमाला के क्रम में प्रो. पंचानंद मिश्र ने (अवकाश ग्रहण के बाद) 13 सितंबर, 1993 को *'मिथ ऑफ राममोहन राय'* विषय पर तीसरा व्याख्यान दिया।

अपने विभागाध्यक्ष काल में प्रो. मिश्र ने विश्वेश्वर प्रसाद व्याख्यानमाला आयोजित करने के लिए अलग से एक फंड कायम कर एक लाख पैंतीस हजार रुपए जमा कर विभाग को अमूल्य देन दे दी। व्याख्यानमाला का यह क्रम इतिहास विभाग आज भी बरकरार रख रहा है।

प्रो. मिश्र के शैक्षणिक प्रेम तथा अथक् प्रयास से स्नातकोत्तर इतिहास विभाग ने *रिसेंट रिसर्चस* नामक शोध जर्नल का प्रकाशन शुरू किया था।

प्रो. पंचानंद मिश्र को 1962-63 में फुलब्राइट स्मिथ मंड स्कॉलरशिप मिला। 1978-79 को ए.सी.एल.एस. फेलोशिप अवार्ड से सम्मानित किए गए तथा उसी वर्ष अमेरिका के पेंसिलवेनिया यूनिवर्सिटी में विजिटिंग फेलो के रूप में गए। 1969 में बनारस हिंदू विश्वविद्यालय में हुए इंडियन कांग्रेस ऑफ अमेरिकन हिस्ट्री के अध्यक्ष बनाए गए। प्रो. मिश्र ने हैदराबाद स्थित अमेरिकन स्टडिज सेंटर तथा

पटना के ए.एन. सिन्हा रिसर्च इंस्टीट्यूट की कार्यकारी समिति के सदस्य पद को भी सुशोभित किया था।

इस बात से इनकार नहीं किया जा सकता है कि उस समय मत भिन्नता नहीं थी। वैचारिक मतभेद थे, गुटबाजी थी। बावजूद इसके प्रो. पंचानंद मिश्र ने सबों को साथ लेकर इतिहास विभाग को बुलंदियों तक पहुंचाया। उनके सहयोगी शिक्षकगण भी विभाग की प्रतिष्ठा को बढ़ाने के लिए अपने-अपने मतभेदों को भुलाकर कार्यक्रम को सफल बनाने में तन-मन-धन से सहयोग करते थे।

प्रो. मिश्र ने *मेकिंग ऑफ दी इंडियन कांस्टीट्यूशन* नामक पुस्तक लिखी जो वर्ष 1974 में प्रकाशक यंग मैन एंड कंपनी, दिल्ली द्वारा प्रकाशित हुई।

पुनः सात लेखकों, क्रमश :

1. डॉ. कृष्ण बिहारी वाजपेयी,
2. सुशील माधव पाठक, रांची
3. डॉ. पंचानंद मिश्र
4. प्रेम नारायण माथुर, जोधपुर
5. रामपाल कौशिक, दिल्ली
6. भगवत कुमार श्रीवास्तव, जे.एन.यू.
7. बी. रमेश बाबू, बंबई ने मिलकर *संयुक्त राज्य अमेरिका का इतिहास : एक शोधपूर्ण अध्ययन* पुस्तक की रचना की। 31 दिसंबर, 1991 को विश्वविद्यालय इतिहास विभाग के विभागाध्यक्ष पद से अवकाश ग्रहण करने के बाद अपनी शैक्षणिक गतिविधि को बनाए रखने हेतु 1992 में विक्रमशिला रिसर्च इंस्टीट्यूट की स्थापना की। उस समय के बिहार के राज्यपाल डॉ. ए.आर. किदवई ने इस संस्था का उद्घाटन किया। संस्था को सोसायटी रजिस्ट्रेशन एक्ट-1860 के अंतर्गत 121/92-93 पंजीकृत कराया गया। प्रो. मिश्र इसके चेयरमैन बने। उनके नेतृत्व में इंस्टीट्यूट ने कई शैक्षणिक गतिविधियों की शुरुआत की जो आज तक बरकरार है। विक्रमशिला रिसर्च इंस्टीट्यूट द्वारा क्रमशः निम्न कार्यक्रम किए गए—

* आई.सी.एच.आर. द्वारा 14-15 मई, 1996 को प्रायोजित *कास्ट, क्लास एंड कम्यूनिटी इन इंडिया विद स्पेशियल रेफ्रेंस टू बिहार*।
* आई.सी.एच.आर. द्वारा 7-8 मार्च, 1999 को प्रायोजित, *अकबर एंड हिज एज* पर सेमिनार।
* आई.सी.एच.आर. द्वारा 15-16 अक्टूबर 2005 को प्रायोजित *आर्क्योलॉजिकल एक्सकेवेशंस एंड रीकंसट्रक्शन ऑफ दी हिस्ट्री ऑफ बिहारा* पर नेशनल सेमिनार।

* दिल्ली के प्रो. श्रीमाली का 21 नवंबर, 2005 को *नेशनल करिकुलम फ्रेम वर्क 2005 एंड टीचिंग ऑफ हिस्ट्री* विषय पर विशेष व्याख्यान।
* 25 जनवरी, 2006 को बी.आर.ए. यूनिवर्सिटी, मुजफ्फरपुर के पूर्वप्रति-कुलपति स्व. विजय कुमार ठाकुर का *आइडिया ऑफ हिस्ट्री इन एंशिएंट इंडिया* विषय पर विशेष व्याख्यान।

प्रो. पंचानंद मिश्र ने अपने इंस्टीट्यूट से *विक्रमशिला जर्नल ऑफ सोशल साइंस* नामक एक उच्च कोटि के अर्धवार्षिक जर्नल का प्रकाशन 2004 (जनवरी-जून) से प्रारंभ किया। तब से लगातार इस जर्नल के अंक (जनवरी-जून) तथा (जुलाई-दिसंबर) नियमित प्रकाशित हो रहे हैं। जर्नल की उत्कृष्टता को देखते हुए आई.सी.एच.आर, नई दिल्ली ने अनुदान भी दिया है।

2. डॉ. पंचानंद मिश्र : भागलपुर की एक शख्सियत

शमीम अफजा कमर

अपने दोस्तों के लिए वह जान की बाजी भी लगा देते थे, उनके करीब के लोग बहुत ज़्यादा नहीं थे, लेकिन चंद-एक जरूर हुआ करते थे, डॉ. कमर तौहीद और सर सुरेंद्र नारायण उनके बहुत अच्छे दोस्त थे, सुरेंद्र नारायण अक्सर उनको पांचू सिन्हा कहा करते थे।

एक वाकिया याद आता है, इसे इत्तफाक ही कहिए कि तौहीद साहब के वी.सी. बनने के बाद अचानक ही प्रॉक्टर के लिए उनके नाम की घोषणा कर दी, ये पोस्ट ओहदा में नीचे आता है लेकिन पंचानंद मिश्र जी बहुत सीनियर थे, बहरहाल ये भूल तो तौहीद साहब से हो गई, लेकिन पंचा बाबू ने इसे मंजूर कर लिया और हमेशा छतरी की तरह साया दिए रहे कि न धूप की तपिश महसूस हो, न ओले पड़े।

एक दूसरा वाकिया याद आता है, प्रति-कुलपति के बहुत से काम पंचानंद मिश्र रोक लिया करते थे क्योंकि इसमें खतरा ही खतरा था, तौहीद साहब की जान मुसीबत में थी। एक दिन मैंने कहा कि 'आप टूर पर जा रहे हैं, बेफिक्र होकर जाइए, मैं प्रति-कुलपति साहब से बात कर लूंगी,' डॉ. तौहीद क़मर ने मुझसे पूछा कि 'तुम क्या करोगी?' मैंने कहा, 'आप फिक्र न करें, मैं कुछ अच्छा ही करूंगी।'

तौहीद साहब चले गए। मैंने प्रति-कुलपति साहब को फोन किया कि मैं आपसे मुलाकात करना चाहती हूं। या तो मैं आपके यहां आ जाऊं या आप मेरे साथ चाय पीजिए। उन्होंने कहा मैं खुद आ जाऊंगा मैडम, आप तकलीफ न करें। शाम को वह आए, मैंने चाय के दौरान कहा कि तौहीद साहब की पूरी जिंदगी भागलपुर में गुजरी। यहां की यूनिवर्सिटी के लोग और सारा शहर उनका दोस्त है। वह कह रहे थे कि मैं वी.सी. की पोस्ट से इस्तीफा देना पसंद करूंगा लेकिन अपने दोस्तों को तकलीफ नहीं

दूंगा। आदमी होशियार थे, इशारा समझ गए। कहने लगे, नहीं, मैं सर के खिलाफ कुछ भी नहीं करूंगा और खुद से मुलाकात कर लूंगा।

डॉ. पंचानंद मिश्र जी भागलपुर यूनिवर्सिटी के इतिहास विभाग के बानी अपने आप में एक बड़ी शख्सियत हैं। आज से पचीस साल पहले पंचानंद मिश्र की झलक देखिए।

वह खुद छोटे कद के लेकिन सिर बड़ा, पेशानी चौड़ी, आंख रोशन, सूट पहने, खूबसूरत टाई बांधे कैंपस में तेज-तेज चलते-फिरते नजर आते। हेड की जिम्मेदारियों को संभालते हुए ज्यादा से ज्यादा क्लास लेते। लड़के उनके क्लास को छोड़ना अपनी भूल समझते थे। जो किसी अच्छे अध्यापक की निशानी है।

डॉ. पंचानंद मिश्र, हिंदुस्तान की दूसरी तमाम बड़ी यूनिवर्सिटियों में बहुत इज्जत से बुलाए जाते थे और देश के तमाम बड़े इसिहासकार से इनकी अच्छी मुलाकात थी। वे किसी काम से इनकार नहीं करते थे और हर मुमकिन कोशिश करते थे कि अपना काम खुशी और ईमानदारी के साथ अंजाम देते। इनकी बातों में असर था, इसलिए लोग इन्हें आसानी से भूल नहीं सकते थे। इनका प्रशासन सख्त था। लेकिन वह अपने स्टाफ और छात्रों से मुहब्बत करते थे। जूनियर प्रोफेसर अक्सर आजादी के साथ छेड़छाड़ भी कर लेते। वह कभी हंसकर दिलचस्पी लेते, कभी मुंह फुलाकर बैठ जाते। पंचा भैया मुंह फुलाते तो फौरन अध्यापक 'बा अदब, बा मुलाहिजा होशियार' हो जाते कि उन्हें कोई तकलीफ न हो।

उन्होंने दो बार अमेरिका का सफर किया। पहलो दफा पी-एच.डी. के लिए और दूसरी बार किसी यूनिवर्सिटी में चंद क्लास लेने के लिए। उनकी एक खूबी और भी थी, वह दूसरों की तकलीफ पर बहुत जल्द पिघल जाते थे। लिहाजा लोग उनसे गलत काम करवाने की कोशिश करते लेकिन सच्चाई का पता लगाने के बाद वह गलत काम से बच निकलते थे।

डॉ. मिश्र एक्ट और स्टैच्यूट को खूब अच्छी तरह जानते थे। इसलिए सीनेट, सिंडीकेट और यूनिवर्सिटी के कामों में सलाहकार थे। जिस जमाने में प्रोफेसर थे, वे यूनिवर्सिटी या तो अपने स्कूटर पर आते थे या रिक्शा पर। डॉ. पंचानंद मिश्र ने नई फिएट कार खरीदी, कभी ड्राइवर नहीं रखा और चंद महीना पहले तक वह कार खुद ही ड्राइव करते थे। वक्त ने उनके घुटनों को बेकार कर दिया है फिर भी हिम्मत नहीं हारे और 'आर्य भट्ट' नाम का स्कूल 10+2 के संरक्षक (गार्जियन) बने। पहले साल जगह की कमी की वजह से सिर्फ दस छात्रों का दाखिला लिया। कहने की जरूरत नहीं कि उन्होंने अच्छे से अच्छे अध्यापक को रखा। परिणाम पहले साल भी अच्छा था, लेकिन वह खुद को इत्मिनान न दिला सके। जम के मेहनत की और अब तो छात्रों की तादाद 40 तक पहुंच गई है। रिजल्ट भी बहुत अच्छा होता है।

आर्यभट्ट स्कूल भागलपुर के बच्चों के लिए एक बेहतरीन तोहफा है।

इतना ही नहीं, उन्होंने एक *विक्रमशिला रिसर्च इंस्टीट्यूट* भी खोल रखा है जिसके जरिया मैगजीन और रिसर्च पेपर शाया होते हैं।

मैं पंचानंद मिश्र जी की बहन कहलाती हूं तो मुझे बेहद खुशी होती है।

[उर्दू से अनुवाद प्रो. (डॉ.) मनाज़िर आशिक हरगानवी,
स्नातकोत्तर उर्दू विभाग, टी.एम. भागलपुर विश्वविद्यालय, भागलपुर]

3. THE GOOD SAMARITAN

Ratneshwar Mishra

Today in a somewhat shattered physical condition owing to pain in his joints and also perhaps owing to his advancing age Dr. Panchanand Mishra still remains a great source of strength and inspiration to his friends, colleagues, students and admirers many of whom occupied high positions and enjoyed successful careers largely because of his guidance and benevolence. I am also obliged to him for lots of things in my life and precisely due to this that I thought I can write about him anything but a historian's dispassionate assessment / account of him which is what I was seemingly asked to write by Dr. Raman Sinha sometime back. Obviously because I felt so close and so indebted to him that instead of attempting to write his life sketch I am just depicting some of my personal encounters with, or should I say obligation, to him. Even that is a difficult task, howsoever nice it may otherwise be. Nevertheless it has to be undertaken primarily because I always thought that a scholarly volume should be brought out in his honour and therein must be some contribution from my side just by way of a public admission of my indebtedness to him.

A celebrated teacher, an acknowledge scholar, an able administrator and above all an exceedingly sociable person Dr. Panchanand Mishra rose in the academic hierarchy of Bhagalpur University braving all sorts of oppositions and insinuations which came his way, mostly undeservingly, from time to time. One such occasion was his appointment as Reader in History in Bhagalpur University in mid 1960, when I was a post-graduate student of History at Patna University and my father, Late Madaneshwar Mishra was the Principal of Purnea College as well as the member of the syndicate of Bhagalpur University and I unintentionally got involved in the matter and unwillingly stood in direct opposition to him at least apparently. It so happened that the Bihar Public Service Commission had recommended two names in order of preference, as per practice then prevalent, for appointment, as Reader, the first being that of late Dr. J. C. Jha, my teacher at Patna University and the second that of Dr. Panchanand Mishra who was to enter into my life in a big way later. Dr. Jha one day asked me to tell my father to help him in the Syndicate to secure the appointment and I faithfully did that little understanding that I was thus opposing someone who, I discovered later, deserved to get the appointment on the strength of his services to the History Department of Bhagalpur University since its inception as also his teaching and research experiences, but was already being opposed by many on some imaginary grounds viz. his Ph. D. degree of an American University was not based on exactly scholarly work, on the period of his absence in America for doing Ph. D. could not be counted as teaching experience, or he, a Shakadwipi Brahmin, belonged to nobody's caste in Bhagalpur and such others. Be that as it may, my father responded to my request to help professor Jha by saying farther enigmatically, "I will see to it." I was not particularly happy with his responce and hesitated to face Dr. Jha for quite sometime but even after Dr. Mishra got the appointment Dr. Jha one day told me to my utter surprise and relief that he was grateful that my father had helped him, unsuccessfully though, but in any case he was expecting to get similar appointment at Patna University and so was not bothered about what happened at Bhagalpur. My father had indeed helped Dr. Mishra and not Dr. Jha but when he told Dr. Mishra just prior to the meeting of the syndicate that he was at a loss to understand as to how he could help him as he had to give weightage to Dr. Jha's request made through his son a third person present there, whose identity I have not been able to establish until today, reported this part of conversation to Dr. Jha and the latter was satisfied. However the relationship between my father and Dr. Panchanand Mishra eversince remained one of unshakable friendship.

After doing my M.A. in 1966 I joined as Lecturer at S.P. College, Dumka, in Bhagalpur University where Dr. Mishra was already Head of the University, Dept. of History. He had indeed got that coveted post quite early in his career when he was only a Lecturer as in the newly established Bhagalpur University he happened to be the senior most man in the Department after the retirement of Late Neelmani Acharya. At Dumka even though I was new to my job I enjoyed the confidence of my Principal Late S. N. Jha and both my senior colleagues in the Deptt. Vandacharan Mishra and Late Devendra Kumar all of whom were admirers of Dr. Mishra's qualities of head and heart and therefore, whenever I organised annual or other functions to project the academic image of my Dept. at University level, I got ready support from all of them. In one of such functions I invited Dr. Mishra to be the Chief guest to which the latter not only agreed readily but came on the appointed day along with other colleagues of his Dept. I remember two of them vividly, they were Dr. Diwakar Pd. Singh and Dr. C. P. N. Sinha both of whom later succeeded Dr. Mishra as Head of the Dept. one by one. What I want to emphasize here is the wonderful speech delivered on that occasion by Dr. Mishra which was characterized by a freshening approach to his subject and not by such oratorial qualities as control and rhythmic punctuation of voice or sarcastic and humorous remarks. He on that day talking on some aspect of historiography, the art and science of history, a subject that had not yet received any perceptible currency in India, less so in this part of the country. Since then I had occasion to hear him many more times but the one that I will like to mention here is when he delivered a memorable lecture on the causes of British withdrawal from India in the University Dept. of History of L.N. Mithila University, Darbhanga, which I had joined by then and had become its Head. Dr. H. S. Shrivastava, the Head of the History Dept. of Gorakhpur University, presided over that meeting and was so impressed by him that he said that on the basis of just that one lecture it could safely be said that Dr. Mishra should have by now gone many places higher than where he was. Dr. Mishra had in fact highlighted the internal compulsion of the British emanating from financial losses and strains and in the process he did not in any way minimise the role of Gandhi and other nationalists or the foreign countries like U.S.A. but viewed their successful role as a corollary to the financial discomfiture of the British in the absence of which they must have clung to India for much longer period.

During my Dumka days from 1967 to 1974 Dr. Mishra was

the University representative of the Governing Body of S. P. College for a year or two when on a particular occasion a couple of teachers of that college went all the way to Bhagalpur to persuade him to attend the G. B. meeting and vote in their favour. An exceedingly congenial and helpful man that he is, he agreed to their proposal even though that might have been antagonistic to the Principal with whom he had no personal reason to pick up a quarrel. He indeed offered them the comfort of travelling in his car which he was himself driving on their journey from Bhagalpur to Dumka. As ill luck would have it a passer by was hit by the car causing him some injury and a case was lodged against Dr. Mishra in a nearby police station. The police officer and other after knowing Dr. Mishra, a hugely influencial person, were ready to help him in finalising the case specially in view of the fact that the accident had occurred not due to the fault of Dr. Mishra but of the victim himself. The irony of the situation, however, reflected in the fact that the S. P. College teachers travelling with him were ready to fish in troubled waters and keep Dr. Mishra implicated or even harm him as during those days he was opposed to some of the leaders in the University politics one of whose casts was the same as that of one of those teachers of S. P. College. Dr. Mishra finally succeeded in extricating himself honourably in spite of their damaging eye-witness statements but what is worth emulating is that Dr. Mishra neither during those days nor ever after harboured any revengeful intentions against them. And all this in spite of the fact that some of his contemporaries, with whom he is known to have love and hate relationship, hold the opinion that like the girl in the nursery rhymes really when he is good he is very very good.

I am, however, at a loss to understand how can a man be bad who always acts as a good Samaritan particularly to those who are retired or in distress. Late Neelmani Acharya, Dr. Mishra's predecessor as Head of the Dept. of History at Bhagalpur University, Late Jagadish Narayan Sarkar, the renowned historian, Late Sushil Ranjan Mukherjee, retired Principal of Murarka College, Sultanganj, to name a few, all remained his concern during their retirement and all of them relied on him for help and assistance, in many cases, more than perhaps their own relatives. I have seen persons, irrespective of their age and status, going to him to seek his help in pulling them out of their perplexities and he instead of indulging in patronizing and sermonizing deeds, straight away started looking for ways to help them without letting them have the feeling of being small and trivial. He really helped any number of Ph. D. seekers either by himself guiding them or by sending them to suitable guides and seeing them through till they got the degree and in the process he saw to it that they were not belittled on any count, poverty, language or basic academic stuff. What he did for Ph. D. seekers he did for others too, viz. job seekers, parents looking for appropriate schools or colleges for their wards or even someone harassed by this or that office in the University or even elsewhere. While thus obliging people he has been able to create a very large circle of friends and well wishers who are not confined to just academics but are spread in different walks of life all around. When I retired from service on 31st January 2005 he without any delay rang up to ask me to send my curriculum-vitae so that he could fix me up somewhere as Visiting Professor or some such thing. If he has not succeeded in spite of his best efforts nothing can be taken away from his goodness because his sincere willingness in this regard is unmistakably there and what is more that he would never let me have the feeling of being helped, rather he would say that 'I am proud of you.'

I do not know why should he be proud of me, of someone who was guided / and supervised in obtaining his Ph. D. degree by him but when that Ph. D. thesis was published in book form no complimentary copy was sent to him, any valid explanation for this lapse notwithstanding or someone who never remembers to have done anything substantial for him or for someone else on his command. He is a busy and innovative person who always keeps on doing something academic and his tremendous resourcefulness ensures success in all his endeavours. When he was in the University he would organise seminars and lectures on grand scale. Even after his retirement he is engaged in such activities. The remarkable thing about him in this respect is that he would utilise these occasions to perpetuate some distinguished memory and to gather his favoured ones together in spite of his known closeness to some of the greats in the world of history. Late Bishweshwar Prasad, a renowned historian of Allahabad school and a former Vice-Chancellor of Bhagalpur University, loved him very much but when he was no more it was Dr. Mishra's turn to repay by getting memorial lecture instituted in his name. One of these lectures was delivered by Deitmar Rothermunnd, a great economic historian, another by Ram Sharan Sharma, the celebrated Indian historian and yet another by Dr. Mishra himself. In one of these lectures he also arranged to felicitate the memory of Late Radha Krishna Choudhary, again a celebrated historian from Bihar, who had been his colleague in the Dept. for sometime and through a quirk of fate had unsuccessfully challenged his seniority and headship.

These days he is busy in the activities of his brainchild, the Vikramshila Research Institute which also brings out a research journal apart from holding seminars, lectures etc. I am priviledged to be invited by him to attend as a participant to all these activities. So much so that when he once organised a seminar on Akbar he sort of forced me to present a paper even though he knew more than anyone else that my chosen field of work was modern Indian history with emphasis on regional history of Bihar. But this is his way to favour his favourites.

My personal contacts with Dr. Mishra have been many and varied which are difficult to be recounted in a brief narrative like this but I wonder if I will ever be able to write a fuller account to show how he from being a friend and admirer of my father switched over with perfect case to being my friend, philosopher and guide and did all that he could to shape my career and stand by me through the thick and thin of my life as indeed of many others, quite a few of whom I know somewhat closely. Personally he himself appears to have been a victim of circumstances in as much as he was sought to he slightingly treated by some of his friends who conveniently turned foes at will on caste ground or some such flimsy grounds when it suited their fancy but Dr. Mishra would still not talk ill of them and would rather like to help them if opportunity was offered to him. As regards charges of being casteist he once told me that how could he be so belonging as he did to a hopelessly minority caste and indeed he considered issues and persons as important and not caste when he was required to allign with this or that person. Even in his bad state of health he is busy with his academic and philanthropic deeds and amid these busy schedules I have never seen him becoming oblivious to his duties to the members of his family, friends and visitors. I am grateful to Ramanjee for providing me the opportunity to put on record my respects for him and due sense of benefits received from him.

4. MY IDEAL AND IDOL:
Dr. Panchanand Mishra

Ajay Kumar Jha

It is a great pleasure to write a few sincere words on one of my most revered teachers at the University level based on personal perception. I came to know Dr. Panchanand Mishra, Prof. & Head, University Dept. of History, T.M. Bhagalpur University, Bhagalpur in 1970 through an article in the American Reporter when I was a B.A. Hons. Student at Munger. It published his photograph along with his article on *Indo-American Relations.* The visage in the photograph and the content of the article gave an inkling of the seriousness of his being and his intellectual acumen. That was my first acquaintance of the person and it created a positive and lasting impression of him.

Later on, when I was admitted to the Post-graduate course in History at Bhagalpur, I could see and know him both as a teacher and a person from close quarters. Endowed with reserved and serious countenance, his presence always evoked an awe among students and colleagues as well. Physically short but heavily built he stood above all in the Dept. and his manner and deportation all had an imperious bearing. He was a classic teacher with a touch of his own. True, we were always in awe of him, still we always wanted classes to be engaged by him. But who could dare to make such a request to the 'Royal Bengal Tiger,' a sobriquet, which we had fondly given him in our circle. What better word could characterize a person whose presence made us speechless and we almost forgot to breathe. Even today I do not feel normal and comfortable before him though he is a vastly changed person.

He was a very busy person in and outside the state. But whenever he was in the town he was very particular about his classes. In the classroom, he was at his best. Who can forget his performances in the class, his step-by step analysis of the historical development of the constitution making in England in the 17th - 18th centuries. His sentences were short, description simple; delivery gentle and the language flawless and very easy and intelligible like the gentle flow of water in the Ganges. We simply marvelled at the teaching—the evolution of political ideas and institutions and its presentation in a logical and sequential manner,—well supported by facts. The elements of Divine Right Theory of kingship and its impact on politics, the execution of king, the Glorious Revolution, the flight of James II from the country—all were told and discussed calmly, gently without any fury and sound. Even in retrospect, his word-sketch of the Restoration and Revolution in England brings an air of romance and we are lost in a reverie. Today I can understand the value of his teaching of history. To him history was not merely a description of bare facts, but also a critical analysis of facts in historical context. Actually, it was he who acquainted us with the 'Why' and 'How' of history. Without being aware of historiography, we could understand the philosophy of history and the practical usefulness of history on the basis of its lessons. As a mater of fact, actually it was he who initiated me into the discipline of 'History' as Dr. K.K. Dutta's book, *An Advanced History of India* and its rendering in a chaste Hindi : by Dr. Yogendra Mishra had created an interest for the subject long back at my school days. For my interest in the subject, I am beholden to my teachers directly, and some scholars of history, indirectly.

Golden moments of University-days were soon over and the M.A. result was out. I was dismayed at my second position in first class in the University. Teaching was my first love for the career but now I wavered a bit and thought of leaving Bhagalpur. But God had willed otherwise for me. One morning, when I was coming out of my residence at Lal Kothi, Tatarpur, I saw Pancha Babu going to the dept. in his car. I paid my respects through the gesture of my hands. His response was instant and affectionate. He stopped his car and asked me to sit in. That was the turning in my career. He asked me to apply for lectureship as well as Research Fellowship for Bhagalpur University, which had been advertised at the moment. I changed my plan for future. Instead of going to Delhi or Patna as planned earlier, I applied for the post and in due course I was selected for lectureship and posted in the University Department of History without any godfather in the University service. It was a great feat to have joined the same institution where one had been himself a student a few months back.

Momentous was, the 15th of January 1975, when I went to join the dept. I submitted my appointment letter. Pancha Babu looked at me non-chalantly as was his wont and feigned ignorance at my appointment and surprised me by asking the purpose of my visit. It was characteristic of him to appear familiar at one moment and distant at the next. He asked me to submit the joining. I seribbled a few sentences hardly legible of reading in excitement and awe before him. Thereafter I was asked to engage class of my choice. I preferred to go to M.A. Previous class to which he agreed. At this hour, sensing the predicament of a raw young man just out of the campus, he asked Prof. Padmesh Pathak to introduce me to the students. After this, he counselled as well as bid me good wishes to be a successful teacher. Now, it was my turn to prove myself before the students, who were eager to tease a new teacher. Shaking and trepidating to the bone, I introduced myself and started speaking to the class. Sure enough, God was on my side. Of course, my teachers' blessing saved me from any embarrassment on the first day. I created a good impression on the class and have been fortunate enough to receive the love and affection of my students in abundance. Pancha Babu was happy at my performance in the class and he complimented me for this in as few a words as possible. But gesture of praise was much enough to inspire me to be confident of me and my abilities.

The years rolled by. Came 1979 and Pancha Babu left for America on sabbatical leave for a year. In the meantime I suffered a setback and had to join T.N.B. College, Bhagalpur on transfer. I had to go because of being the junior-most in the Department. It was the rule and of course, in those days rules were meant to be followed. I stayed at T.N.B. College for long 19 years and learnt many things of life. There I had the opportunity to interact with a good number of teachers of different subjects. I was happy at the College and never thought of coming back to the Dept. where many junior teachers remained posted. After many years of languishing in worldly affairs, I thought of doing research and got myself registered under Pancha Babu on a subject suggested by him. I did not know anything about research, its methodology nor the academic benefits that accrued to its pursuers. Many of my friends had got the degree without any apparent improvement in their academic excellence or quality. Pancha Babu appeared a hard taskmaster and asked me to write a summary of Dr. Tarachand's book. *The Influence of Islam on Indian Culture*, which I readily did without little realizing its value in research. I thought he was not much interested and was avoiding me. He was happy and satisfied at the summary of the book and advised me to undertake the work earnestly. Though he was always short of time, he remained available to me and my task became easy. Fortunes again smiled on me and one day in one of his cheerful moods he gave me certain tips, which were to prove in the end important key to research. Diverse source- materials, collection of facts, their collation, the systematic presentation of facts under different sub-titles; their analysis and the writing of conclusion etc. formed the essentials of research. It was good enough a direction to move into the labyrinth of research which I gladly undertook and for two years I dreamt research and nothing else. Here I must admit that I have not grown much what I learnt at the moment under his guidance.

I still remember the suspense when I gave the draft of my thesis to him for perusal. He took a week to go through it and I cannot describe my happiness when he approved every word of it and patted me profusely for the work. I stumbled again as ever at the writing of the conclusion. I requested him to salvage and bring me out of the impasse. How can I be ungrateful and forget his contribution in making me what I am today. He wrote a few sentences in his own hand that concluded the essence of my study. I was exultant at the completion of my academic dream, more so at his fatherly love and praise clearly visible in his moist eyes. The date for the Ph.D. viva having failed twice, I was naturally anxious about it. Finally, it was fixed at Delhi at my request but unfortunately Pancha Babu fell seriously ill and he suffered excruciating pain in the abdomen. Pancha Babu did not care for his illness and readily agreed to go to Delhi. We travelled to Delhi where the viva-voce was held at Jamia Milia Islamic University. We were warmly greeted by Prof. S.N. Sinha who praised me for the excellent work. I stood speechless and forget to reciprocate.

We stayed in Delhi together for a couple of days where I had the opportunity to know Pancha Babu intimately as a person. I came back to Bhagalpur with fond memories of his association and the kind feelings that he had for me. I do not know how to redeem the debt that I owe to him.

The debt grew in proportion as time passed by I became Reader and subsequently Professor knowing full well my abilities and shortcomings. I believe it has been his good wishes and blessings that brought me distinctions in career.

Pancha Babu retired from service in 1991 and even after retirement he remained concerned for the Dept which had deteriorated much since then due to many reasons. His concern for the Dept. was obvious. He had created the Dept. from the scratch, recruited most of the teachers for it and despite handicaps, he had brought the Dept. on the national map. The annual conference of Indian History Congress was organized at Bhagalpur in 1968 largely due to his efforts. Thereafter, he organized many ICHR-sponsored Seminars and Conferences and invited many well known scholars to Bhagalpur. Dr. A.L. Basham, Dr. R.S. Sharma, Dr. J.N. Sarkar, Dr. D.C. Sarkar, Prof. Bisheshwar Prasad and Prof. Ruthermund of Germany to name only a few—all came down to Bhagalpur and delivered lectures. I have seen him speaking all extempore in the midst of a galaxy of scholars without a ruffle. His organizational skill, academic interest, wide contacts and domineering figure- all made his profile complete and colourful and brought him envious success. He was the talk of the times and the city. He remained a force in the University administration and he used to solve the intricate situations by a sleigh of his hand. All the bigwigs in the university came to him for parleys. His manoeuvrability was superb which made him either friend or foe to his peers. He was a past master in establishing good personal rapport with most of the acclaimed scholars and others which made him unbelievably resourceful to undertake any seemingly difficult academic venture. In 1997 when I joined the Dept. once again I always felt the absence of his towering personality. It was now the autumn in the Dept. and dwarfs had the heyday. How could one be great without grace and greatness? Despite his growing age and failing health, Pancha Babu has the heart of a lion and will as strong as iron. This was evident when his long cherished dream the 'Vikramshila Research Institute' came into existence in Feb. 1992 and was inaugurated by His Excellency the Governor of Bihar, Dr. A.R. Kidwai. It was under its aegis that he ventured the publication of The *Vikramshila Journal of Social Sciences*. The publication of academic journal from a small place like Bhagalpur appeared almost impossible not because of fund only but more because of the decline of the academic interest even among the academicians. He managed the fund partly through donations and invested a good deal of personal fortunes in it only for the sake of academic interest. He had made possible the impossible and septics were given a good rebuff. The journal is being published regularly and I hope it to grow as his favourite child. It has been a welcome academic initiative and I have been fortunate enough to have been actively associated with it.

Born on 8th of August 1928 Pancha Babu is today 79. Though physical ailment has weakened him but it has not diminished his spirit a bit. He takes active interest in the Arybhatta plus-2 School of which he happens to be the patron. It has been because of his inspiration that 'Arybhatta' is today recognized as an excellent Centre of learning. Keeping himself useful to the society through association with the 'Arybhatta' and 'Vikramshila' Research Institute in the evening of his life, he deserves our salute. He has been a patriarch to many at Bhagalpur to whom we used to run hastily for counselling at any moment of crisis. Disillusioned though he has been at falling standards in life all-around, we wish him to live longer and healthy for our own sake and for the good of the society. Who would like to loose such a useful person?

It has been my good luck and privilege to grow and mature under his guidance and inspiration. A teacher has a great role in making and moulding his student and the student grows in imitation of his idol knowingly or sometimes unknowingly. I can claim to have imbibed some of his inimitable teaching style knowing full well that imitation cannot have the flavour of the original. As a person he has been unique and matchless, he helped anybody who came to him asking for it. He had no consideration of caste and creed. He had been a good Samaritan throughout and no one could miss his generous hospitality. A thorough gentleman and conscious of self-respect, a conspicuous streak of his nature has been his dictatorial temperament. As a matter of fact, he commands respect, because of his generosity and helping attitude. I remember my days as a young lecturer when he used to drop at my non-descript address and demanded good tea out of his sheer love and affection for me. Even today, whenever I am ill, he enquires about my welfare and shows interest in my affairs. This makes him different from the general mass of people. A person of serious disposition, he has the heart of a child-full of innocent emotions. I have seen him happy and melancholy, laughing and crying. My love and respect to him has been for a teacher which has grown in course of time. He himself has been a grateful student to his eminent college-teacher Prof. Nilmani Acharya, whom he still remembers with fondness and respect. He carries with him a particular tradition, a scholarship which will be wanting in the days to come. He remained stuck at Bhagalpur because of it being his birthplace, had he moved to a bigger place, he would have grown taller and attained a higher stature. Even in professional circle, he remained free, unattached to any 'ism or ideology' which is more often used by a lesser mortal as a ladder for upward journey in career. Controversial and a man of envy among his peers because of his bearing and living, Pancha Babu has been a prominent figure among the gentry at Bhagalpur and a well-known figure in the history-circle throughout the country. His interpretative acumen led him to the study of Indian Constitution and writes *The Making of Indian Republic* based on constitutional debates. A widely travelled man, rich in years and experiences; it is a privilege to enjoy his association. He is a man of many parts. One may criticize him but he couldn't be ignored. We wish him a long innings to get benefits from his presence. At times I have experienced his reference as forceful and fruitful as his presence. A man of untiring intellectual energy, he has been an embodiment of success despite odds and opposition. This could have been possible because he faced life himself—a self made man in all aspects. He has been inspiring, emulative and ideal in many ways to admire and adore.

Succeeding in life with elan, he embodies all the failings of a human being. A trusted friend to count among his circle, he never forgot his enemies. Anger and revenge was there in plenty, which, though, could be calmed and forgiven with sincere apology. A deeply religious man with rational outlook in personal life, he is firmly involved in the world with the conviction of a yogi who undauntedly faces the world and its ups and downs. In a word, worldly man with full religiosity, coupled with humanism is our Pancha Babu—with a lingering flavour distinctly of his own. His ideas and deeds all make him creditable and give a credence to the truism that even an individual with determination can end our mental-torpor and put his signature on the fleeting moments of times. I have put my mentor-musings in black and white with feeling and these ought to be appreciated as such.

5. DR. PANCHANAND MISHRA:
A Constructive Genius

Jagdishwar Jha

To write about Dr. Panchanand Mishra who has been so near and dear to me is rather difficult. A very successful teacher, a great organiser of the Bhagalpur University Department of History, a natural orator and a lucid writer, he was probably the first learned man in Bihar who understood the importance of American History teaching which became a separate Paper in Post-Graduate Syllabus in Bhagalpur University and later on in almost all the University of Bihar. The chief quality of Dr. Mishra during his tenure as Head of the University Department of History and even after his retirement is that he has always nourished great and noble ideas and has successfully implemented them.

To enumerate his works and achievements briefly as recorded in the Silver Jubilee Session (1989) of the Deptt. of History, Bhagalpur University. The Department under Dr. Mishra successfully organised the thirtieth session of the All India History Congress in 1968. Three years earlier in 1965 a workshop on American History was organised by the History Deptt. In 1968 again the third session of the All India Congress of American History was hosted by the History Deptt. of Bhagalpur University. The department organised a small museum. The Department Constituted 'Dr. Bisheswar Prasad Memorial Lecture' and the first lecture was delivered by Prof. Dr. Rothermund of Germany and the second was delivered by Dr. R. S. Sharma. During the period when he was the Head of the Department about 100 scholars were admitted to Ph. D. / D. Litt degrees of whom about

40 scholars were guided by Dr. Mishra and rest by other teachers of the Deptt. With his untiring energy he would hold annual functions of the History Deptt. persided over by such eminent Historians as Dr. Kalikinkar Dutta, Dr. A.C. Banerjee, Dr. Bisheshwar Prasad, Dr. S. V. Sohoni and others. Thus by the time he retired in 1992, the University Department of History became a star studded Deptt. and probably the best Department in Bhagalpur University.

Even after retirement he remains engaged in noble academic activities. He has successfully edited and published the *Vikramshila Journal of Social Sciences,* which has been acclaimed as a world class journal. Besides he, along with some like minded persons has established a high class higher secondary school namely *Aryabhat* CBSE School which has gained name and fame within a very short time. Now a lofty idea of establishing Vikramshila University is engaging his mind. I fervently hope this venture will also he successful. So he contiues to plan, cherish and nourish noble ideas and then he tries to give concrete shape to them.

Such a great person rests cosily in my heart. Although our long association of about 62 years we have been very close friends. From Intermediate, and Degree classes in T.N.J. College, Bhagalpur to Post Graduate class in Patna College and even in the P.G. Hostel, Patna, we were together. After our student career we joined the same profession of lecturers in History, ofcourse in two colleges T.N. J. College, Bhagalpur and Saharsa College, Saharsa. Dr. Mishra was my guide also and the Research topic was. 'Trade Relations between India and America in the 18th and 19th Centuries.' Dr. Mishra did his best to help me get Ph.D. degree. He took me to Madras to consult State Archive for necessary materials there. Then in 1969 he nominated me to represent the Bhagalpur University in the American History Seminar held at Hyderabad for a month. Then again the U.S.I.S. organised a week long Seminar on American History at Calcutta, I was again selected by Dr. Mishra to be one of the seven delegates from Bhagalpur University. All these activities gave me a deep insight in the History of U.S.A. But alas! my appointment as principal deprived me of the Ph.D. degree. However, we remained close to each other till we retired from services. And I remember that once he requested me to join the University Deptt. of History, which I politely refused due to my home sickness and love for Saharsa College, Saharsa.

In the end I remember a line of a very famous poem by Rastrakavi Dinkar "बड़ा वह आदमी जो जिन्दगी भर काम करता है।" It aptly applied to Dr. Panchanand Mishra who, in spite of his ailments, continues to strive for all sorts of noble works.

May God bless him with long life and with sound and good health.

My Sincere love and blessings to Dr. Panchanand Mishra.

6. DR. MISHRA: THE HUMANIST

Rakesh Kumar

Dr. Panchanand Mishra is universally acknowledged to be one of the giants of Indian History and can truly be considered as precursor of Indian renaissance. Dr. Mishra earned his name and fame through his writings, research works, work culture in his profession. It is said that Dr. Mishra during his Headship of the Department of History, was not given due recognition rightfully. This is not true because as recognition is concerned he is rather fortunate among his contemporaries. Almost all his works were published during his tenúre as a professor and became much sought after. Later all writings are of great historical importance.

It is very difficult for me to write a few words about a personality who is so great. However I am writing about an emotional scene in which he proved himself as an example of Indian culture during his farewell by his teacher in America. Dr. Mishra proved a living example of Indian culture, a culture whose foundations were laid on the highest moral values and empathy and brotherhood. The values and principles through which he learnt to love whole manking irrespective of caste and creed. He keeps these values close to his heart and even during the most testing times in America, he never compromised his faith in humanity. His lecture during his farewell *I love whole mankind of Muslim, Hindu and Christian and consider them my brothers and sisters. No matter what others say.* Proves that he is above any mankind of Parochialism. His work depicts the best, the most serene and the most exalted emotions of humanity in general. It also creates a human character which has the courage of conviction to stand up to society, the powers that be and above all God.

An often quoted incident bears testimony to his characteristic nature, his self-esteem and the feudal etiquette which was so dear to him. It was a difficult time when, after the end of the academic session, his Professor invited all Students for dinner. Friends told Dr. Mishra that drink would be offered and if he denied, they would take ill of it and his (Dr. Mishra) career may be ruined. It did happen like that. The Professor's wife came and offered drink first to Dr. Mishra which be politely refused. She felt insulted and left the room angrily. His colleagues abused him as uncivilized as he had insulted the hostess. The Professor came out and was very hurt. Dr. Mishra requested the Professor to call his wife and she came with great reluctance. Dr. Mishra told her that before coming to the States his mother had taken a promise that he would never drink and not marry an American girl. And his mother had died out of burn injuries. However, he told her that he treated her (Professor's wife) as his mother and if she still asked him to drink he would drink. The hostess was overwhelmed and had a great respect for him and asked him not to drink at all. The atmosphere was again pleasant and so much so that he was invited to come again to her house. The situation expreses the Indian Culture.

In my view, may I concise the philosophy by saying :

He is one
Above all rituals
Above all dogma
Above all customs.
It is only
Where these paths cease
Does true faith begin.

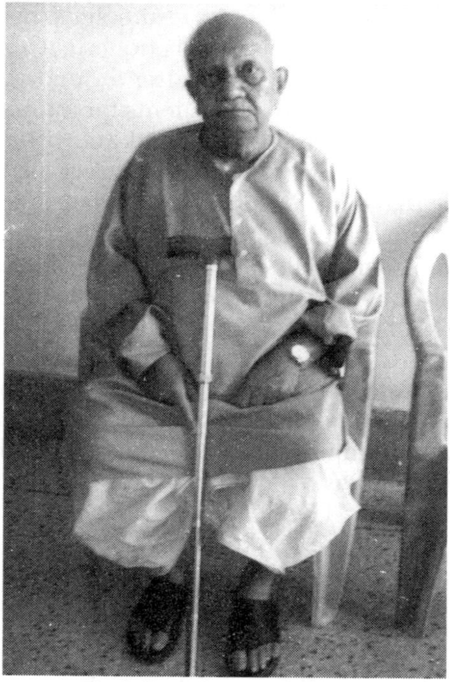

Prof. Panchanand Mishra

Prof. Panchanand Mishra and wife Smt. Hemlata Devi

Prof. Mishra on the occassion of national seminar

Prof. Panchanand Mishra on the function of I.C.H.R sponsored National Seminar

Prof K. M. Shrimali delivered lecture on–
"National Curriculam Framework 2005 and Teaching of History",
dated 21 November 2005

Mrs. Jeena Biswas, Director, All India Radio, Bhagalpur,
Chief Guest of the function.

Prof. Panchanand Mishra gives thanks on special lecture on– "Idea of History in Ancient India", dated 25 January 2006. Prof Vijay Kumar Thakur sitting left.

Prof. Vijay Kumar Thakur Releases "Vikramshila Journal of Social Sciences", dated 25 January 2006

PART II

7. NATURAL HISTORY OF KOSI RIVER BASIN

J.S. Datta Munshi

Abstract

There are more than seventy wetlands (chaurs) spreading all over the Kosi river of North Bihar, India. They are fed by about small channels called *Dhars,* originating from the Kosi, Burhi Gandak, Baghmati, Balan rivers which are tributaries of the Ganges. Hydrological studies along with the physico-chemical factors of waters of Kosi river and Berela chaur (swamp) of Kusheswarsthan, Darbhanga have been conducted. In summer months, the Kosi river gets water supply from the glaciers, but drastic depletion of water in most of these wetlands occur as they lose their connections with the riverine source. The peripheral regions of the wetlands dry up due to rapid transpiration of water by macrophytes. In the rainy season they get flooded with water of the adjoining rivers. The formation of wetlands and chaurs and their hydrological cycles depend mainly on the annual flush floods of the rivers and partly on the monsoon rain during the period May to September. In this paper the hydrological features, drainage pattern, water discharge, sediment load, formation of Dhars and wetlands and conservation of their biota and their production potentiality, fisheries and the present status of subsidiary industries like, mother of pearl (MOP) button and lime industries have been evaluated. The management strategy for sustainable hydrological cycle of the river basin lies in the construction of a network of canals and reservoirs to control the annual devastating flood and drought. The wetlands and chaurs of North Bihar are some of the most productive aquatic systems of the world, which sustain the life of millions of people.

Acknowledgements

The financial assistances from the Indian Council of Agricultural Research and the Council of Scientific and Industrial Research, Govt. of India under project No. 37/0904/96 are gratefully acknowledged.

Keywords: wetland, hydrological cycle, conservation.

The river Kosi or the 'Kausik of the legends, drains the southern slopes of the Nepal Himalayan terrain (25° 20' to 29° 0' N Lat. and 85° 20' to 89° 0' E long,) sprawled over a catchment area of 70,409 km² covering the territory of two countries viz. Nepal (59, 570 Km²) and India (10, 839 Km², North Bihar). The river originates from the glaciers of the Mount Gasainthan (8,013 m), the Mount Everest (8,848 m) and the Kanchanjunga (8,579 m) in the form of three main different streams Viz., the *Sun Kosi*, the *Arun Kosi* and the *Tamar Kosi* respectively, all joining together at *Tribeni*—10 miles upstream off Chatra. In addition to these, the Indravati, Bhote, Likhu and the *Dudh Kosi* join the *Sun Kosi* from the north. Thus, this mighty Himalyan river, a combination of seven streams assumes its popular Nepali name, the *Sapt Kosi*, at *Tribeni*. It has the highest rate of siltation among the rivers of the world causing land degradation, heavy silt concentration in the run off and formation of wetlands in North Bihar. Due to strong current and heavy sediment load this flushy hill torrent, as it reaches the plains, has oscillated its course over a vast tract of land since 1736. The hydrological features, drainage pattern, water discharge, sediment load, formation of dhars and wetlands and production potentiality of the Kosi river system have also been described.

The river Kosi or the *'Kausiki'* of the legends is the wildest and the most notorious and uncertain among the Indian rivers. It drains the southern slopes of the Nepal Himalayas (25° 20' to 29° 0' N Lat. and 85° 20' to 89° 0' E long,) extending from *Gasainthan* (8.013m) in the west to *Kanchanjunga* (8,579m) in the east. With a catchment area of 70,409 Km² covering the territory of two countries viz., Nepal (59,570 Km²) and India (10,839 Km², North Bihar), the Kosi basin is the third largest (in area) in the whole of India, ranking next to those of the Indus

(3.06,655 Km²) and the Brahmaputra (2,56,930 Km²). Compared to the Ganges length of 2,575 km arising from 3,950 m high Gangotri, the river Kosi is only 965 km long, originating from 5,490m high Tibetan plateau. It also has the highest rate of siltation among the rivers of the world. From the above physical characteristics, it is evident that the Kosi is a violent river in the mountains that has a catchment area too large for its relatively shorter course. The Kosi, due to these topographical and meteorological features, is rated as one of the problematic rivers of the world.

Derivation of the name

'Kosi': The Kausiki or Kosi

The Kosi known for its antiquity has some myths behind it. It is mentioned as Kausiki in epics, such as, the *Skandha Puran, Matsyapuran, Balmiki Ramayan,* and the *Mahabharta*, etc. In ancient literature, the river has been described as a large, powerful and sacred stream for holy bath. According to *Skandha Puran*, Kosi is said to be the daughter of *Kausiki Raja,* a celebrated Kshatriya King of Gadhi. The legendary semidivine maiden (*Nymph*) Kausiki had a brother named *Vishwamitra,* a worshipper of *Para Barhma*, or the Supreme God. His sister *Kausiki*, though Kshatriya by birth, was wedded to a Brahamin sage, *Richik* by name, who had attained perfection by virtue of worshipping gods. The saint later on, got furious with his wife, for his son, unlike his father, rose against worshsipping of gods. *Richik* cursed his wife and prayed God to convert his wife (*Kausik*) into a river (*vide Buchanan, 1928*).

Kausiki, according to another mythical writing, was a mermaid goddess, a sea woman having the head and body of a lovely lady and her waist ending as the tail of a fish. She was worshipped by the people inhabiting the *Matsyadesha*, the land of fishes. The Kingdom by that time was delimited between the old beds of Brahmaputra and the Karatoyo to which the Kosi was connected by a water way.

In the epic Balmiki Ramayana, the *Kausiki* is associated with the *Vishwamitra Satyavati* episode. Satyavati, the elder sister of the sage, was married to a saint *Rehika*. She followed her husband to the heaven from where she was transformed into a river, later to be known as the '*Kausiki*,' and, it was on its banks that *Vishwamitra* built up his hermitage and used to live.

Much like the Ganga, the Yamuna, the Saraswati and the Brahmaputra, the Kosi too has its own religious importance. People of the area take holy bath in this river during festivals. Several temples have been built up on the banks of the river, of which the following deserve special mention—temples of *Barraha Mahadeo* (8 Km downstream of Tribeni), *Koka Mukh*, both on the Nepal Hills, *Dewanbaba Temple* (Nauhatta), *Karubaba Temple* (Mahishi) and *Katyanisthan* (Salkhua). All these temples are in Saharsa district of Bihar.

Origin of Kosi

The river originates from the glaciers of Mount Gasainthan (8,013 m), the Mount Everest (8,848 m) and the Kanchenjunga (8,579 m) in the form of three different main streams viz., Sun Kosi, the Arun Kosi and the Tamar Kosi respectively, all confluencing together at Tribeni 10 miles uphill of Chatra town. In the upper catchment basin, the main feeders of Arun are the *Phungchu, Bhangchu, Menchu, Shichu, Dzakarchu, Chiblungchu* and *Yaruchu* (chu is a local term for a stream in Tibet.) In addition to these, the *Indravati, Bhote, Likhu* and the *Dudh Kosi* join the *Sun Kosi* from the north. Thus, the Kosi becomes one of the mighty Himalayan rivers comprising of seven streams. It is for this fact that the united stream assumes its popular Nepali name, '*The Sapt Kosi*' at Tribeni. As it enters the plains at Chatra (Nepal), it assumes the name of '*Kosi.*'

The total catchment of the Kosi, above Chatra in Nepal, is about 59,570 Km^2 out of which 5770 Km^2 is above the snow line (Table 1).

Glaciers

A large part of the Kosi catchment (5770 km^2) is covered with permanent glaciers of the Himalayas. This accounts for heavy water discharge in the river during the summer. Some of the important glaciers are the *Kanchanjunga* (10 miles), *Yalung* (13 miles). *Zemu* (16 miles), *Rongbuck* (14 miles) and the *Kyebark* (11 miles).

Shifting courses of the river

The river Kosi is well known for profuse branching into many interlacing channels in its course. It does not remain static in a

Table 1
Catchments of different principal tributaries forming the Sapt Kosi at Chatra

River	Catchment (km^2)	Percentage to total
Tamar	5,770.1	10%
Sun Kosi	18,985.7	32%
Arun	34,524.7	58%
Sapt Kosi (Below Tribeni upto Chatra)	290.0	Negligible
Total	59,570.5	100%

fixed channel for a long time. Since ancient times, it has been oscillating over a vast tract of North Bihar. This wild movement of the river has neither been steady nor continuous, rather it has been taking sudden jumps from one channel to another. In this process, it deserts the previous ones which still hold on some water (Chibber, 1949), leading to the formation of swamps and wetlands. The only comparable river in this respect is the "Hwang-Ho of China" (Ahmed, 1947).

Causes of shifting tendency

The oscillating character is associated only with the Kosi and no other river of the region. The causes of oscillation have puzzled hydrobiologists, geographers and geologists. Furthermore, the westward shifting tendency of the Kosi as against the natural slope (North-west to South-east) and configuration of the region is more amazing. Several explanations have been given by different authorities from time to time. However, the most common and widely accepted explanation given by Das (1968) and Singh (1986) deserves special attention. According to these authors, situation, rapid water discharge and bed slopes of the Kosi flood plan, are responsible for ever-shifting nature of the river.

History of Shifting courses

In the early part of the 18th century, the Kosi flowed down the town of Purnea but it has worked west-ward across 120 km upto Saharsa-Darbhanga border. The left out channel at Purnea is now known as *Kalikosi.* During the period, the Kosi after issuing forth from Chatra turned east and southeast through Purnea and met the Ganga near Manihari and later on in its neighbourhood of Karhagola (1856). Since then, the river has been known to have curved out numerous parallel channels during its westward migration from Purnea (1736) to Nirmali (1950). The oscillating shifting nature and its rate of movement is clear.

The Kosi river harbours more than 110 species of teleostean fishes of 66 genera belonging to 27 families and 10 orders (Datta, Munshi and Srivastava, 1988). Best quality fish spawns of major carps come from the Kosi river during the first flush flood (Jhingram, 1975). The swamps, chaurs and wetlands are the natural abode of about 15 species of air-breathing fishes which are very well adapted to the physico-chemical conditions of these derelict water bodies. Several workshops were held on air-breathing fish culture of which the sixth one was held at CIFRI, Barrackpore, Calcutta, in December, 1982 (Dutta, Munshi and Choudhary, 1996).

Production potentiality of wetlands/swamps

Shell-fisheries and Mother of pearl Button Industries

Shell fisheries has been considered as one of the important aspects of the riverine-fisheries of North Bihar, in which such mollusks (*as Bivalves and Gastropods*) are collected from the Kosi river basin which form raw materials for the *mother of pearl* (MOP), button industries, and ornaments.

Recently, we have surveyed the different types of aquatic beds of the Kosi river systems to identify various mollusk collecting centres of North Bihar. Molluscan species so far collected from different aquatic systems of this area have been systematically identified and their commercial importance was evaluated, (Sharma et. al., 1983). Out of 19 species of Parreysia favidens, P. favidens var. *pinax, marcens, delete and Lamellidens corrianus* cater the requirements of MOP button industires. The empty shells after sun dried are processed for the production or lime, poultry feeds, mosaic tiles, fertilizers and chemicals (CaCo3) in these industries.

Present status of MOP button industries of North Bihar

The shell-fisheries in this belt had a glorious past because of the availability of raw materials in sufficient amount. The number of these industries declined from 3.50 to 151 tonne by 1940 which declined further to 103. Presently only 84 registered units (industries) run in the area which can hardly work for a few months in a year due to less supply of raw materials. These industries now have started manufacturing "Shell-ornaments" of different colours and varieties.

From the bivalve landing data obtained for the period of 1957 to 1971 from different sources such as CSO at Mehsi, we could assess the present status of MOP button indusries in this belt. The landing data of bivalves reflect their population structure in terms of biomass in the area.

A histogram of the annual landing data (1957-1971) of bivalves was plotted in which 5 spikes (2+1+2) of bivalve biomass (ton) were discernible at intervals of 2,3 and 4 years in a time span of 15 years. The appearance of spikes only at specific intervals of time is difficult to explain. The spikes and the curves (representing the biomass of the shells obtained in clusters of year) obey the general exponential equation $y = ae^{LK}$. Where a constant (321.23 ton) L is a factor indicating together, we had a straight line indicating steep declination of the bivalve population.

Production of Gastropods and lime Industries

The gastropod molluscs are eaten by common people, the shell of mollusks are used for manufacturing lime indigenously. Lime so manufactured by this process is consumed with tobacco and betel by local people.

Integrated aquaculture

In the country about 0.6 x 10^6 ha of water area is supposed to be swampy and unutilisable due to its weed infestation and derelict ecology. The culture of air-breathing fishes like Channa punctatus (garai), Anabas testudineus (Koi), Heteropneustes fossilis (singhi), clarias batrachus (magur), is usually integrated with the raising of aquatic cash crops much as makhana (Euryale ferox) or singhara (Trapa bispinosa). These operations considerably enhance the income of the farmers. A production of 1200 kg of air-breathing fishes and 3200 kg of Makhana per hectare during a season in Gunsar fish farm Darbhanga (Bihar) has been demostrated by the local farmers and authorities. Apart from these paddy-cum-fish culture is an age-old practice in these swamps. Vast lowlands are being used for paddy-cum-fish culture. The paddy which is grown in the marshy lands are hydrophytic in nature (Table 1) (Dehadrai, 1982)

The production of *makhana* (Euryale ferox) is produced from one acre of Jalkar (water bodies of different types). As per the recent survey report of the Central Bank of India, about 2,500 such types of Jalkars are located in Darbhanga district alone (Laal, 1981).

This unique freshwater system seems to be highly productive which could be developed further by innovating new eco-developmental strategies with the best utilization of the production potentialities of the area for the upliftment of the socio-economic condition of the inhabitants and for the prosperity of the region.

Studies show that the bio-geochemical cycle operating in the wetland / swamps is more complex owing to its specific pattern of transportation of nutrients. Hydrologic pathways include import of nutrients from the surface runoff and discharge from the rivers Kosi, Bagmati and Burhi Gandak in Biological monsoon. Biologic inputs include carbon and nitrogen fixation by benthic autotophs. Excreta of animals of the offshore region and birds guano add nutrients to the wetlands. This lends to eutrophication of the swamps which are bio-geochemically closed. Due to siltation, eutrophication of wetland/swamps and human habitation surrounding the water systems, there is terrestrialization of the large wetlands and chaurs in the region.

A series of reservoirs and canals are to be constructed in the upper reaches of the rivers for control of flood as well as drought. The dead river channels of the region may be converted into permanent canals to feed the chaurs and wetlands.

During drought season feeding of swamps / chaurs with water is essential. For this a series of reservoirs are to be constructed in the uppear reaches of the Kosi river. The *Maradhars* (deud Channels) are to be converted into permanent canals for feeding the chaurs.

REFERENCES

Choudhary, L. K. (1996): *Eco-biology of fishes and the status of fisheries of the river Kosi*. Ph.D. Thesis, Bhagalpur University, Bhagalpur, (Bihar) India.

Das, K. N. (1968): *Soil erosion and the problem of silting in the Kosi catchment*, J. Wat. Cons., India 16 (3-4), pp. 62-64.

Datta Munshi, J.S., J.ayashree Datta, L.K. Choudhary and P.K. Thakur, (1991): *Physiography of the Kosi river basin and formation of wetlands in north Bihar,* A unique freshwater system, J. Freshwater, Biol.3(2), pp. 105-122.

Datta Munshi, J.S. and M.P. Srivastava (1988): *Natural History of fishes and systematics of freshwater fishes of India*, Narendra Publishing House, Delhi, pp. 403.

Datta Munshi J.S. and S. Choudhary, (1996): *Ecology of Heteropneustes fossilis (Bloch) and air-breathing catfish*, South-East Asia, Narendra Publishing House, Delhi, pp. 174.

Datta Munshi, J.S and G.M. Hughes (1992): *Air-breathing fishes of India, their structure, function and life history,* Oxford and IBH publishing Co. Ltd., New Delhi, pp. 338.

Dehadrai, P.V. (1982): *Progress of the work on the techniques of culture of air-breathing fishes in swamps in Bihar*, Assam and Mysore centres of the Project, Second workshop held at Patna. Dec. 20-21, pp. 1-26

Jhingram, V.G. (1979): *Fish and fisheries of India*, Hindustan Publishing Corporation, Delhi, India, pp. 954.

Laal, A.K. (1981): *Studies on the ecology and productivity of swamps in North Bihar in relation to production of fishes and other agricultural commodities*, Ph.D. thesis, Bhagalpur University, pp. 163.

Rai, D.N. and J.S. Datta Munshi (1979): *Observations on diurnal changes of some physico-chemical factors of three swamps of Darbhanga Comp*, Physicol. Ecol 4(3): pp. 52-55.

Rai, D.N. (1980): *Ecological structure of certain swamps of Darbhanga* (Bihar) Ph.D. Thesis, Bhagalpur University, India.

Rai, D.N. and J. Datta Munshi (1979): *The influence of thick floating vegetation (water hyacinth: Eichhornia crassipes) on the physio-chemical environment of a freshwater wetland*, Hydrobiologia, 62, pp. 65-69.

Rai, D.N., P.K. Verma and J. Datta Munshi (1980): *Interactions between floating Trapa bispinosa and subermerged vegetation community in a fish pond of Bhagalpur*, Polskie archiwum Hydrobiology 27, pp. 137-142.

Rai, D.N. and J. Datta Munshi (1982): 'Ecological characteristics of Chaurs of North Bihar.' *In Wetlands II: Ecology and management*, Gopal B., Turner, R.E., Wetzal R.G. and Whigham, D.F. (eds) Int. Sci Rubi and Nat. Instt Ecol. Jaipur, India 89-95.

Singh, A.K. (1986): *Characteristics of silt deposition in the Kosi river basin*, Nat. Geo. 21 (1), pp. 107-115.

Sharma, V.P., S.P. Roy and D.N. Rai (1983): *Aquatic mollusks of Bhagalpur*, Biol. Bull. India 5 (2), pp. 147-155.

8. JAGADIS CHANDRA AND ENVIRONMENT

Chittabrata Palit

Patrick Geddes, biographer of Jagadis Chandra has written that he was a lover of nature in his boyhood. When he entered St. Xavier's College, he had intended to study Botany Honours on account of his inclination. However, he took Physics Honours on the advice of his favourite professor, Fr. Eugene Lafont.[1] He obtained Tripos in Physics, Chemistry and Mathematics from Cambridge University qualified in the IES. Later, he became a teacher of Physics at Presidency College. During this phase he engaged himself in research in Physics until 1916. He was awarded D. Sc. from London University in 1896 without oral examination on account of his fundamental Physics papers. Although his work was theoretically sound, there were shortcomings in the equipment used by him for exhibiting the applications due to adverse circumstances of colonial rule. He had to fabricate his equipment using local artisans. In 1901, he showed the application of his theory at the Royal Society in 1901. Marconi's demonstration of the same application was related free from blemish. Later, Marconi patented his discovery and was awarded Nobel Prize. Although, Jagadis Chandra was the pioneer, he was not interested in patenting his discovery. After this, Jagadis Chandra turned his attention to Botany. Ashis Nandy has written that he switched over to Botany after realising his limitations as a Physicist.[2] This is not correct. He was always attracted by Botany. There was scope for research in Botany in our agrarian country. His attention was diverted towards Botany possibly for this reason. However, he did not dissociate himself completely from Physics. He tried to detect life and pulsation of plants with the aid of electromagnetic waves. He fabricated his famous equipment, Crescograph, on this basis. He could have obtained Nobel Prize for this discovery but he never tried for it.

Study of plant genetics enables us to conserve, spread and control production. Jagadis Chandra's subsequent research was directed towards development of a variety of seeds through hybridisation. What he had set down in his research papers in English, he explained in simple terms in Bengali in his popular science book *Abyakta* ('Unsaid'). He wrote in *Gachher Katha* ('Story of Tree')—

> গাছেরা কি কিছু বলে? অনেকে বলিবেন, এ অবার কেমন প্রশ্ন? গাছ কি কোনদিন কথা কহিয়া থাকে? মানুষে কি সব কথা ফুটিয়া বলে? আর যা ফুটিয়া বলে না, তাহা কি কথা নয়? আমাদের একটি খোকা আছে, সে সব কথা ফুটিয়া বলতে পারেনা; আবার ফুটিয়া যে দুই চারিটি কথা বলে, তাহাও এমন আধো আধো ও ভাঙা ভাষা যে, অপরের সাধ্য নাই তাহার অর্থ বুঝিতে পারে। কেবল তাহা নয়। বলে না : চক্ষু, মুখ ও হাত নাড়া, মাথা নাড়া প্রভৃতির দ্বারা আকার ইঙ্গিতে অনেক কথা বলে, আমরা তাহাও বুঝিতে পারি, অন্যে বুঝিতে পারে না।
>
> ....
>
> আগে যখন একা মাঠে কিংবা পাহাড়ে বেড়াইতে যাইতাম, তখন সব খালি খালি লাগিত। তারপর গাছ, পাখি, কীট-পতঙ্গদিগকে ভালোবাসিতে শিখিয়াছি, সে অবধি তাহাদের অনেক কথা বুঝিতে পারি, আগে যাহা পারিতাম না। এই যে গাছগুলি কোনো কথা বলে না, ইহাদের যে আবার একটা জীবন আছে, আমাদের মতো আহার করে, দিন দিন বাড়ে, আগে এ সব কিছুই জানিতাম না। এখন বুঝিতে পারিতেছি। এখন ইহাদের মধ্যেও আমাদের মতো অভাব, দুঃখ-কষ্ট দেখিতে পাই। জীবন ধারণ করিবার জন্য ইহাদিগকেও সর্বদা ব্যস্ত থাকিতে হয়। [3]

A summary of the extract of the above article is given below:

Do trees speak? Humans do not always express themselves merely through speech. A little child expresses himself not merely by the few words he can lisp but by his articulation ... We come to realise that, they always can not speak. Trees are living organism who eat, grow and feel like us.

We cannot consider trees to be inanimate, after reading

Jagadis Chandra's sympathetic treatment. He has spoken about conservation of plant life in this fashion. Jagadis Chandra has further clarified the relationship of trees with our environment in his article *Udbhider Janma O Mrityu* ('Life and Death of Plant').

'আমরা যখন শ্বাস-প্রশ্বাস গ্রহণ করি, প্রশ্বাসের সঙ্গে একপ্রকার বিষাক্ত বায়ু বাহির হইয়া যায় তাহাকে অঙ্গারক বায়ু বলে। ইহা যদি পৃথিবীতে জমিতে থাকে তবে সকল জীবজন্তু অল্প দিনের মধ্যে এই বিষাক্ত বায়ু গ্রহণ করিয়া মরিয়া যাইতে পারে। বিধাতার করুণার কথা ভাবিয়া দেখ। যাহা জীবজন্তুর পক্ষে বিষ, গাছ তাহাই আহার করিয়া বাতাস পরিষ্কার করিয়া দেয়। গাছের পাতার উপর যখন সূর্যের আলোক পড়ে, তখন পাতাগুলি সূর্যের তেজের সাহায্যে অঙ্গারক বায়ু হইতে অঙ্গার বাহির করিয়া গাছকে বাড়াইতে থাকে।[4]

A summary of the extract of the above article is given below:

The poison we exhale would have killed all animal life on earth but this poison (Carbon Dioxide) is a food for trees which they remove from the atmosphere when the Sun shines every day.

The above extract expresses the cleansing role of trees for human benefit. The role of trees in our preservation by ridding environmental pollution has been expressed by Jagadis Chandra. Our complimentary relationship with trees has been well expressed by Jagadis Chandra in his article *Udbhider Janma O Mrityu* ('Life and Death of Plant').

এখন বুঝিতে পারিতেছি, আলোই জীবনের মূল। সূর্যের কিরণ শরীরে ধারণ করিয়াই গাছ বাড়িতে থাকে। গাছের শরীরে সূর্যের কিরণ আবদ্ধ হইয়া আছে। কাঠে আগুণ ধরাইয়া দিলে যে আলো ও তাপ বাহির হয় তাহা সূর্যেরই তেজ। গাছ ও শস্য আলো ধরিবার ফাঁদ। জন্তুরা গাছ খাইয়া প্রাণ ধারণ করে; গাছে যে সূর্যের তেজ আছে তাহা এই প্রকারে আবার জন্তুর শরীরে প্রবেশ করে। শস্য আহার না করিলে আমরাও বাঁচিতে পারিতাম না। ভাবিয়া দেখিতে গেলে আমরাও আলো আহার করিয়া বাঁচিয়া আছি।[5]

A summary of the extract of the above article is given below:

Light is the source of life. Trees absorb sunlight. Heat produced by burning wood is actually solar energy, which is entrapped by plant life. Animals feed on plants and the solar energy of plants enter animal body. As a matter of tree, we live by absorbing sunlight.

The above extract does not merely explain the complementary nature of relationship and the unity between plant and animal kingdom, it also interprets the life and death of plants and their thirst for light. We shall discuss later his interpretation of the process of plants extracting light as food also called photosynthesis. He has also explained in greater detail about the mystery of plant life in his article *Nirbak Jeeban* ('Silent Life').

> গাছের প্রকৃত ইতিহাস সমুদ্ধার করিতে হইলে গাছের নিকটই যাইতে হইবে। সেই ইতিহাস অতি জটিল এবং বহু রহস্যপূর্ণ। সেই ইতিহাস উদ্ধার করিতে হইলে বৃক্ষ ও যন্ত্রের সাহায্যে জন্ম হইতে মৃত্যু পর্যন্ত মুহূর্তে তাহার ক্রিয়াকলাপ লিপিবদ্ধ করিতে হইবে। লিপি বৃক্ষের স্বলিখিত এবং স্বাক্ষরিত হওয়া চাই। ইহাতে মানুষের কোনো হাত থাকিবে না; কারণ মানুষ তাহার স্বপ্রণোদিত ভাব দ্বারা অনেক সময় প্রতারিত হয়।[6]

A summary of the extract of the above article is given below:

To understand a tree it is necessary to record the history of its lifetime with a suitable equipment. The result must be authenticated by the tree itself, for humans are often misguided by preconceived motions.

In this article he has informed us how he measured the duration of sensation the flow of excitement and involuntary pulsation plants, shy or otherwise, with the aid of crescograph. He has thus explained plants genetics in simple terms. His description of the dance of Banchandal is faultless. Jagadis Bose wrote—

> বনচাঁড়াল গাছ দিয়া উদ্ভিদের স্পন্দনশীলতা অনায়াসে দেখা যাইতে পারে। ইহার ক্ষুদ্র পাতাগুলি আপনা-আপনি নৃত্য করে। লোকের বিশ্বাস যে, হাতের তুড়ি দিলেই নৃত্য আরম্ভ হয়। গাছের সংগীতবোধ আছে কি না বলিতে পারিতনা, কিন্তু বনচাঁড়ালের নৃত্যের সহিত তুড়ির কোনো সম্বন্ধ নাই। তরুস্পন্দনের সাড়ালিপি পাঠ করিয়া জন্তু ও উদ্ভিদের স্পন্দন যে একই নিয়মে নিয়মিত তাহা নিশ্চয়রূপে বলিতে পারিতেছে।[7]

A summary of the above extract is given below —

Pulsation of plants is easily observable in Banchandal whose leaves dance on their own. It is not true that they start dancing at the snap of fingers as people say. By studying the pulsation of the plant, he was convinced of the similarity of the pulsation of plants and animals by studying recording of responses to stimuli on the plant.

In a similar fashion, the indication of death of a plant has also been detected. He told us about the creation, conservation and death of a plant in this manner. I conclude this topic with the following extract —

> এই আমাদের মূক সঙ্গী, আমাদের দ্বারের পার্শ্বে নিঃশব্দে যাহাদের জীবনের লীলা চলিতেছে তাহাদের গভীর মর্মের কথা তাহারা ভাষাহীন অক্ষরে লিপিবদ্ধ করিয়া দিল এবং তাহাদের জীবনের চাঞ্চল্য ও মরণের আক্ষেপ আজ আমাদের দৃষ্টির সম্মুখে প্রকাশিত করিল। জীব ও উদ্ভিদের মধ্যে যে কৃত্রিম ব্যবধান রচিত হইয়াছিল তাহা দূরীভূত হইল। কল্পনার ও অতীত অনেকগুলি সংবাদ আজ বিজ্ঞান স্পষ্ট ভাষায় ঘোষণা করিয়া বহুত্বের ভিতরে একত্ব প্রমাণ করিল। [৪]

A summary of the extract of the above article is given below:

Our dumb companions, who live next to our doorstep have expressed their profound secret in their speechless language. The excitement of their life and throes of their death stand revealed. The artificial barrier between plant and animal life has been removed. Science has announced clearly the unity in diversity, which was hitherto in the realm of imagination.

His reflections on environment were not restricted to life and death of plants. He conceived our unity with the cosmos. We can give an example from his scientific and philosophical article *Akash Spandan O Akash Sambhab* Jagat ('Sky Tremor and Sky Originated World').

> সূর্যকিরণ লালিত উদ্ভিদ ভোজন করিয়াই প্রাণিগণ জীবন ধারণ করিতেছে ও বর্ধিত হইতেছে। তবে দেখা যায় যে, এই ভূপৃষ্ঠের প্রায় সর্ব গতির মূলে সূর্যকিরণ। আকাশের স্পন্দন দ্বারাই পৃথিবী স্পন্দিত হইতেছে জীবনের স্রোত বহিতেছে। .... জীবনের চরমোৎকর্ষ

মানব। এ কথা সর্ব সময়ের জন্য ঠিক নয়। যে শক্তি আদিম জীববিন্দুকে মনুষ্যে উন্নীত করিয়াছে, যাহার উচ্ছ্বাসে নিরাকার মহাশূন্য হইতে এই বহুরূপী জগৎ ও তদবৎ বিস্ময়কর জীবন উৎপন্ন হইয়াছে, আজিও সেই মহাশক্তি সমভাবে প্রবাহিত হইতেছে। উর্ধ্বাভিমুখেই সৃষ্টির গতি। আর সম্মুখে অন্তহীন কাল এবং অনন্ত উন্নতি প্রসারিত।[৭]

A summary of the extract of the above article is given below:

Animals live and grow eating plants nourished by sunlight. It is observed that sunlight is behind all movement on earth. The current of life flows as earth moves impelled by the tremor of the sky. Man is the model of living organisms. However, this is not universally true. The primeval energy which has raised man from microscopic organisms, whose upsurge has created this picturesque world and wondrous life—the same energy is still flowing with equal vigour. Creation always moves in upward direction. And, ahead extends infinite time and boundless progress.

He has explained this primeval energy in a different way in another article. He had imagined this energy as Mahadeb. In the article *Bhagirathir Utsa Sandhane* ('In search of the source of Bhagirathi'), Jagadis Chandra has made the river utter that it has originated in the matted hair of Mahadeb. He went to the source of the river while travelling in the Himalayas. He gained an impression of the matted hair of Mahadeb from the Nanda Debi and Trishul peaks. He felt that the cloud rising from the cluster of rays on the Nanda Debi peak was the matted hair of Mahadeb. He had no doubt that the river rose here. He has written —

শিব ও রুদ্র! রক্ষক ও সংহারক। এখন ইহার অর্থ বুঝিতে পারিলাম। মানসচক্ষে উৎস হইতে বারিকণার সাগরোদ্দেশে যাত্রা ও পুনরায় উৎসে প্রত্যাবর্তন স্পষ্ট দেখিতে পাইলাম, এই মহাচক্রপ্রবাহিত স্রোতে সৃষ্টি ও প্রলয়-রূপ পরস্পরের পার্শ্বে স্থাপিত দেখিলাম।

সম্মুখে আকাশভেদী যে পর্বতশ্রেণী দেখিতেছি, হিমানূরূপ বারিকণা উহাদের শরীরাভ্যন্তরে প্রবেশ করিতেছে। প্রবেশ করিয়া মহাবিক্রমে উহাদের দেহ বিদীর্ণ করিতেছে। চ্যুত শিখর বজ্রনিনাদে নিম্নে পতিত হইতেছে।

সম্মুখে আকাশভেদী যে পর্বতশ্রেণী দেখিতেছি, হিমাণুরূপ বারিকণারাই নিম্নে শুভ্র তুষার-শয্যা রচনা করিয়া রাখিয়াছে|ভগ্ন শৈল এই তুষার শয্যায় শায়িত হইল। তখন কণাগুলি একে অন্যকে ডাকিয়া বলিল, "আইস, আমরা ইহার অস্থি দিয়া পৃথিবীর দেহ নতুন করিয়া নির্মাণ করি।[10]

A summary of the extract of the above article is given below:

He visualised *Shib* and *Rudra* respectively, as the protector and destroyer of the cosmos in the cycle of the river from its source to the sea and its return to its source as icy droplets on the mountain range.

The writer wanted to know the source of the river and he was able to get the reply. The present question, however, is to whom does the river belong. There is tremendous water dispute and selfishness among states and nations through which Ganga flows. Although the problem is due to pressure of population, but the beneficial aspect of the river has been a prey to this selfishness, which has revealed the problem of environment.

Jagadis Chandra had also involved himself in another environmental problem. In the 1920s, the people as also the government got worried about the problem of water hyacinth. Water hyacinth created not only stagnant swamps, but also breeding ground for mosquitoes. It is closely associated with malarial epidemic. It destroys the fertility of land and harms agriculture. Water Hyacinth Committee was formed to examine the problem. Jagadis Chandra was elected the chairman of the Committee in 1921.[11] The Committee's work was to suggest means for preventing extension and rooting out water hyacinth. Meetings were held at Bose Institute. At the meeting on August 16, 1921, he said that it was necessary to pass an enactment for removal and destruction of water hyacinth. Secondly, it was necessary to find out a method for eradication. It was necessary to examine the efficacy of the patent spray invented by Griffith, as there was some doubt as to whether it could root out water hyacinth and the quantum of poison was not known. It was necessary to conduct scientific research regarding the life and death of this floating plant as all plants have a period of degeneration which had to be determined. There should be an enactment for population support. It would be necessary to explain to the people the ill effects of water hyacinth including its capacity to harm agriculture and fishery, its obstacle to navigability and its role in the spread of malaria. In another meeting of February 21, 1922, he said that it was expensive to destroy water hyacinth by burning. It would be preferable to bury the plant instead as it would act as manure. Destruction by poison or steam was not possible. It was necessary to find out alternative methods. For the present existing methods might continue. We may hear the rest from an article by Jagadananda Roy, published in Ashwin 1329 issue of *Prabasi*.

Jagadis Chandra felt that there were four ways of destroying water hyacinth, viz.,

(i) Destruction by stimulating the growth of fungus like organism.
(ii) Destruction by steam.
(iii) Destruction by sprinkling poison.
(iv) Destruction by uprooting the plants from water.

According to Jagadis Chandra, it is not possible to destroy the roots of water hyacinth by the first three methods. Although time and money is required, the fourth method is the best as water hyacinth is rooted out . Jagadis had suggested production of manure or paper pulp from water hyacinth for meeting expenses. Research in this area had been undertaken at Bose Institute. Jagadis Chandra had appealed both to the state and the people to exert to the utmost to eradicate this menace. [12]

The environmental problems associated with water hyacinth did not escape Jagadis Chandra's notice. This is the final observation on Jagadis Chandra's concern with ecological issues.

NOTES AND REFERENCES

1. Patrick Geddes, *The Life and Work of Sir Jagadish C. Bose*, Longmans, Green & Co., London, 1920.
2. Ashis Nandy, *Alternative Sciences*, Oxford University Press, Delhi, 1995.
3. *Abyakta*, J. C. Bose, Bangiya Vigyan Parishad, Cal. 1921, Article: 'Gachher Katha,' pp. 12, 13.
4. *Abyakta*, J. C. Bose, Article: 'Udbhider Janma O' Mrityu,' pp. 17.
5. *Abyakta*, J. C. Bose, Article: 'Udbhider Janma O' Mrityu,' pp. 18.

6. *Abyakta*, J. C. Bose, Article: 'Nirbak Jeeban,' pp. 66, 67.
7. *Abyakta*, J. C. Bose, Article: 'Nirbak Jeeban,' Sub-topic: pp. 72.
8. *Abyakta*, J. C. Bose, Article: 'Nirbak Jeeban,' Sub-topic: pp. 74.
9. *Abyakta*, J. C. Bose, Article: *Akash Spandan O' Akash Sambhab Jagat*, pp. 7.
10. *Abyakta*, J. C. Bose, Article: *Bhagirathir Utsa Sandhane*, pp. 52.
11. Bengal, Water Hyacinth Committee, 1921.
12. Jagadananda Roy, *Kachuri Pana, Prabasi*, Ashwin, 1329.

9. ENVIRONMENTAL ETHICS:
Great Future

Debashis Guha

For most of us, the members of civil states who remain civil or at least wants to be so, "environmental crises" is a dreaded expression because the raging Apocalypse around us mostly by virtue of our acts is surely not welcome. Hence, apart from many mind boggling physical solutions to prevent the dreaded event, we are now at hand another one, the theoretical and the practical effort to stop the Apocalypse for now (or for a longer period). We are speaking about "environmental crises" which presses on us its call to stop the crises. Can it really do so? To answer this we ought to remember that the way of looking at "environment" from *our* way of looking at things, its "beyondness" amounts to some kind of a "disconnectedness" whereas the truth may be an "involvedness" or a "organic relation"—some sort of "oneness" if we like to be more metaphorical but not metaphysical. From this angle, "environment" appears not as an Indian or Pakistani or American would explain, or in the way you and me or he or she or they might explain, for *us* "environment" is an "integrity" notion. We shall further see that this "integrity" notion does help us in empathizing with agonies of the environment or of earth at least, lest, "environmental crises" is a dreaded notion.

Keeping these technical (not so metaphorical) and implicit (most hopefully metaphorical but not metaphysical) meaning of "environment" we may now explain "environmental science" as a systematic and scientific study of human environment and their role in it. On the other hand, "Environmental studies," a little different from the science, deals with several environmental topics as broad as including social aspects of the environment. Such concern is not unscientific rather, *trans-scientific* as it covers the concerns of non-scientists as well. Now if we bring in "ecology" as a science here for a contrast, it studies the intricately manifold relationships between all living entities and their environment. We have seen that such a study is predominantly biological. Environmental science, in its extremely "broad" notion does reveal the close affinity with ecological science and at times one has a feeling that 'trans-human' notion of environmental science is hardly any different from ecological science. Yet, a thin line a difference may be that the broadest sense of environmental science need not be taken as predominantly biological for it covers social and other non-biological aspects as well. In this sense, environmental science may be looked upon as more broad in its task or subject matter than ecological science. Truly, environmental studies as we have seen just now, appears to be broader than a purely scientifically oriented ecological and environmental science. We do realize that environmental issues and environmental crises may be as broad as to what purely scientific issues might not touch upon. Hence, we maintain henceforth that within the broader context of environmental studies in "environmental ethics" makes a special mark because it is often thought as one good aid to resolve crises in ecological and environmental sciences. It seriously takes up the crises caused by the great manipulator and marauder—the Homo sapiens. What we get is that the deliberate or intentionally acting human beings with their "junkyard" philosophy of life are placed crucial in serious environmental crises in modern times. It is here that we doubly realize why ethical matters creep in environmental science and environmental studies. We will now analyze the notion, "environmental ethics" and also "ecological ethics."

In order to perform our task of clarifying the meaning of "environmental ethics" we can either propose a definition of the same, which we believe is more or less satisfactory enough or else we do not propose logical or other types of definition. Instead, we try to analyze first the meaning of the components of the expression: "environmental ethics." There is no doubt that we should first start analyzing the meaning of "ethics" and then "ethics" in "environmental ethics."

To clarify what is "ethics," a strict or logical definition is not needed at all because formal or non-formal definitions are either incomplete assertions of what are the tasks of ethics or are unsatisfactory statements of what one thinks ethics should be like. The latter efforts are more injurious to ethics as they resulted into several misconceptions like; ethics is nothing but moral science and study of social and personal morality. Whereas the former effort, a little less subjective but myopic, ends up in leaving out same task or the other. A careful reader of the subject finds quite often than not that the practical; the professional and the virtue ethical tasks are left out. It is desirable therefore that we become more careful qua analysts of the various tasks of ethics and thereby construct a normative definition of "ethics" if that is at all needed after so much of painstaking.

First is to mention that ethics is a branch of study within the broad field of philosophy, which attempts at doing many important things barring constructing prohibitions of sex and dos' and don'ts in personal life. Rather, ethics is concerned with three major tasks of analyzing the *truth and meaning of ethical language*, which is to clarify the sense of important ethical notions like good, right, justice, duty, obligation etc. We call this the *metaethical* task of ethics, which also includes the discussion about *justifications* of ethical standards or norms. With this, we come to *normative* ethics or discussion about the *bases* of *ethical judgments* of intentional human actions having far-reaching social and personal impacts. The explanations of the standards, their various implications and use all come in this purview. The case of having a norm is also related to arguments for not having one or any such norms as is with the former task of ethics where we question the meaningfulness and truth of ethical language. In this context we often talk about *ethical scepticism*, its logic and its limits. Such scepticism is about norms, language and the practical application of ethical norms as well. Defying scepticism we now say that apart from the normative and the metaethical tasks, *practical or applied* task of ethics is equally important in which, we find out ways to resolve value-laden ethical problems of practical life. Apart from these three tasks, we have some other tasks of ethics. One among them, which is arguably old but lost in the controversy of philosophy or psychology, is to analyze the *psychological bases* of ethics. It is believed that without proper clarification of the psychological sphere in ethics one cannot realize what it is to speak about 'motives,' 'intentions,' 'free will,' voluntariness and non-voluntariness in actions, and also about moral development and moral evolution in human beings. Closely related to this is another old but forgotten task called the virtue oriented discussion or simply, virtue-ethics, which is concerned with the nature, kinds and inculcation of basic ethical virtues in place of being theory-laden. Moreover, we now speak of occupational ethics and professional ethics within ethics because we realize that both the forms of human life need serious consideration about the ethically just, right and good as well as facing the value-crises in decision-making leading to pertinent resolution and formulations for guidance in social life. We will shortly realize that *environmental ethics* is also within ethics or that among many tasks that ethics performs; one is to deal with ethical concern in environmental studies (and also ecological studies). Ethics has become so wonderfully vibrant a subject within philosophy that it has perhaps become as unpredictable as the sciences to crystallize in exact terms what it could do any more. The performatives of ethics being so dynamic that it would be a little foolish to put a bracket here and say that these are the tasks and if you have understood them, you have known what ethics is. Yet, one might be satisfied enough to know what a general statement of "ethics," "ethical" and "ethicality" means.

We should keep in mind that an ethical discussion is "what pertains to ethics" and not simply moral churning of some moralists as moral philosophy or ethics is neither moral science of fashionable ethicists nor mere casuistry of Church fathers. Nor is it handmaiden of moralists who have taken the sacred task of building great individual and national characters by dint of formulating what to do and what not to do. We need to remember that any misgiving about environmental ethics might arise out of not understanding what ethical philosophy does and what it does not attempt at all. Another question may be that ethics is not truly ethics if it has nothing to do with metaphysics and religion. We shall remind here that ethics, metaphysics and religion are different categories altogether for their nature and tasks are different. Hence, they are not one and the same but that does not mean that they are completely unrelated. In fact, history of ethics is a testimony to the relation of ethics, metaphysics and religion, but the question is what purpose does the relation serve? We should understand that there is no room for confusing ethics and religion, and ethics and metaphysics. Truly speaking, there are metaphysical ethics and religious ethics as also metaphysical and/or religious environmental ethics, but we have to peruse into what they do or strive to do, and the way they contribute or they do not contribute in any way to the growth of ethics and environmental ethics.

It is proper now that we correlate "environment" and "ethics" in "environmental ethics" to reveal what is its nature and what are its functions. We should also discuss what the significance of putting together "ecology" and "ethics" in "ecological ethics" is. Precisely now we should state that for all practical purposes we have resorted to the use of "environmental ethics" rather than "ecological ethics" because we know that both the conceptions are quite different but closely related, and that a *study* of environment in its extremely *broader significance* does cover a study of ecology as a science to a great extent. However, the unique 'biological' overtone of ecological study, which is not predominantly oriented towards social, economic, political and other factors, does not rule out or even neglect to smallest extent the ethical orientation. Hence, it would be equally important to speak of "ecological ethics" separately but the unique 'biological' concerns in ecology that permeates ethical scrutiny is adequately taken care of by environmental ethical concerns. A separate biologically oriented ethical discussion may not be redundant or even superfluous but well covered under a much broader discussion, which we take as "environmental ethics" where it simply means any *ethical discussion pertaining to environmental matters or matters concerning the biotic world, the inanimate world, the components covering this animate and inanimate world and the manipulated and modified world of the human beings.*

It is here that we have to realize what the meaning of "pertaining to ethics" is. This is now not at all a difficult matter for us to understand because what pertains to ethical discussion has been unequivocally stated before. The main problem is does it make any sense if we now place the environmental study in this context. Or, we may ask, is it sensible to juxtapose environmental concerns and ethical concerns? It is sensible no doubt, for the reasons are fairly simple. First, we have to accept the argument that any discussion within the field of ethics need not be so broad as to cover all the tasks of ethics. No body would accuse us of a gravity of mistake if we discuss metaphysics and epistemology and yet justify that such discussion "pertain to philosophy." Similarly, no one accuses us of not doing something "pertaining to ethics" if we merely discuss about norms and practicability of norms. Going by this reasoning we ought to realize that unique way of discussing ethics within the fold of environmental studies (and also ecological studies) should not be conceived as undertaking all the tasks of ethics which we have enlisted earlier on. Second part is that what pertains to ethics in environmental studies is to find out how relevant is the question of *ethical values* in environmental studies. More precisely, do some environmental practical problems raise problems of ethical value as well? It is here we have to realize that *ethically* good, right, just, obligatory, dutiful are some crucial value notions, which does emerge prominently while we consider some environmental problems of concern in modern times. At this point one is reminded of an important problem to be resolved, that is, about the human centred understanding of the ethical values. Do we have to speak of right, good etc. only in terms of human good, right and so on or does it make sense to understand them in a broader perspective of life? However, in so far as intentional acts of man and evaluations are concerned, we do speak of ethical values of such actions only but those decisions and actions as influencing other animate and inanimate beings and things, raises question about the validity of the good and the right of these beings and things. Similarly, the question of value of human beings vis-à-vis the value of other beings and things make some prominence, which is understandably unavoidable. We have to consider this problem as well at a proper place. Third, we should realize that *metaethical* concern like the clarification of the *sense* of "environmental ethics" and the *justification* of or *possibility* of an environmental ethics does make a sense or else what we have been doing thus far would be labelled as sheer nonsense. Fourth, an inquiry about the possibility of ecological norms (environmental so to say) or ecological principles along with well framed ecological codes as forming an independent and important part of the body of ethical norms or principles should be thoroughly taken care of. There is, however, some controversy and to my mind some misconceptions about ecological principles and codes forming by themselves a body of ethical principle or ethical norm. However, there is no doubt in my mind about ethical first principle like deontology and teleology and some secondary principles of morality like compassionate and emphatic acts have been found proactive in the context of the real life dynamics of applying ethics. Again, in this context it would be a good case to analyze whether or not ecological principles and codes as so-called independent bases of morality are themselves proactive. Here we have to inquire about the soundness of calling environmental ethics as a branch of applying ethics. Or, should we treat it as an independent branch in ethical studies as we treat professional and occupational ethics as distinct from applied or practical ethics? Finally, we have the possibility of discussing about basic virtues forming a part of human character (by virtue of being acquired dispositions or traits) which are deemed essential for the resolution of any ethically charged environmental problem. It is a pertinent question to ask whether or not without being a virtuous person first, someone can at all apply ethical knowledge of principles and codes to resolve value crises in environmental studies. Such discussion about virtues and virtuosity avoids to a great extent a reference to ethical norms but it is academically interesting to find out whether or not such an attempt to avoid certain things are possible.

In any case, what I was trying to justify is clear by now. In my mind there is absolutely no doubt about the involvement of ethics as a branch of philosophy dealing with the important tasks it performs, in the field of environmental studies and ecology. To be precise, many issues in environmental and ecological studies are not merely scientific and practical they also raise questions of ethical values (of goodness and rightness etc.), norms, application of norms and virtues. We should remember one important thing in this context that many matters in environmental studies are in fact *interdisciplinary* in nature as it gets related to not only ecology, geography, botany, forestry and so on but with sociology, economics, politics and also philosophy and ethics. Hence, it is not difficult to justify that the problem of "environmental refugees" and their rehabilitation owing to construction of mega multipurpose river projects remains unresolved if we do not take care of the ethical value questions apart from many other questions. We have to remember that the big question of ethical ought or should or, what we call ethically *desirable* should be properly addressed to because practical problems of urgency does not get resolved without an ethical face. If we boast to be civilized, it is not merely material and mental, it is something more, it asks about whether or not we are ethically right, just and good, that is, whether or not we take care of ethical values as well. We should also remember that practical decision-making in the fields of environment and ecology is a queer phenomenon for such decision-making, apart from scientific feedbacks, some concern about what is desirable or ought to be done is most important. From this, we find that there are at least three important problems regarding the "justification" of environmental ethics as an independent field of study. Before moving on to consider some extremely important issues in environmental ethics, we would like to provide some reasons behind the evolution of ethics-talk in environmental studies. This will give us a glimpse of what concerns ethicists and environmentalists alike to come together for an active resolution for the welfare of the existential. Indirectly, this discussion would reveal the value of the study of environmental ethics.

Jorgen Randers and Donnelly Meadows in their excellent essay on "The Carrying Capacity of Our Global Environment: A Look at the Alternatives" in *Western man and environmental ethics* edited by J. G. Barbour goes like this: "Because our environment—the earth—is finite, growth of human population and industrialization cannot continue indefinitely... but its consequences pose an unprecedented challenge to mankind... In deciding on the ethical bases for making the trade-offs which will confront us in near future because in a limited world we cannot masteries everything for everyone".[1] Randers and Meadows write these lines keeping in mind that if man did not exist on earth, importantly there will be perhaps no one to cry about environment and environmental ethics. Yet, we should be equally concerned about the way man is going in this limited space, with limited resources at hand. The authors are also concerned about earth ethics in particular and the future of the next progeny in terms of their welfare. The authors have thus a strong basis to justify that environmental ethics (earth ethics in particular), is possible if and only if the finiteness of earth environment is a truism and our urge to grow, develop and be happy for generations to come not so limited. Hence, one grave ethical concern is the way we should at present encounter and use our limited environment for welfare. The authors have meticulously shown in their essay that agricultural land, forests, and minerals everything is limited and our means for material growth has been utterly exploitative. The question is should we continue this way? Should we not take care for the future generations? Interestingly, here are bare remarks about the welfare of animals, plants and inanimate objects; though one can understand that ethics is basically a human affair and its different tasks need not avoid the questions concerning human beings.

If we are not immediately so fussy about such human centeredness, we may accept the truth the much ethical concern about desirability of decisions taken by man in limited earth resources boils down to the following things:

(a) Our continuous current *growth practices* would certainly lead us to an environmental crunch including a cultural and economic denomination of the human race;
(b) Our objective is to *maximize* the physical *benefits* of the *people alive today* would lead us to reject concerns for people infesting the earth in future and
(c) Our present actions influencing the physical conditions of earth tend to a "global non-equilibrium" tending to a global catastrophe.

From these we have fairly clear idea about three natural human aspirations. One cannot easily denounce them as unethical on face value because there is no point in "non-growth," "non-maximization of benefits" and "individual and local no-growth." What is unethical is that "short term objectives" of human beings are *only desirable* and "global equilibrium" is a *mere utopia*. It is therefore that ethics-talk or the talk of the "desirable," the "just" and the "good" of "long term objectives" and "global equilibrium" comes to the fore. Equally true is that the so-called 'unethical' things as stated above needs to be justified as 'unethical' in clear terms or else our convictions cannot be taken to be justified on face value. The unethicality of the short-term objectives of human beings depends on the *criteria of unethicality*. In environmental ethics the broad criteria fixed for calling short term benefits of man on earth at the present time as "unethical" is general welfare or simply "welfarism." Though "welfarism" appears to be an economical concept and despite the close relation between ecology and economy (the oikos terms), it should be understood in the context of ethical criterion as *the maximization of good over evil in the overall existential situations*. This would cover the situation or the environment in which we live and in which other animate and inanimate beings and things exists as being enveloped by the essential elements around them to a great limit beyond earth, which sustains or help sustain life and things on earth. But this is an extremely broad conception of "welfare." People prefer to avoid vagueness in the conception by replacing "good over evil" in more concrete terms as we find in "well-being." However, what is "well-being" is often blurred by several misconceptions ranging from physical prosperity to solace of soul. It cannot be comfortably replaced by older concepts like "happiness" unless a more blunt "benefit" is not used as an alternative. So it would stand as "what is beneficial" to the existence as whole, notwithstanding human needs and aspirations. Some people clarify it more by saying it should primarily keep in mind the need of the neediest among human beings notwithstanding human urge to grow and develop along with other beings on earth.

Whatever may be the vagueness in "welfare," the "beneficial" (if it is a clearer notion), need not be taken merely as either economically beneficial or physically beneficial or materially beneficial. Most of the modern environmental ethicists tend to transcend gross conception of "benefit" or "well-being" and without being necessarily metaphysical, holds that some material advantages might be downplayed under the idea of "quality of life." Is this a clear conception of well-being?

Many people harping on "quality-of-life" as the mantra of well-being think that a non-metaphysical conception is altogether impossible because its main proponents have exactly in mind the metaphysically oriented life as "qualitative." Some would hold that first it is important to conceive the whole existence as becoming of Pure Being, which is essentially "One," and as such, the existence in itself is complete, harmonious and good. If human life is led in accordance with the "sustenance" of the "pureness," "harmony," "goodness" and "Completeness of Being," it is "qualitative," therefore, "well being" of the person is guaranteed. Such "well being" is thus inextricably bound with many *non-metaphysical* conceptions as well says the metaphysicians. Others who are more soaked in such philosophy of life advocate divinization of the existence as such and avoid such veiled assertions like Absolute Being or Pure Being because "Being and being" duality of the Heideggerian legacy had its own non-metaphysical (even anti-metaphysical) import. A clear divinization would tend to almost the same idea of "sustenance" of the perennial "one." Yet, the non-metaphysical and anti-metaphysical ways of interpreting "quality-of-life" may have a different conception of "sustenance" altogether. The claimants of "scientific sustenance" of the whole of existence would speak in another relatively understandable language. They would speak about the growth and development of human beings with other beings in a fine-tuned equilibrium or a state from where a conception of nature in entirety tending to a thermodynamic equilibrium or entropic state is not conceivable in far future thus assuring the *long-term objective* of *liveable life for future*. It has to be mentioned here that the objective of a "liveable life for future" or what is a scientific way of qualitative life or well-being cannot and need not be refuted by the metaphysicians. The metaphysician and the proponents of divinization base their arguments differently as their presuppositions about man and nature are radically different from the material conception of man and nature.

In any case the metaphysicians, the scientists and the anti-metaphysicians as well derive several "qualitative' ways to live a life on earth. It is believed that *unnecessary* infliction of pain or harm on animate and inanimate existence is adverse to 'qualitative life' on earth. Though one animal does consume another animal and one animal does consume other life-forms, which need not be reversed by whims. In any case, hermits' ethics of rigorism does not find a suitable place on earth as that might be too good for us to live. It is equally believed by the metaphysicians, non-metaphysicians and anti-metaphysicians that all people who live today on earth are as valuable as all people to infest earth henceforth (and hopefully for another millennium), therefore, we ought to use and reuse the limited resources on earth and around it in a manner so that growth and development of the human race in future is not hindered or gets poor in any way.

Keeping these things in mind, we are now in a position to say that in environmental ethics, we do not conceive of one basis of or one criterion of ethicality and unethicality, we conceive of many criteria. Though "welfarism" or the theory of "well-being" appears to be the criterion, it becomes a cluster of criteria in reality if the metaphysical and the non-metaphysical sense well-being are kept in mind, though in itself, none is absolutely true. To be sweeping, welfaristic criteria are two, not one, the metaphysical and the non-metaphysical, which commonly speaks about *sustenance of existence among milieu of growth and development avoiding unnecessary suffering and a care for life now and then.* This says many things. The ethical bases we find in environmental studies are as plural as they could be and appears to be different from the deontological and the teleological norms taken from our traditional ethical basket. However, we have to peruse into the reason for such claim. For now, it is enough to say that ethical questions in environmental studies are of some worth at least because without it, we live a life but do not live an ethically charged life. Such life is desirable in itself or else tries to imagine its corollary if that suits a being called 'man.' Here it is important to point out that if relativists argue about the non-fixity of an ethically charged life because ethicality is subject to change, I do not believe that they will accept that at a point of time unethical life is better than ethical life to sound like sophist Thrasymachus of Plato's "Republic" fame.

With this we close this discussion by saying that environmental ethics has its unique value to compel us to realize that if human beings are not so capable as to sustain their life all alone and if life on earth is valuable for times to come, our deliberate act that goes against sustenance of the whole of environment in general, should be questioned for "desirability" or scrutiny of ethical goodness. We are now at hand a fairly clear statement of the nature of "environmental ethics" in terms of the tasks it performs. To be precise, it has a task of clarification of important value concepts as well as justification of environmental ethics as within ethics but independent of applied ethics. It has also the task of justifying the ethical norm or norms to be applied in resolution of environmental things. It is also important to see whether such norms, like "welfarism" bear different sense than the one we are acquainted in traditional normative ethics. It is thus important to find out whether or not traditional normative ethics is sufficient for norm related environmental ethical discussion. Finally, it deals with the way value-laden decision-making rules needs to be formulated following resolution of value crises in environmental matters.

REFERENCES

1. Randers, J. and Meadows, D. in J. G. Barbour edited, *Western Man and Environmental Ethics*, p. 253.

10. AGRICULTURE AND CONCEPT OF ENVIRONMENT IN HIGHER EDUCATION IN INDIA, 1937-57

S.M. Mishra

Reputation of the Indians for higher knowledge and learning goes back to the days of remote antiquity. Indeed, as Mr. Thomas observed: 'there is no country where the love of learning had so early an origin or has exercised so lasting and powerful an influence.[1]

Thomas Babington Macaulay (1800-1859), first Baron of Rothley, in his four-year stay in India, helped establish a system of education and the criminal code for *universal* application in colonial India. He wished to found "an empire exempt from all natural causes of decay. These triumphs are the pacific triumphs of reason over barbarism: that empire is the imperishable empire of our arts and our morals, our literature and our laws."[2] Accordingly, therefore, the purpose of the Educational (Wood's) Despatch[3] of July 1854 was "the diffusion of the improved arts, science, philosophy and literature of Europe; in short, of European knowledge in India."

In seeing how this came to pass, one can begin with mindsets, and in particular with the mindset brought into being by James Mill's (1773-1836) *History of India* in which a principal theme was that Indian society had remained unchanged since remote antiquity. Serving as required reading for all East India Company and later British government employees going out to India, it was doubtless a reason why in official reports coming out of India the phrase "customs dating from time immemorial" was so frequently used. Translated into general policy, this code-phrase meant that Indians themselves were intellectually somnolent, decadent, and stood in urgent need of the moral uplift which the conquering British alone could provide.[4]

Nature of Education in Colonial India: An Overview

And, therefore, that Empire could be established by three means: (a) attributing cognitive authority to the bearers of Western culture in the colonies, (b) centralization of the function of production of knowledge in the imperial metropolis, as distinct from limited knowledge-transmission functions which were carried on in the schools and colleges in the colony, (c) the marginalisation, tantamount to de-legitimation, of knowledge systems and educational institutions indigenous to the colony.[5]

It is a truism that science and its applications are potentially *universal*, but so are arts and morals, literature and laws potentially *universal*. For example, Euclid was already, as elsewhere, universal in India, irrespective of Queen Victoria's approval. The need was to make loyalty to the *person* of the English Crown, and other related English values *universal* in India: *values* of the ruled *ought* to be identical with those of the rulers for the *convenience* of the latter.

However, as Kalidasa, so Shakespeare: separated in space and time, both were staunch supporters of the "divine right of kingship" i.e. *rajatantra*, though the one Indian, the other English in thought, expression, belief, faith, worship, and choice of characters for his plays. Therefore, *not* Euclid, *not* science, but *the* arts; not Kalidasa, *but* Shakespeare and Milton and Bentham and John Stuart Mill were fit and proper study-material for colonial India. "The ruling ideas of each age have ever been the ideas of its ruling class."

Curriculum for Colonial Hegemony

Therefore, if the Sun was *not* to set on the British Empire, the courses and facilities, policies and procedures, requirements and opportunities—some of the tools with which a given society in history educated its young—of the colonial educational process geared to that end; *any* diversion was discouraged. For example, the Patna Division Commissioner, Mr. W. Tayler, entrusted with the educational operations in his division for about two years

(1856-57) was discredited and censured by the Government for his scheme of an Industrial Institution at Patna,[6] for practical instruction in Agriculture, Horticulture, the establishment of schools of elementary art and industry, of a museum, library, printing press and Vernacular school.[7] The British Government would foster Western learning alone. In colonial India, therefore, education was an instrument of colonial hegemony.[8]

In fact, in countries under colonial rule, the metropolitan power shaped and guided the educational policy and the educational institutions promoted the needs of the colonizer, ignoring for the most part the aspirations of the colonized.[9] For example, the Charter Act of 1813 directed the East India Company government of India to spend at least one lakh of rupees per annum over the education of the people of this country—to undertake the education and moral uplift of the Indian people. but appointed no separate machinery for the administration of the funds. Wherever a college was to be established (as one Hindu College proposed at Bhaur in Tirhut in Bihar, 1811-17) a local committee for superintending that institution was formed. On the creation of the General Committee of Public Instruction (1823) all matters relating to education were sent to this body for necessary action. This arrangement continued until the years 1842, when certain considerations led the Government to replace it by a Council of Education that, in turn, dissolved on the creation of the Education Department in 1854.[10]

An 'Eton' in India: Education in British Raj-tantra

Under British rule, there were two kinds of elitist schools in India: those for the hereditary aristocracy, called the Chiefs' Colleges; and those for the newly emerging professional classes, called European or English schools (including English-teaching schools and armed forces schools that taught all subjects in English). Both kinds of institutions served political and social purposes. The Chiefs' Colleges were meant to anglicize young rulers, to encourage loyalty to the crown, and preclude events like those of 1857. This was the principle of "indirect rule" discussed by J.M. Mangan in some detail in the context of schooling.[11] In keeping with the "white man's burden" theory, the idea was, as Captain F.K.M. Walter—the agent of the Bharatpur—put it in his report of 1869-70, to "establish an Eton in India" to help the princes come up to the level of the British and thus become "promoters of peace, prosperity and progress among their own peoples and hearty supporters of British authority." Six major "Chiefs" Colleges were established: Rajkumar College (1870) at Rajkot; Mayo College (1872) at Ajmer for Rajputana; Rajkumar College (1871) Nowgong for Bundelkhand; Daly College (1876) at Indore for Central India; and Aitchison College at Lahore (1886) for the chiefs of the Punjab. There were lesser schools for the landed gentry too, the most notable among them being: Colvin Taluqedar School, Lucknow; Rajkumar College, Raipur; Nizam College, Hyderabad; Taluqedar School at Sadra, Gujrat; etc. Here the emphasis was on English as the central symbol and tool in the process of Anglicization. Lord Curzon, the Viceroy of India (1898-1905), believed that the young chiefs who were supposed to "learn the English language, and [become] sufficiently familiar with English customs, literature, science, mode of thought, standards of truth and honour," would be allies of the British. The assumption that these English values and norms of conduct were intrinsically superior was, of course, part of Curzon's worldview, as it was of most Englishmen. The political motive of making the chiefs loyal to the Crown and so consolidating the empire was justified on the assumption that it was morally necessary to civilize Indians.[12]

Education in India: 1937-1947

It is said that education makes a people easy to lead, but difficult to drive; easy to govern but impossible to enslave. By the 1930s, nationalism had gathered strength, and thanks to the movement's demand for total indigenisation, the British government could conveniently leave the core sectors of agriculture, health, and education in Indian hands. Indian leaders and government now vied to raise development issues.[13] Therefore, Education, a provincial subject, was one of the most important and difficult problems, which the Congress ministries faced after they assumed office after the 1937 elections under the Government of India Act 1935. There was no uniformity in the system of education and the schools and colleges of the provinces were not under a single administration, as they remained affiliated to different institutions under different administrations. For example, until 1936, in Orissa, the schools and colleges of north Orissa affiliated to the Patna University and those of south Orissa to Andhra University. With such a system prevailing then, the syllabus, examinations and other related matters were bound to differ and consequently suffer. Therefore, integration and reorganization of the educational-administrative machinery to a working order was of primary importance and the Congress Ministries wanted to overcome it at the earliest. The secondary education in the provinces was in no way better than that of primary education. The divergent conditions in the two parts of the province of Orissa, for example, hindered the scope of uniformity in secondary education.[14]

Education in India: 1947-57

The first decades of independent India unfold the story of the main educational developments as one of substantial advance. The total number of recognised educational institutions in the country rose from 2,18,171 in 1946-47 to 4,13,656 in 1958-59. The total enrolment in recognised educational institutions rose from 1,82,46,784 (boys 1,39,48,999 and girls 42,97,785) in 1946-47 to 4,14,26,749 (boys 2,96,11,798 and girls 1,18,14,951) in 1958-59. The total expenditure in education rose from Rs. 576.6 million in 1946-47 to Rs. 2,600 million in 1958-59. This stupendous increase, perhaps, had no precedent in the educational history of this country, nor perhaps had many parallels outside. The expansion was probably most rapid in higher education. The number of universities increased from 19 in 1946-47 to 46 by 1960-61. In 1946-47, there were 297 arts and science colleges, 199 intermediate colleges and 140 professional and technical colleges. By 1960-61, there were 462 university departments, 228 constituent colleges, 1,316 affiliated colleges and 83 recognised research institutions. There were 15 Boards of Secondary and Intermediate Education to which 988 intermediate colleges were affiliated. In addition, there were 581 institutions of higher education that were not affiliated to any university. The increase in the number of students was equally impressive. Enrolment in arts and science colleges increased from 212, 000 in 1946-47 to 840,000 in 1960-61. Enrolment in colleges of professional and special education increased from 44, 000 in 1946-47 to 275,000 in 1960-61. Equally great expansion took place in agricultural, veterinary and medical education. In 1947, there were only 38 institutions for degree courses in engineering and technology (with admission capacity of 2,940 students) and only 53 institutions for diploma courses (with admission capacity of 2,670 students). By 1960-61, the number of institutions offering degree courses increased to 100 and their admission capacity to 13,860. The number of institutions offering diploma courses during the same period increased to 196 and their admission capacity to 25,570. Measures to improve the quality of higher education were also taken.[15]

University Grants Commission (1953)

The Constitution classified the "co-operation and determination of standards in universities" as a Central function. The University Grants Commission was the principal agency created to discharge this constitutional responsibility. The University Education Commission observed that a committee or commission for allocating both recurring and capital grants to universities from the Centre was fundamental to its proposals for improving and developing university education in India and proposed setting up such an organisation. This recommendation was generally endorsed by the Central Advisory Board of Education in India and by the Inter-University Board. Accordingly, "to make provision for the co-ordination and determination of standards in universities and for that purpose, to establish a University Grants Commission," the University Grants Commission was set up in 1953 and under the provisions of the University Grants Commission Act, 1956, the first University Grants Commission was constituted with Dr. C.D. Deshmukh as its Chairman.[16]

With substantial assistance from the Commission, the State Governments and the public, a large number of tuitional buildings, hostels, libraries, laboratories and staff quarters were constructed. Facilities for post-graduate teaching and research increased several-fold and more attention was paid to student welfare and guidance. The promotion of scientific and technological research was given a very high priority and a large number of research institutions, including 20 national laboratories and 3 regional research centres, were established. The research departments of universities were considerably strengthened and a strong scientific and technical organisation built up.[17]

Education of Girls

There was a great advance in the education of girls. The total enrolment of girls in all educational institutions increased from 4.3 million in 1946-47 to 13.0 million in 1960-61. The gap between the education of boys and girls bridged and special facilities were provided for expanding the education of girls at every stage, particularly by increasing the number of women teachers in primary schools.[18]

Modern Indian Universities: Colonial Model

The colonial model of the educational process was essentially about managing and disseminating knowledge rather than about its production. (This continues largely to be the template for India's higher education system.) Universities set up by the colonial state in mid-19th century laid down the syllabi, conducted examinations and regulated affiliated colleges. Research found expression outside colleges and universities, in the proceedings of learned societies. Universities were state apparatuses and their personnel, government servants.[19]

In addition, for example, during the second quarter of the 20th century, Calcutta University expanded rather too fast for its old and outmoded framework. Existing institutions could not bear the strain of the increasing rush on their rolls. While the number of students multiplied from year to year, the arrangements and methods of teaching remained the same. The classes were overcrowded; the atmosphere was noisy and disturbing. The teacher was a talking machine and the student a dumb receiving box. As C.F. Andrews observed in his address to the Convocation of 1938, "The crowded class room is sub-personal, sub-human, herdlike. It does not carry men forward into that sphere of 'plain living and high thinking,' which alone can produce the scholar, the artist, the thinker, and the man of affairs."[20]

Similarly, until the passing of the Indian Universities Act of 1904, the Bombay University for example, in common with the others, was limited to the function of examining candidates and arranging for the courses of study, which led up to their degrees. Under this Act, it acquired the right of organizing teaching, arranging for University extension lectures and of publishing such works as were necessary for the direct educational work it was to carry on.[21] This situation obtained in 1937-38, at the beginning of our twenty-year study.

However, perhaps, these universities could not have become a purely research university. Perhaps, it was as true then of Indian universities, as today (2005) of the University of Cambridge: "If we didn't get to inspire undergraduates, where would tomorrow's researchers come from? Teaching contributes to our research strength."[22]

Transformation in Higher Education in Agricultural Sciences

By 1900, Indian agriculture was widely documented by the colonial State, and analyzed in addition by scientific and political organizations, sponsored by the colonial elite and devoted to the progress of India's rural masses. In 1901, for example, Congress praised European scientific agriculture and urged government to adopt recommendations by John Voelckar, Consulting Chemist of the Royal Agricultural Society, who toured India in 1890. Congress repeated its praise of scientific agriculture often. Even Gandhian critics of western industrialism left its agricultural application unscathed.[23] Congress agreed with government that agricultural progress required programmes such as catalogued by the Royal Commission. In 1929, the *Report of the Royal Commission on Agriculture* emerged as a textual monument to empire, to make agrarian India appear as a field for progress and as a production system under scientific management.[24]

"Increased agricultural production obtained by the application of science and technology in the utilization of the available resources in the country." It was with this aim that the establishment of agricultural colleges, agricultural experiment stations and extension organizations in agriculture conceived and developed gradually since 1892 [John Voelckar's Report] in India.[25] For example, during the period of our study, the Agricultural Institute at Barrackpore started work in 1939, with seven students. The two years' certificate course of study included dairy, poultry and industrial training. Fishery was included the following year in its curriculum. The Institute became a casualty of the Second World War when the Army commandeered its premises. It maintained a skeleton existence in hired premises. After the war, as the problem of feeding the ever-growing population of the country became more and more acute, Calcutta University revived the idea of starting a college of agriculture. In 1947, it decided to enlarge the old course by introducing I.Sc. and B.Sc. courses in

Agriculture. A research section opened from 1948 with funds from the Khaira Endowment under the Khaira Professor of Agriculture. A Chair of Agricultural Chemistry was also set up with donation of Rupees two lakhs made by Professor Nilratan Dhar, a distinguished alumnus of the University. In 1949, the young Raja of Jhargram (Midnapore) at the request of the Vice-Chancellor Pramathanath Banerjee made a bequest of Rupees 1 lakh and 450 *bighas* of land for an agricultural college at Jhargram. The building was raised in 1951, and the Jhargram Agricultural College promoted to the degree standard with a two years' B.Sc. course. However, the University could not meet its financial requirements, and in 1953, the college was made over to the Government of West Bengal with the teaching of Agriculture retained only up to the I.Sc. standard with teaching of B.Sc. in Agriculture taken over by the Government Agricultural College at Tollygunge.[26]

Agriculture & Higher Education

However, little attention was paid to agricultural education in the beginning of the 19th century. Madras had an agricultural farm established in 1854, to which was attached a school of agriculture in 1886. The engineering college at Poona (Kirkee) too had an agricultural wing in 1879. The Agricultural Conference held in 1888 stressed the importance of agricultural education. Dr. J.A. Voelcker of the British Royal Agricultural Society made a number of suggestions in order to improve upon the agricultural education and practices in 1893. Even so, it was only in 1897 that the government accorded the rightful place to agricultural education, in the same way as it did for other subjects. In the closing decades of the 19th century, agricultural schools were opened at Coimbatore, Nagpur and Kanpur. The Sibpur Engineering College also developed an agricultural wing, while the Madras Agricultural School soon became a college. However, the Bombay University was the first to recognize agriculture as a separate subject for degree examination.[27]

Thus, for example, in 1947, there were only 29 agricultural colleges with less than 5,000 pupils in them. Even in these, the courses had little reference to the practical needs of Indian agriculture. There were hardly any institutions for teaching dairy or poultry farming, horticulture or veterinary science.[28]

Therefore, perhaps, Mahatma Gandhi bemoaned almost a

decade earlier in the *Harijan* of 31.7.1937: "I have a painful experience of some agricultural graduates. Their knowledge is superficial. They lack practical experience. But if they had their apprenticeship on farms which are self-sustained and answer the requirements of the country, they would not have to gain experience after getting their degrees and at the expense of their employers."[29]

Nevertheless, by 1937 there were 18 universities in India, including that of Rangoon, and 12 centres of higher learning, including the Bose Research Institute, Calcutta, Forest Research Institute and College, Dehra Dun, the Imperial Council of Agricultural Research (ICAR), the Imperial Agricultural Research Institute (IARI), New Delhi, etc. On the eve of Independence, India had 22 universities, including those of Ceylon and Rangoon, though the total number of centres of higher learning remained at 12 as before. By the close of our period of study, i.e., by 1957, with the foundation of the University of Gorakhpur in 1956, there were 33 universities, including those of Burma and Rangoon. Several of the Indian universities taught agricultural science, as one of the many major courses offered, which included agricultural engineering and veterinary hygiene, agricultural chemistry, agricultural botany, agricultural zoology, economic and commercial geography, botany with plant pathology, botany with plant breeding, botany with horticulture, zoology with entomology and parasitology, zoology with animal breeding, rural economics, crop and cropping scheme, internal morphology—study of the form of animals and plants, crop systematic and physiology, soils plant chemistry, fertilizers and manures, agricultural entomology, plant pathology including bacteriology, animal husbandry and veterinary science, agricultural economics, farm management, soil management and field experimentation, farm machinery, dairying, horticulture, genetics and plant breeding, dairy chemistry and animal nutrition, agriculture extension, etc.[30]

Yet by 1938, three of the 18 universities, those of Bombay (founded 1857), Nagpur (1923), and Punjab (1882); and by 1948, nine universities out of the 22, those of Agra (1927), Allahabad (1887), Andhra (1931), Banaras (1916), Bombay (1857), Calcutta (1857), Madras (1857), and Mysore (1933; the University of Mysore was the first University to be founded in the Indian States), and Nagpur (1923) taught agricultural science.[31]

The U.P. Agricultural University established at the Terai State Farm, Pant Nagar, was the first Agricultural University in the country and as approved and developed as a Second (1955-60) Five Year Plan project[32] in 1960.

Thus under the existing system of agricultural education in India, at Independence, Education, Research and Extension were completely divorced from each other and the training imparted to the agricultural graduates was mostly theoretical. The Land Grant Universities in U.S.A. which had an integrated system of teaching, research and extension had made a very substantial contribution towards the development of agriculture in that country and provided a pattern which was considered for adoption at suitable centres in India with advantage. That necessitated, however, the reorientation of the existing system of education and research in the country.[33]

Overturning the British Raj Curriculum

The weak system of higher education in India did not go unnoticed after Independence. The dawn of Independence underlined the need of developing the resources of the country. A new educational plan and re-organization of the scientific studies became the paramount necessity. Jawaharlal Nehru dilated upon this in his address to the Calcutta University Convocation in 1946. He exhorted the University authorities to think of educating the human material for free India, "of the kind of social structure which will have to be raised, of feeding, clothing and housing every citizen and of training the future citizens for the new order." In 1949, India became a sovereign republic having a constitution with adult suffrage as its basis. About seventeen crores of men and women got the vote of whom about only 10 per cent. were literate. The supreme task was to educate the masses of the country. A radical re-orientation of the educational pattern became the crying need of the hour.[34]

Overturning the British Raj curriculum was required to create a new mind set compatible with the values of the Republic of India where Indians *must not* beg for leave "to subsist in their own land, to think their own thoughts, to sing their own songs, and to garner the fruits of their own labours." For, curriculum is the point of contact between the intentions, which initiate educational reform, and the reality of the teaching-learning encounters, which ultimately determine the success of the changes attempted. A well-developed curriculum is the most potent instrument of educational reconstruction, which can justify and contribute to the meaning and possibilities of the total system. Against this description, planning a curriculum in any discipline becomes a complex and a highly professional duty. The work of curriculum development is completed only when the curriculum enters the classroom. Change is not effected by direction, only through participation.[35]

Curriculum in the Republic of India

In the Republic of India, education was for republican hegemony, although what it inherited in terms of an educational system was based on British policy or British Raj-tantra whose aim, according to Lord Macaulay, was to produce a group of people to serve as interpreters between the rulers and the ruled—in other words government servants of a specific aptitude.

The development of the new system of higher education in free India was owing to the awakening created by the University Education Commission in 1948 for a new system of higher education for agriculture and rural needs.[36] The idea of establishing agricultural universities was contained in the report of the seven-member First Education Commission headed by Dr. S. Radhakrishnan that was also recommended by the Indo-U.S. teams. The concept of an agricultural university was based on the promise that research, teaching and extension activities should be fully integrated and geared towards the solution of the farmers' problems.[37]

Agriculture in University Education in Independent India

During our period of study, however, the various post-war development plans of the Centre and of the Provinces and States involved a large demand for Agricultural graduates. The requirements of the Centre alone came to about 500 graduates. Despite the expansion of facilities for training in the then existing colleges in the larger Provinces, the increases barely met their own requirements. The smaller provinces, the Centrally Administered Areas and the Indian States experienced difficulty in arranging for the proper training of agricultural graduates to meet their own needs. The Governing Body of the ICAR recommended in 1944 that suitable steps be taken to meet the situation. Enquiries from areas that had no colleges then revealed that their requirements came to over 200 students a year. It was, therefore, decided to set up an Agricultural College at Delhi with aid from the Central Government. There were about 26 students from the Centrally administered areas studying in the college then. It was also proposed to conduct a farmer's training course of six months in the college. The College was not meant for research work.[38]

Vestiges of Raj-tantra: Aversion to Manual Labour

As indicated above, higher education in agriculture had a low status at the time of Independence, as manual labour was considered a social disgrace in India, as elsewhere also, during this period. In 1948, there were only 17 state agricultural colleges and 4 veterinary colleges, producing about 2,000 graduates per year and facilities for only 160 students for training in post-graduate work.[39] In 1949-50, the number of agricultural institutions in India, of both College and School standard, were 15 and 39 with enrolment strength of 4,538 and 1,882 respectively;[40] by 1953, there were 19 recognised Agricultural Colleges with 4,529 enrolments as per 1950-51 records, and 35 recognised Agricultural Schools with 1,854 enrolments accorded during 1950-51 in the States in India,[41] and by 1958-59, the number was 29 and 102 with the enrolment strength of 10,871 and 7,411 respectively. In the field of Veterinary Science, in 1949-50, the number of institutions of College standard was 10 with 1,486 enrolments; by 1958-59, the number of veterinary institutions of College and School standards was 17 and 10 with enrolments of 5,137 and 1,093 respectively.[42]

Reorganisation of Agricultural Education in Independent India

However, the reform of university education was one of the earliest problems to attract the attention of the Government of free India. This was due partly to the basic significance of the subject to the development of the country and partly to the fact that no comprehensive survey of university education had been held in India after 1917-19. A University Education Commission was, therefore, set up in 1948 under the chairmanship of Dr. S. Radhakrishnan. The report of the Commission was a very comprehensive document that had far-reaching influence on the reconstruction of university education in independent India. The

Government of India amended the Acts of Incorporation of the Central Universities in keeping with the recommendations of this Commission. Thus, the Visva-Bharati at Shantiniketan, established by Gurudev Rabindranath Tagore "to study the mind of man in the realisation of different aspects of truth from diverse points of view," was constituted as a Central University in 1951.[43]

In addition, the question of reorganisation of agricultural education at the University stage was under the consideration of the free Government of India and the idea of suitable Agricultural Universities in different parts of the country actively canvassed in this connection. The establishment of Rural (Agricultural) Universities, as originally suggested by the University Education Commission under the Chairmanship of Dr. S. Radhakrishnan, visualised a Rural University as a "Ring of small, resident under-graduate Colleges with specialised and University facilities in the centre." The First Joint Indo-American Team on Agricultural Education set up by the Ministry of Food and Agriculture in 1954 further clarified this recommendation and made practical suggestions for its implementation. The Team recommended as a first step, the setting up of a nucleus comprising a College of Agriculture, and a College of Veterinary Science to which, in due course, could be added a College of Home Science and a College of Agricultural Engineering and Technology. The University would use the villages in its neighbourhood for research and experiments and provide a comprehensive type of education with special emphasis on Agriculture and allied subjects. A blueprint of such University, prepared by Mr. H.W. Hannah, Dean of the University of Illinois in order to give a concrete shape to this idea, was circulated to all the State Governments with Department of Agriculture's letter No. F-4-22/56–Edn. III dated the 1st November 1956. A proposal for setting up of an Agricultural University at Rudrapur on the lines of the blueprint prepared by Dean H.W. Hannah received from the Government of U.P. in September 1956 and some other States in the country showed their desire to go ahead with the idea. After discussion with the Planning Commission, it was, however, decided that:

(i) Only one such University should be set up during the Second Five Year Plan as an experimental measure and its progress watched before proceeding with the establishment of similar other Universities.

(ii) As the only concrete scheme was that submitted by the U.P.Government, the State Government might be assisted to set up an Agricultural University at Rudrapur.[44]

Agriculture in Higher Education in the Republic of India

Appointed on 4 November 1948 by the Government of India in the Ministry of Education, the Radhakrishnan Commission in its report expressed its concern over the inadequate number of faculty and researchers, the overall quality of teaching and research, and the lack of social relevance in higher education and the lack of autonomy given to the universities. The Commission specifically addressed the lack of higher education for rural people and advocated the creation of rural universities to meet the needs. They recommended for the university a common core of liberal education as for other universities, though the methods used in teaching and learning may be different. The common core was to include substantial introduction to the physical, natural and social sciences and humanities. And to advanced and specialized subjects, the Commission recommended that no field of human concern was to be foreign to the rural universities. The curriculum was to be made to fit the needs of individuals and not the studies made to an arbitrary curriculum. For implementing this bold concept and departure from the then existing system the United States Land-Grant-University was discussed as a possible model for the rural university. However, no action followed to implement the recommendations of the University Education Commission to set up rural universities. The absence of a department or agency at the centre responsible either for co-ordinating agricultural education in the country or assisting agricultural and veterinary colleges to equip themselves adequately for high standard of teaching was keenly felt.[45]

Indian Council of Agricultural Education: 1952

The Agricultural Education Committee of the Central Advisory Board of Education suggested that the ICAR might set up a council of agricultural education (including animal husbandry and dairy) for this purpose. Accordingly, the setting up of the Indian Council of Agricultural Education was notified on 27 February 1952. The functions of the council were to be purely advisory and to co-ordinate so that a uniform standard of agricultural education might be achieved in the country and that model syllabi for adoption in the various teaching institutions was to be prepared. This was approved in a conference convened by ICAR of the State Ministers of Agriculture, Vice-Chancellors and Deans of the faculty of agriculture at New Delhi on 3-4 November 1951.[46]

Grow More Food: 1952

In 1952, the Grow More Food Enquiry Committee came to the conclusion that the lesson to be derived from failure of programmes of increasing food production was that all aspects of rural life were inter-related and that no lasting results could be achieved if aspects of it were dealt with in isolation.[47]

Efforts & Results: Community Development Block

These views and recommendations led Government of India to set up a national extension service and a new unit development administration known as the Community Development Block. This programme received support from the Ford Foundation and United States Agency for International Development (USAID) from its inception since 1961. This period also brought about the first linkage between Indian and the United States Land-Grant-Universities through programme supported by USAID. The Universities of Illinois, Ohio State, Missouri, Kansas State and Tennessee entered into a technical assistance agreement in 1955 to assist agricultural and veterinary education in the country. For this purpose India was divided into five regions for operational convenience. This programme mainly helped in the training of some Indian nationals in some specialized subjects including post-graduate degrees in the collaborating U.S. universities, provision of equipment and books and journals.[48]

However, confusion abounded, as neither Americans nor Indians were quite sure as to what their roles were in this collaboration. The Ministry of Agriculture and its attached office of the Indian Council of Agricultural Research oversaw this arrangement. In 1955, in an agreement between the Government of India and the USAID, a joint Indo-American Committee was constituted to examine the entire field of agricultural education and research and to recommend improvements. An Indian delegation spent 3 months in the United States studying the Land-Grant-Universities and their role in agriculture in that country, while an American Team examined the situation in India. The Joint Team urged that agricultural universities similar to those in the USA i.e., Land-Grant-Universities be established. This was the first effective step recommended for the implementation of the *'rural university'* concept made in 1948 by the University Education Commission. However, the name adopted later was agricultural university and not rural university owing to lack of agreement between the Ministry of Education and the Ministry of Agriculture. The Government of India, accepting the project submitted by the state Government of Uttar Pradesh, and with the approval of the Planning Commission, decided to establish, as a completely new venture on a state farm of 16,000 acres in a forest reclaimed area of tarai, one such university as an experimental measure in Uttar Pradesh under the provision made in the Second Five-Year Plan (1955-60). Thus, the first Agriculture University was enacted in Uttar Pradesh in 1958.[49] Following which the Govind Ballabh Pant University of Agriculture and Technology, Pantnagar was established in 1960.

Precursors of Environmental & Ecological Studies in India

During the period of this study, the now pervasive term *environment* was never employed, though nature and the place of humans within the natural world were conceptualised and contextualised. Writers sometimes referred, as in Europe, to the *environs* of a town or village. The term *ecology* was similarly not used in scientific literature in India before the 1900s. What we in the late twentieth and early twenty-first centuries have come to identify and integrate as *the environment* coalesced in India, and elsewhere, around rather different visual, experiential and conceptual nodes—around *climate* (in a broader and generally more determined sense than we would recognise today) and its neo-Hippocratic linkages with health and disease; around ideas of natural history and "nature"; around agriculture and "improvement"; and, not least, around ideas of landscape and scenery.[50]

Therefore, it is interesting to note that of the subjects for the Entrance Examination for admission to the University of Calcutta (founded 24 January 1857) were: (1) Languages, including English and one of the following: Greek, Latin, Arabic, Persian, Hebrew,

Sanskrit, Bengali, Oriya, Hindi, Urdu and Burmese; (2) History and Geography, including outlines of General History, outline of Indian History, a general knowledge of Geography and a knowledge of the Geography of India; (3) Mathematics and Natural Philosophy, including Arithmetic, Algebra, Geometry and elementary knowledge of Mechanics; (4) Natural History which included general knowledge of the habits and characteristics of vertebrated animals and general economy of vegetation and simple or elementary organs of plants. Nevertheless, it is speculative as to why the Senate at its meeting on 10 July 1858 adopted certain changes in the courses of studies for the Entrance Examination. The provision for oral examination in the Languages was omitted, and *Natural History* was deleted from the course. Mechanics too was omitted from the paper on Mathematics and Natural Philosophy. Though, when the University decided to hold in January 1874, the first examination in the new Science course (known as B course) for the degree of B.A., four papers were—Chemistry, Physical Geography, and two optional subjects in Physical Science.[51]

A perusal of the *Handbook of Indian Universities* (1938) shows that Indian universities like Agra, founded 1st July 1927, were already giving courses on geography, botany, zoology, agriculture, agricultural chemistry, botany with plant pathology, botany with plant breeding, botany with horticulture, zoology with entomology and parasitology, zoology with animal breeding, rural economics, with practical examination in each subject; the Aligarh Muslim University, founded 1920, offered courses on geography, botany, zoology, while the University of Allahabad offered courses on botany, zoology, agriculture including agricultural engineering and veterinary hygiene, agricultural chemistry, agricultural botany, agricultural zoology, economic and commercial geography; the Andhra University, founded 1st July 1931, taught geography, botany, zoology, geology, economic geography and agriculture. And, besides many other subjects, Bombay University offered courses on Agriculture for the *Intermediate Examination*, Bachelor's and Master's of Agriculture: (i) *Intermediate Examination:* The course of study extended over two academic years after passing the Matriculation Examination except in the case of Bachelors of Science of this University with Chemistry and Botany, who were exempted from this Examination. Candidates were examined in

(1) Agriculture (including Geology) (two papers and a practical examination), (2) Chemistry (two papers and a practical examination), (3) Botany (one paper and a practical examination), and (4) Mathematics and Elementary Physics (one paper and a practical examination). (ii) *Bachelor of Agriculture*:—The course extended over two years subsequent to passing the Intermediate Examination in Agriculture, or subsequent to passing the B.Sc. Examination of this University with Chemistry and Botany. Candidates were examined in the following subjects: (1) Agriculture (four papers and two practical examinations), (2) Chemistry of Agriculture (one paper and a practical examination), (3) Agricultural Botany and Horticulture (one paper and a practical examination), (4) Plant Pathology (one paper and a practical examination), (5) Agricultural Engineering (one paper and a practical examination), and one of the following special subjects (one paper and a practical examination):—(a) Intensive Study of Certain Crops, (b) Advanced Plant Breeding, (c) Advanced Agricultural Chemistry, (d) Advanced Animal Husbandry and Dairying, (e) Advanced Agricultural Economics, (f) Advanced Horticulture, and (g) Advanced Plant Pathology. (iii) *Master of Agriculture*:—Each candidate for this Degree was to be a Graduate or a Licentiate in Agriculture of this University of not less than 3 year's standing and was to have been engaged in the practice of Agriculture or Work of research in connection with Agriculture for a period of at least 3 years after receiving the Degree of Bachelor or Licentiate in Agriculture. Each candidate was to submit a report of work or research of an original character in the Agricultural field subsequent to his graduation and was, if the examiners so desire, to submit himself to an oral examination; University of Gorakhpur (founded June 1956) taught agricultural science, as one of the many courses offered, which included crop and cropping scheme, internal morphology—study of the form of animals and plants, crop systematic and physiology, soils plant chemistry, fertilizers and manures, agricultural entomology, plant pathology including bacteriology, animal husbandry and veterinary science, agricultural economics, farm management, soil management and field experimentation, farm machinery, dairying, horticulture, genetics and plant breeding, dairy chemistry and animal nutrition, and agriculture extension.[52]

Agricultural Implements

Published in 1901, a three-volume textbook on Indian agriculture was 'arranged to meet the requirements of the Syllabus of the Bombay University for the Degree in Agriculture.' The contents of Volume I on Soils, Manures, and Implements, for example, show scientific awareness of world standard. On agricultural implements, it maintained that indigenous implements were generally suitable to the conditions of Indian agriculture. "The best of the indigenous kinds—the most effective at work—might with advantage be more widely known in the country and the same might be said of other indigenous implements, but there is certainly no need to go out of the country for the ordinary tillage implements which are required."[53]

All these subjects of study, perhaps, were the precursors of the more modern environmental and ecological studies, in the same sense, as the first telephone was the precursor of modern communications networks. In any case, the issue of environment and development did not receive any significant recognition in the Indian planning process until 1968. The Fourth Five Year Plan (1969-74) observed that planning for harmonious development was possible only when based on comprehensive appraisal of environmental issues. It was necessary therefore to introduce the environmental aspects into our planning and development.[54] Nevertheless, all this is much beyond our present brief that covers only the period 1937-57.

Agricultural Education Impacts Environment

No society can ever exist without economic activity. It must carry on the production process even with a view to maintaining the bare physical existence of its members. To be able to produce, that is to transform elements of nature into forms suitable for meeting the needs of men, it must gather an understanding of Nature i.e. it must achieve scientific knowledge. It is in the process of social practice of man for biological existence that mechanics, physics, chemistry, agronomy and other sciences developed. Men, associated in big or small groups, applied this scientific knowledge and evolved technology i.e. such means of production as the plough and the tools of the handicraft industry, and such modern means of production as machinery driven by steam, electricity and even by atomic energy.[55] All knowledge is historically conditioned. Though growing, it is finite at a given moment, and its depth and extent depend upon the level of social development, which a people have reached.[56] There is always some element of scientific knowledge in every society. For, society to exist must produce and production presupposes technology and scientific knowledge, however, meagre. Otherwise, no society can survive.[57]

In sum, however, as observed by David Ludden: "Though many old texts from India contain knowledge about farms and farming, they do not depict agriculture as a distinctive subject of study'; and that 'colonialism created agriculture as a subject of study, an object of observation, analysis, and manipulation by the social classes whose written legacy dominates the historical record.'[58] As far back as 1930, Mahatma Gandhi perspicaciously said that Indian agriculture would continue to stagnate unless brain and brawn are married in the countryside. He made his remarks because of the very low social prestige attached to rural professions with the consequent migration of the educated persons to town and to city. Agriculture in those days was regarded as a profession mainly of the illiterate. The only exceptions related to plantation and commercial crops where the interests of industry and foreign trade were involved, as indicated in the previous two chapters. The Mahatma also said that the most serious form of brain drain is the migration of both brains and financial resources from the villages to the cities.[59]

Nevertheless, though the Indian agriculturist—perhaps like his counterpart elsewhere—was largely illiterate during the period of our study, he knew his profession very well. He was not able to read and write but he knew what crops were good for what soils and he was not inclined to waste his money and labour where he was not to get a proper return. By the experience that he and his forefathers had gained, he had become wiser and knew what crops are good for what climate.[60] After all, agriculture has been the vital industry of India since ancient times. The Indian farmer knew various techniques relating to agricultural practice. He made selection and preparation of both his soil and seeds according to planned techniques. His method of sowing seeds was equally remarkable. Besides, the Indian cultivator practiced the rotation system, though in a different way, to increase his production. He was also aware of the importance of using manure in the fields. Therefore, his agricultural production was quite impressive under the existing conditions.[61]

The agriculturists as a class consisted, as elsewhere, of people tied to the customs and usages and traditions built around food production, i.e. agriculture facilitated by manual technology, which were not easy or perhaps even possible to forsake. In fact, the method of cultivation adopted by Indian peasants did not change much with the passage of time, including during the period of our study. They were guided by nature and tradition in carrying out their profession. Nevertheless, the skill and ingenuity of humanity upset the 'balance of nature' since agriculture largely destroyed the forest and turned to bush or grassland in recorded history.[62] Of all human activities, therefore, agriculture leaves the biggest footprint on Earth.

REFERENCES

1. F.W. Thomas, (1979): 'History and Prospects of British Education in India' quoted in Jata Shankar Jha, *Education in Bihar*, K.P. Jyaswal Research Institute, Patna, p. 1.
2. Quoted in the *Address* by Dr. S. Radhakrishnan at the Centenary Celebrations of the University of Calcutta, 1957.
3. Named after the then President of the Board of Control, Sir Charles Wood (afterwards Lord Halifax).
4. Sheldon Watts, (1997): *Epidemics and History, Disease, Power and Imperialism*, Yale University Press, p. 175.
5. Sabyasachi Bhattacharya, (2003): 'Introduction' to Sabyasachi Bhattacharya, Joseph Bara, Chinna Rao Yagati ed., *Educating the Nation, Documents on the Discourse of National Education in India, 1880-1920*, Kanishka Publishers, Distributors, New Delhi, p. x.
6. Jata Shakar Jha, op. cit, p. iv.
7. Jata Shankar Jha, Ibid, p. 291.
8. Sabyasachi Bhattacharya, op. cit, p. x.
9. Aparna Basu, (1982): *Essays in the History of Indian Education*, Concept Publishing Company, New Delhi, p. 60.
10. Jata Shankar Jha, op. cit., pp. ii-iii.
11. *The Games Ethic and Imperialism,* Viking Penguion, New York, 1986, p. 125.
12. Tariq Rahman, (2004): *Denizens of Alien Worlds, A Study of Education, Inequality and Polarization in Pakistan*, Oxford, pp. 43-4.
13. Deepak Kumar, (2000): 'Reconstructing India: Disunity in the Science and Technology for Development Discouse, 1900-1947,' Roy Macleod, ed., *Nature and Empire: Science and the Colonial Enterprise, Osiris*, Second Series, Volume 15, 255-56.

14. P.K. Som, (2005): 'Education in Orissa and the First Congress,' *The Journal of Orissan History*, Vol. XVIII, pp. 101-9.
15. Prem Kripal, (1961): 'Foreword' to *A Review of Education in India (1947-61), First Year Book of Education,* National Council of Educational Research and Training, Ministry of Education, New Delhi, pp. vi-ix.
16. Ibid. 28.
17. Ibid. vi-ix.
18. Ibid.
19. 'Reward Research, Rid The University Of The Raj' in *The Economic Times,* Friday 17 June, 2005, 14.
20. *Hundred Years of the University of Calcutta, A History of the University issued in commemoration of the centenary celebrations*, University of Calcutta, 1957, 416.
21. *Handbook of Indian Universities,* Inter-University Board, India, 1938, 120.
22. Ian Leslie, (2005): 'Why does innovation matter?' in *CAM Cambridge Alumni Magazine*, No. 45 Easter Term. p. 9.
23. David Ludden, (ed.), (1994): *Agricultural Production and Indian History*, OUP, pp. 4-11.
24. David Ludden, Ibid. 7.
25. *Progress Report of Committee on Agricultural Universities,* March 1962, Government of India, Ministry of Food and Agriculture, Department of Education (ICAR), New Delhi. 1.
26. *Hundred Years of the University of Calcutta, A History of the University issued in commemoration of the centenary celebrations*, University of Calcutta, 1957, 373.
27. O.P. Jaggi, History of Science, Technology and Medicine in India, Vol. IX, *Science in Modern India*, Atma Ram & Sons, Delhi, pp. 58-9.
28. Aparna Basu, (1982): *Essays in the History of Indian Education*, Concept Publishing Company, New Delhi, p. 18.
29. M.K. Gandhi, (1947): *India of My Dreams*, Navjivan Publishing House, Ahmedabad, p. 190.
30. *Handbook of Indian Universities,* Inter-University Board India, Association of Indian Universities, 1938, 1948 & 1958.
31. Ibid.
32. *Progress Report of Committee on Agricultural Universities,* March, 1962, Goverment of India, Ministry of Food and Agriculture, Department of Education (ICAR), New Delhi, p. 22.
33. Appendix — I, Letter to the State Governments, etc. from Shri V. Shankar, Special Secretary, Goverment of India, No.20 (22)/ 60-Edn.II, dated 22.8.1961, to *Progress Report of Committee on Agricultural Universities*, March 1962, p. 27.
34. *Hundred Years of the University of Calcutta: A History of the University*

issued in commemoration of the centenary celebrations, University of Calcutta, 1957, 406-18.

35. Vasantha Ramkumar, National Co-ordinator, UGC Curriculum Development Centre, National policy on education 1986, *Programme of Action*, 1992, Government of India, Ministry of Human Resource Development, Department of Education, i-v.
36. N.K. Anant Rao, (1989): 'Evolution of a New System of Higher Education for Agriculture in India and Its Impact on Manpower Development,' *40 Years of Agricultural Research and Education in India*, ICAR, p. 231.
37. N.S. Randhawa, *'Agricultural Research and Education for productive Agriculture,'* Ibid. 17.
38. Reply by Shri Jairamdas Doulatram to 'Q. No. 660 *Re. Representations by students of Central College of Agriculture, Delhi* by Shri R.R. Diwakar, Constituent Assembly Debates, 10.3.1948, 1792-93.
39. N.K. Anant Rao, *Evolution of a New System of Higher Education for Agriculture in India and Its Impact on Manpower Development*, op. cit., p. 230.
40. 'Table No. V, 1&12' in *A Review of Education in India (1947-61) First Year Book of Education,* National Council of Educational Research and Training, Ministry of Education, New Delhi, 1961. p. 816.
41. Annexure No. 10 *Vide* Answer to Q. No. 162 Re. *Statistics of Recognised Agricultural Colleges in States in India,* and Annexure No. 11 *Vide* Answer to Q.No. 163 (a) and (b) Re. *Statistics of recognised Agricultural Schools in States in India,* Appendix II to House of the People Debates, Third Session, 1953, pp. 94-95.
42. 'Table No. V, 1' in *A Review of Education in India (1947-61) First Year Book of Education*, op. cit.
43. *A Review of Education in India (1947-61), First Year Book of Education*, National Council of Educational Research and Training Ministry of Education, New Delhi, 1961, p. 27.
44. Appendix—I, Letter to the State Goverments, etc. from Shri V. Shankar, Special Secretary, Government of India, No.20 (22)/ 60-Edn.II, dated 22.8.1961, to *Progress Report of Committee on Agricultural Universities*, March 1962, p. 27.
45. N.K. Anant Rao, (1989): 'Evolution of a New System of Higher Education for Agriculture in India and Its Impact on Manpower Development' in *40 Years of Agricultural Research and Education in India*, ICAR, pp. 211-13.
46. N.K. Anant Rao, Ibid.
47. N.K. Anant Rao, Ibid.
48. N.K. Anant Rao, Ibid.
49. N.K. Anant Rao, Ibid.

50. David Arnold, (2005): *The Tropics and the Travelling Gaze, India, Landscape, And Science, 1800-1856,* permanent black, p. 4.
51. *Hundred Years of the University of Calcutta,* University of Calcutta, 1957, 63-87.
52. *Handbook of Indian Universities,* 1938, Inter-University Board, India.
53. J. Mollison, A Text-Book on Indian Agriculture, Vol, I, Soils, *Manures, Implements*, Goverment of Bombay, Bombay, 1901, 135.
54. Shekhar Singh (ed.), (1984): *Environmental Policy in India*, IIPA, New Delhi, p. 58.
55. A.R. Desai, Ibid, 135.
56. A.R. Desai, Ibid, 136.
57. A.R. Desai, Ibid, 137.
58. David Ludden, (ed.), (1994): *Agricultural Production and Indian History*, OUP, pp. 1-3.
59. M.S. Swaminathan, (1989): 'Achievements in Agricultural Research and Education' in *40 Years of Agricultural Research and Education in India*, ICAR, New Delhi, p. 1.
60. Govind V. Deshmukh, *A Non-Muhammadan Member from Nagpur Division in the Legislative Assembly on 10th March 1943,* Legislative Assembly Debates, 942.
61. Satpal Sangwan, (1991): *Science, Technology and Colonisation, An Indian Experience, 1757-1857*, Anamika Prakashan, Delhi, p. 4.
62. Joan Robinson, (1970): *Freedom & Necessity, an introduction to the study of society,* George Allen & Unwin (India), pp.367.54.

11. DE-FORESTATION AND ANNIHILATION OF HILL MEN:
The Colonial Tragedy in Jungle Terai-Santhal Parganas (1770-1880)

Surendra Jha

The deepening awareness in recent years of fragility of the earth's ecology and its grave implications for human survival has made possible from within modern discourse a qualitatively different kind of attention to the Nature. The significant pre-modern facts, survival of human species, as an ineliminable concern, basic to the human condition, has re-acquired something of its immemorial relevance. In India, we find a tremendous diversity in geographical and ecological zones and diversity of human cultures corresponding to different agro-climatic or vegetative zones, which exhibit diverse technology of resource-use and also of social modes of resource-control. These modes range from stone age hunter-gatherers, shifting cultivators, nomadic pastoralists, subsistence and cash crop agriculturists and planters as well as every form of industrial enterprise-from artisanal production to the most modern electronic factory.

However, in spite of this diversity, the country is facing an acute natural resource crisis in the recent years. There are shortages of prey for hunters and fishermen, of land for shifting cultivators, of grazing ground for pastoralists, of fuel, fodder and manure for subsistence plough-cultivators, of power and water for cash-crop agriculturists, of power, water and raw materials for industry. Inevitably such shortages strongly affect the quality both of human life and the natural environment. The problems are becoming acute and defy solution.

These contemporary concerns have led several scholars to try to reconstruct Indian history using insights derived from human ecology. It has been rightly suggested that the colonial rule marks "an important watershed in the ecological history of India."[1] This was because of the fact that India had to encounter a technologically advanced and modern 'culture.' Modern transformation in human history sprang from *Renaissance*—a term coined by Jules Michelet[2] in his well Known *History of France* (1855)—propagating the basic principle of Man as the center of Universe (the so-called *Humanism*). This concept led to the development of the principle of linear progress in history. This 'Modern' discourse, makes its starting point, not Man but the physical material world. This signified a fundamental shift of outlook—reshaping man through reshaping Nature. Modern discourse is sustained by a deep axiomatic faith in the inherent ability of Man to re-shape the material world. Progress is the sovereign from of modern civilization and modern discourse is pivoted on the certainty that Man has at last been able to shatter the cosmic fetters that has set limits, virtually inflexible, to human freedom.[3] Nature, in this vision, is perceived as a forbidding constraint on Man's yearning to live in freedom. The Nature is seen as an immense hostile presence to be tamed and mastered. The belief is that Nature untouched by Man is devoid of worth and purpose, for it is the human outlook which imparts value and purpose to the Nature.

In India, the modern discourse was mediated by colonial conquest. The values of modern discourse steadily came to be the final referent upon which all categories of description and judgment were sought to be predicated. It was in this sense that technologically advanced and aggressively dynamic culture of the British ruler gave rise to profound dislocations at various levels of Indian society and this is an already acknowledged fact. However, the co-relation between and interdependence of ecological and social changes that came in the wake of colonial rule has not been studied in detail. The British agrarian history of India has been structured almost exclusively on social relations around land, its ownership, and conflicts over the distribution of its produce. The ecological context of agriculture—for example, forests, grazing land, fishing etc.—and colonial exploitation in this sphere has been neglected. Such studies, therefore, exclude a substantial area covered by hills and forests and vast wooded estates of the British. The conflicts around forest resources between the state and its subjects has also not been studied[4] in detail. Reasons for the almost universal neglect of Indian ecological history have not been, yet, adequately analyzed. However, it is clear, as Ram Chandra Guha opines, that it 'stems from both methodological and theoretical limitations.'[5] It is beyond the scope of this study to analyse the reasons for the neglect of ecological history. Suffice it to say that this study is concerned with the impact of colonial policies on the utilization pattern of natural resources and the resultant impact on the tribal life, with particular reference to extinguishing tribe of the Paharias of Jungle—Terai Santal Parganas.

The *Paharias* are/were the original tribe of this region. During the early rule of the East India Company, the Paharias were the first to raise the standard of revolt against the British rule.[6] The *Paharias* were a primitive tribe living in jungle and hilly areas of present Santal Parganas, Birbhum and some portions of Hazaribagh from time immemorial. They lived on slash and burn cultivation or shifting cultivation, and hunting and food-gathering from the forests. Captain Browne and L.T. Shaw, two contemporary writers, inform us that during the Mughal rule, the Paharias were leading a peaceful life.[7] They were bound with semi-feudal relations with the local Zamindars and were the custodians of the military passes (Ghats). Each Hill Tappa was under a chief Manjhi to whom all the Manjhis were obliged to show obedience. If any robbery took place, the chief Manjhi was "obliged to trace it and bring the thieves into justice."[8] All the chowkies or the passes were managed by the Hill people. Their duty was to prevent any body or people from the inner hills passing through the Ghats towards the plain country.[9] Browne further informs us that so long as this system was in vogue "no robberies were committed," "the hill people were happy and quiet" and "low country people were safe from depredations."[10]

However, the anarchy after the battle of Plassey (1757-1772) affected this region seriously because Rajmahal was the field of hectic activity.[11] The grip of Nawabs (Mir Jafar, Mir Qasim and Nizamudaulah) became weak; Zamindars became refractory and did not pay[12] revenue and lawlessness prevailed everywhere. So, the Paharias also became contemptuous of their superiors. The great famine of 1770 drove them to dire distress and they began to plunder the passengers passing through the Ghats and plainsmen.[13]

The Paharias, described in early British records as 'mountaineers' and Hillmen and painted in deep black colour as '*savages*,'[14] '*robbers*' etc. have been more sinned against than sinning. The Britishers first hunted them like wild beasts[15] and then under Warren Hastings, an elaborate military plan was executed under Captain Brooke, Captain Browne and Augustus Cleeveland to control and appease them.

This brings us again to the motives and outlook of the colonial rulers in Jungle Terai.[16] As already indicated, the colonial rulers earnestly believed that the British rule is given the historic mission to posit Man as the active, supreme and self-conscious principle in Man-Nature dialectic, this inevitably nurtured a sense of awesome responsibility (or "*whitemen's burden*")—extending the dynamic of modern civilization, into a realm stubbornly unreceptive, to a profound promise of progress. The colonial conquest in modern age was basically different from other pre-modern conquests. Whereas the principal object of pre-modern conquest was to secure control over less powerful human groups; colonial conquest as a modern enterprise sought mastery over the 'resources' or things. From this cognitive vantage colonial administrators conceived civilization as concomitant with the possession of things. The native tribals were so little removed from Nature and possessed so few things that they were perceived as "Noble Savage" living in a state of Arcadian[17] simplicity In India, the anthropological and ethnographical details were mainly collected by the officials of the company who played a key role. The basic presumption of these officers was that tribal communities were isolated. The deterioration in their condition was attributed to "the sanskritization of semi-tribal chiefs and vulnerability of their character." This attitude is quite unhistorical but the portrayal of a tribal as a "Noble savage" led to build up the myth of the company rule as the protector of the tribals.[18]

Thus, the colonial perception of the tribals in India, quite unlike the European perception of the Red Indians or Australian aborigines, was mediated by a third presence[19]—this third party was variously described as Hindu, Mughal or Maratha, In our area of study, it was characterized as the 'Dikkus' (outsider and trouble mongers, etymologically). The "remorse of the west" so brilliantly expressed by Levi—Strauss[20] (for the backwardness of the tribals) was directed towards third party (and not to the colonial rulers). Hence, we find the perception of colonial rule as the protector and saviour of powerless marginal communities like the tribals. This simplistic model also tried to justify the Raj and the role of missionaries as the protector of the tribals against non-tribals.[21]

In the eyes of the colonialists, the tribal hinterland signified a social space least touched by purposive human activity. It was perceived as a romantic virgin field, somewhat akin to the state of man and things in Europe of thousand years[22] ago. It was further conceived that that this frozen lineage of human trajectory was manifestly incapable of self-movement towards something higher and better. They could be pushed towards 'civilization' only by the coercive power of the compelling rule. The compelling and immediate reason for altering the sensibility and social reality of the tribal native stemmed from the need to secure acceptance of the colonial rule.

The political system of tribal India was based on the concept of direct rule. Unlike Africa, which adopted the system of indirect rule through the traditional chiefs, a large part of tribal population in India were integrated within the province of British India. However, there were areas of tribal concentration which were enclaved "*to reclaim to civilization*" the tribes who often rebelled. Jungle terai (Santal Parganas after 1855) was one of those enclaves.

The colonial policy of control as enunciated by early British administrators in Jungle-Terai represented these above mentioned outlook. The colonial policy was objectively reflected in the system of Robert Brooke, James Browne and Augustus Cleveland. Robert Brooke (1772-1774) undertook serious military expeditions to suppress the rebellion of Hill chiefs and was only partially successful. At the same time, he laid down a policy which was adopted by Browne and later more vigorously by Cleveland. The policy, as narrated by Robert Brooke in his report to the president' Board of Revenue of the whole council on 6th September 1773, advocated to instill the "Terror of English Power" among the Hill chiefs but he frankly admitted that only military coercion was not enough. Therefore, a "steady prosecution of a concerted plan of conquest[23] " must be pursued. The basic purpose of the colonialist rule was to convert the Paharias to settled agricultural society so that the company may get revenue. The efforts of Brooke met with success in the beginning, and he claimed to have established 283 villages of the Paharias on lowland[24] by 1774. Warren Hastings wrote to the Board of Directors that "Jungle-Terry ... has been reduced to government, the inhabitants civilized and not only the reduction of revenues ... prevented but some revenue yielded from the country itself which a prosecution of the same measures[25] will improve." Mr. Browne also continued the policy of suppression and appeasement. On one hand, he granted *sanads* for Jagirs to Hill chiefs, on the other hand he made a plan for distribution of large tracts of plain land to the "invalid" or retired sepoys of the company. This was meant for "encircling" the Paharias and to demonstrate them the benefits of settled agriculture.

Mr. Cleveland, acclaimed as a hero, was the shrewdest colonialist. He elaborated the system by making provisions for monthly pensions or stipends for Paharia Sardars.[26] This step had two purposes—(i) to bind the Paharia chief to loyalty and (ii) to introduce money economy instead of barter economy in this area This is clear from his following statement—"The disbursement and, of course, the circulation of money in the hills by the government appears to be the most likely bait to ensure the attachment of chiefs, and at the same time nothing will be so conducive to the civilization of the inhabitants as to employ a number of them in our service."[27]

It was neither philanthropy nor humanism but sheer colonial tactics of control for which Cleveland proposed that the Paharias should be "furnished with means of subsistence."[28] Mr. Cleveland urged for a basic change in the policy in order to change their way of life and their mode of cultivation.

Powerful Kingdoms and empires in the past sought to extend control over the tribal contiguity but the maximum that the pre-British conquest could exact was nominal submission. Such submission meant the toleration of an enclosed fort-like structure in remote areas like *Lakargarh* in Jungle-Terai,[29] and a nominal annual tribute. The strategic significance of the region, being located on the high road between Patna and Bengal compelled serious notice for the rulers. Viability of direct conquest depended, however, upon the certainty of regular and substantial yields of revenue. The fluid configurations of settled cultivation within the areas of tribal concentration like the Rajmahal hills and Manjhwe valley exerted severe constraints on the ability of rulers to collect revenue with any regularity. Moreover, the fact that hill chiefs, could without much exertion, harass and disrupt the movement of Dak, passengers and traders meant that the rulers could not overlook it. Hence we find the confined reach of imperial control, which in pre-modern situation could never be anything more than nominal submission and nominal tribute.[30]

Moreover, conquests whether of medieval or modern kind, never happen in the absence of evident and certain prospects of gain—such gain could be in the form of plunder of accumulated wealth; (which in the case of Jungle-Terai was not possible) or it could be in the form of regular extraction of local surplus as revenue. At the bare minimum such extraction had to be costs of conquest and governance.

To achieve this, might alone would never suffice. For the colonial experiment to endure, it was imperative that the basis of livelihood of the Paharias be recast. Shifting cultivation must be replaced by settled cultivation and barter economy be replaced by market-economy in Jungle-Terai.

On 29th August 1783, Cleveland, in a letter to Warren Hastings from Bhagalpur, wrote about a basic change in the policy in order to change the way of life of the Paharias as their mode of cultivation. The "general outline of the plan was" as Sutherland informs us, "to encourage the mountaineers to desert their hills and to get them 'established' on the plains by assigning them large tracts of waste lands lying at the foot of the hills on long leases." Cleveland also advocated remission of taxes for the first ten years and then equitable taxation.[31] However, the plan could not succeed as Cleveland died on 20 July, 1784.

The Paharias could not be persuaded to change the pattern of their life and mode of shifting cultivation. The Paharias are not alone in sticking to shifting cultivation. The 'Baigas' of central provinces and the 'Agarias' of Bastar, the 'chenchus' of Andhra Pradesh have stuck (or tried to stick) to this natural mode of cultivation.[32]

Shifting cultivation is indeed inefficient and wasteful in the sense that crop yields per acre are considerably lower when compared to settled cultivation.[33] For basic sustenance it requires a larger area. However, it must be made clear that shifting cultivation had never been a threat to Forests or to Environment.

It is affirmed in a simple historical detail—Forests have survived best in regions of shifting cultivation.[34]

Perception of shifting cultivation in the modern world has been connected with two historical views. One, in Europe, nothing like shifting cultivation seems to have been ever practiced The European term '*swidden agriculture*' is related to old Norse practice of setting large virgin forests on fire to clear land for tillage and regular[35] cultivation. In sharp contrast, shifting cultivators set fire to small forest patches and in an effectively controlled way.[36]

However, the colonial perception of the shifting cultivation has been that of "an impediment" which blocks the effective exploitation of forest and other resources in the hinterland. In fact, the only thing that was of use and benefit to the colonial rulers was virtually untouched wealth of Nature in these inaccessible regions, notably timber and minerals. In colonial perception, the exploitation of land for settled cultivation was the first priority to raise revenue.[37] It was the basis of Cleveland's scheme. The philanthropic motive was simply a temporary,[38] device to lure the Paharias into settled cultivation. However, the colonialists were unsuccessful in wooing the Paharias. Shifting cultivation as a way of life had special significance in the ethos of the concerned people, their set of social relationships, as well as cultural values, Even the mythical beliefs have, at times, been found associated with the practice of shifting cultivation.[39]

Our colonial rulers took the first definitive step for control of the tribal hinterland by discouraging and outlawing[40] slash-and burn cultivation. This trend was put on a solid footing by the creation and consolidation of the institution of private property as envisaged in permanent settlement (1793).[41]

Very soon, the 'philanthropic' British rulers of Jungle-Terai were dissatisfied with the Hill men who would not "quit the Hills and settle on[42] the plains." *Fombelle*, the Collector of Bhagalpur expressed grave doubts about the Paharias. However, the merchant rulers were hell-bent on raising revenue by destroying the jungles and encouraging settled cultivation.

It is now a well established fact that the imperatives of colonial forestry were essentially commercial. Different shifts in colonial forest policy had no concern for environmental and ecological imbalance.[43] Therefore, during the early rule of the company the colonial state was quite indifferent to forest conservancy. In early decades of 19th century, the forests were viewed by administrators as an impediment to the expansion of cultivation. With the state committed to agricultural expansion as its major source of revenue, the early decades of colonial rule witnessed a "fierce[44] onslaught" on India's forests, in general, and on Jungle-Terai's forests in particular. This region had to bear the first invasion on the forests because the company rule was first established in this region.

The process of cutting the forests began as early as the last decade of 18th century. Zamindars were encouraged to employ "wood-cutters and wood[45]-merchants" who were given "pattas" and this led to a conflict between the Zamindar and the Hillmen in Madhuban Pargana in Manjhwe valley (presently the area lies between Barhet P.S. and Borio P.S. in Sahibganj district).

Very soon, Britishers began to encourage the settlement of '*Sontar*' (Santal) who were adept in wood-cutting. As a result, "an immense[46] expanse of forests" were cleared by them near the border of Kharagpur Estate leading to a dispute between the Paharias and the Santals and their patron Zamindar. The same pattern of conflict occurred in *Pargana Handwe* (near Nonihat, Dumka). Sutherland reports that "very considerable tracts of extensive forests which here existed have been brought into cultivation by industrious *Sontars* who emigrated from Beerbhoom and Ramgurh districts."[47] This led to a quarrel between the Zamindar of Handwe Jhabban Singh and 39 manjhis (Sardars) of the Paharias.[48] Considerable sums were derived from the removal of timber and charcoal and the rents were charged on such activities as well which became a bone of contention between Hill chiefs of Belpatta on one side and Bechu Kunwar and Sumer Singh (Zamindars) on the other side.

With the abuses becoming rampant in the hill-system of Cleveland, Sutherland, Asstt. Magistrate at Bhagalpur was deputed to make an enquiry. Mr. Sutherland's Report submitted in December 1819 advocated the creation of special tract of encircled land to be called *Damin-i-Koh* (Skirt of the Hill) and that this tract of land be declared as Government Estate. Sutherland writes—"That it be declared under the authority of the superme government that the Hills and generally the Hilly tracts occupied by the Hilly people, are the property of ruling power alone, dependent on whom the Hill people hold their possessions."[49] The government accepted the proposal of Sutherland of creating a government estate. This has been interpreted by British writers as one of the measures adopted for the protection of the Paharias.[50] The colonial government posed itself as the 'protector of hill men' and they tried to control the entry of outsiders in the Damin-i-Koh.[51]

I fear to submit that I do not agree with this classical view of Damin-i-Koh propagated by the British and endorsed by Indian historians[52] as well. As a matter of fact, the land-space encircled by pillars as Damin-i-Koh was the space utilized by the Paharias unhindered where they enjoyed the fruits of Nature sensitively from time immemorial but by a stroke of pen, the land of Paharias was declared as a Government Estate and the rights of the Paharias became subservient to the colonial interests. Above all, the same British official Mr. Sutherland—advised to invite "husbandmen of other races," particulary the Santals to till the lands of the plain if the Paharias did not change their attitude towards cultivation.[53] Sutherland further recommended the resources of the Estate should be increased by whatever revenue might be derived from the forest and arable part of Hilly tract, including the Skirt of Hills"[54]. It is indeed true that the Hill men were not required to pay rent but "all land within the pillars was claimed by the government given over to hill men to be held by them as long as they behaved in an orderly manner.[55] "But as Captain Sherwill informs us "as the hill-men could not be induced to cultivate the valley ..... Government permitted a wandering race of people named Sonthals whose territory extends from Cuttack, Manbhum, Chotanagpur, Hazaribagh, Palamow to Rewah, to locate themselves on the land repudiated by hill men" paying at the same time a light land-tax for the ground so occupied."[56]

As a matter of fact the Santals were setting in Zamindari estates of Handwe (Lakerdiwani) and Barkop as early as the Survey of Buchanan[57] (1810-11) but in Damin–i–Koh they were deliberately infiltrated by some British officials. Mr. John Petty Ward, the officer deputed to demarcate the area of Damin i-Koh, was very enthusiastic about the Santhals and he permitted them and "issued pattas in the teeth of government orders."[58]

Very soon, the Santhals increased in number, both by births and immigration, and in 1838 Mr. Pontet took charge as the superintendent of Damin-I-Koh. Mr. Pontet had nothing to do with the hills and hillmen "but only with the culturable slopes and valleys."[59] He had been appointed to guard the interests of the government "by making favourable land-settlements with the

Santhals and to collect the rent."[60] Mr. Pontent was obviously successful on both the scores. The number of Santhal villages increased from about forty (40) in 1838 to 1473 villages in 1851. Population of Santals increased from 31,000 in 1838 to 82,795 in 1851 and the Rent increased[61] from Rs. 2000/- in 1838 to Rs. 43,918/- 13 Annas 51/2 paise in 1851.

But all the achievement of Mr. Pontet was at the cost of Nature and ecological balance. The forests were mercilessly cut by the Santals who were actually wood-busters. An intelligent and keen observer, Buchanan, saw the Santals settling in Lakerdiwani in 1800. Buchanan writes—"they (Santals) are very expert in clearling forests and bringing them into cultivation but seldom endure to pay any considerable rent and whenever the land has been brought into full cultivation and the customary rent is demanded, they retire to wastes belonging to some other Zamindar."[62] Obviously having destroyed a jungle and having cultivated it for a few years, they proceeded further to destroy another jungle in order to avoid 'full rent.' This was one of the important reasons for their migration from Birbhum. They had been hired by the Zamindars of Birbhum "for the purposes of clearing their estates of jungle and wild beasts after 1795, the year in which the single zamindari of Birbhum was being split up into numerous estates and put to sale-spree and rack renting."[63] Thus, the Santals were a tribe who took delight in cutting forests and killing wild animals.

This region was full of forest in 18th and early decades of 19th century. This is clear from the references in Ancient and Mughal history as well as from the account of Martin[64]. Martin tells us that the district of Bhagalpur (including Santal Parganas) was an excellent field for a botanist and in most part of the district of Bhagalpur the whole land was called 'jungle.'[65] The pre-dominant tree in the district was the *sal or sakhua* (Shorea Robusta). Besides this valuable timber-tree, the other main trees were *Asan* (Terminalia Tomentosa), *Harre* (Terminalia chebula) *Bahera* (Terminalia Belerica), *Piar* (Buchanania Latibolia), *Bamboos*, *Marga* (Ptero carpus marsupium), *Satsal* (Dal—Bergia Latifolia), *Gamhar or Kasomar* (Gemelina Arborea), *Khajur, Banyan, Pipal, Neem, Palas* (Butea Frondosa), *Kend, Jamuri Nimbu* (citrus decumena), *Nimbu* (Citrus Limon), *Mango, Tamarind* (Tamarindus Indica), *Jamun* (Engenia Jambolana) *Goose Berry* (Kamranga—Averto caramfota),

Papita (Carica Papaya), *Bair, Anar* (Punica Granatum). Thus the region was very rich in forest wealth. A tract of woodland started near River Chandan and ran by Jaipur along the whole (present) Santal Parganas' boundary to Laxmipur near Bounsi in Banka (present) district.[66]

The region was rich not only in flora but also in fauna. The leopards, bears[67], wolves rhinoceros and elephants[68] were in abundance. In addition to these big animals, Capt. Sherwill, the revenue surveyor, has enumerated many other species. Captain Sherwill writes "there is an abundance of insect life and fish... consisting of fishing eagles, crows ravens, paddy-birds, mohoka, golden oriole, snipe, mina, Koel, larks, crested bulbuls Jaennas, sparrow-hawks, pewit, plover, king-crow, hoopoe, brahminee kite, king-fishers, storks, kites, snippets, pharaoh's chickens, whistling teals, grey and black patridge terns, finch, pondicherry vultures, brown vulture, swallow, pagla, wagtail, bee-eater, woodpecker, blue pigeon, kokleet, doves, jay horon, cormorants, and numerous wild fowls."[69]

Thus, we may safely conclude that region was very rich in flora and fauna. This ecological setting provided by Nature was the mainstay of the life of the Paharias who lived on slash and burn cultivation, food-gathering, and hunting. The method of shifting cultivation as practised by the Paharias has been described by Sherwill. Sherwill informs us that the hill-men, being basically lazy, did not clear the forests for his crops. They (hill-men) generally chose "the most precipitous hill sites as the ground best fitted for his crops." In these spots, they used "an iron shod staff or a pointed stick hardened by charring" instead of "a plough." With the implement, they made "holes" in the soil at the distance of a foot or less from each other and dropped a mixture of "following seeds, Indian corn, Janera, bora beans and the seeds of several small pulses." The tall and robust Indian corn and Janera formed an ample support to twining born bean, which in turn afforded a beneficial shade to the more delicate pulses at the feet."[70]

This practice, claimed to be the first system of food-production, is said to date back to the lower Paleolithic period.[71] A significant feature of the system was communal property ownership. Under this system, each household unit had rights over the natural resources as a member of the village.[72]

This was deliberately destroyed by injecting the virus of

private property among the Paharias. Captain Browen issued 'Sanads' or grant of land to the Hill chiefs and Cleveland gave them pecuniary allowances and lastly Cornwallis introduced fully the concept of private property in[73] 1793.

Resource-management in the technique of shifting cultivation was oriented to protect natural resources while reaping its fruits. We do not have exact historical data to confirm this claim, but practices among tribes dwelling in forest regions today as well as anthropological data point strongly to such a system in the past. In other words, there was a close relation between nature and culture, oriented to maintaining a sustainable balance between human beings and nature.

Geographers explain this situation by the concept of "cultural ecology"[74] According to this concept, Environmental Balance or stability exist when human populations co-exist in congruence with the natural environment that sustains them. A culture is developed which defines, the nature of exploitation and imposes rules regarding such exploitation. The logic of nature, in fact, governed the entire character of tribal handling of the natural resources. To maintain the cultural ecological balance, slash and burn cultivation or jhoom or kurao of the Paharias was practised in such a way that the maximum was extracted from the forests, without disturbing their productive potential.

However, this cultural ecological balance was deliberately disturbed by revenue hungry merchant rulers and their sponsored tribe, the Santals who were passing through tribe-peasant continuum. Basically a wandering tribe, about the origin of which there are a number[75] of theories, the Santals had become a post-primitive tribe before coming to the Jungle-Terai.[76] As they (The Santals) were a wandering' race they could not develop that sense of cultural ecology, which could have prevented them from committing excess atrocities on flora and fauna of the region leading to denundation of forests and problems of survival for the Paharias. Mr. Petty Ward, who made the entry of the Santals into Damin-i-Koh possible in the "teeth of government orders," writes about the basic qualities of the Santals as such—"From choice they select the most wild spots and so great is their predilection for the wildest places that they are seldom known to remain at one station longer than it takes to clear and bring into cultivation."[77] In other words, the migrant Santals acted as "free-riders" on the common natural resources of the *Damin-i-Koh*. This resulted in a tragic 'deforestation' in Jungle-Terai. A few verbal pictures of the situation are available from an eye-witness, Captain Sherwill, the revenue surveyor.

Sherwill writes that "after a great deal of trouble, the boundary of *Damin-i-Koh* was demarcated but soon the Sonthals from the south were admitted; "before whose axes the forest disappeared in a few years; the wild beasts... were soon destroyed by the arrows of the omnivorous Sonthal...."[78] Again, while Sherwill was crossing the Gumani River (in Sahibganj district) he chanced upon to enter a valley, where the "Scenery" was particularly pleasing and at the top of hills there were large trees, and the plain was also "beautifully wooded with large trees that have escaped being felled by the Sonthals when clearing the forests."[79]

On going further captain Sherwill met an old Paharia chief, Kesoo Sardar. The old Paharia chief took him to the summit and pointed out a number of trees of "finest quality" cut for purpose of erecting a building for the missionaries. However, the missionaries got the trees felled and left the place. They did not return on the hills, there remained Kesoo Sardar and his men to mourn and tell Captain Sherwill that though the "trees had been felled in one day, they had taken fifty years to grow."[80] The hill men along with Kesoo Sardar complained "bitterly" that "the Sonthals were occupying all their vallies, were very saucy and would not leave their clearings alleging that they had received leases from Mr. Pontet and move they would not."[81] Moving further, Captain Sherwill saw at Narganjo (near Kathikund bazar in Dumka district at present) the unmindful and tragic deforestation. Sherwill writes—"At Sonthal clearing of Narganjo now a twelve month old, it was distressing to see the enormous waste of valuable timber, the large trees of many feet diameter were prostrate in every direction, hundreds of still larger trees stood erect but withered, being too large for the small Sonthal axe to cut entirely through, they had been merely girdled, which operation consists of cutting a deep notch of four inches or more in width and depth completely round the tree."[82]... This process of girdling was like slow-poisoning of the trees and in a few months the trees withered, all smaller branches disappeared leaving the main stem standing dry and erect. These attenuated trees were lifted by the Santals later.

Further Captain Sherwill noticed that "fifty-five timber trees" which had been girdled, "stood in this naked condition" in one field and the scene offered "a melancholy and curious contrast to the neighboring green and luxurious forest, with which the field was entirely enclosed."[83] This led the Captain to make a sad and terse comment—"In a few years, not a tree will be left in these now timber crowded valleys, (vallies) almost the whole of the large sal forests have already perished under the operation of girdling for the production[84] of resin known as Dhoomna."

From the above account of an eye-witness (that too British official) like Captain Sherwill, it is crystal clear that indiscriminate cutting of trees took place under the British patronage. The Santals acted as the agents of this deforestation.

The way of life evolved by forest-dwelling primitive tribes, like the Paharias of Jungle—Terai, was woven around the forest ecology. The primitive tribes also ensured that the forest was protected against the depredations of men and nature.[85] This symbiotic relationship suffered a setback during the British rule when the forest was looked upon not as a vital link between human habitat and the larger environment, Rather, the forests were looked upon only as a source of maximization of profit. This led to the ecological imbalance and everything became topsy-turvy for the primitive tribe.

The tribals managed the forest as a resource for fulfilling their basic needs and drives and to optimize its use *as a balanced productive eco-system*. Shifting cultivation (*Jhoom or Kurao*) ensured that there was no famine for the Primitives. The swiddeners produced a variety of crops like maize, millet, pulses, vegetables, chilli, ginger and turmeric in their mixed farming on the same plot. Even if one crop failed, the other produce was available for consumption. Thus, there was no danger of famine for them.[86] Even the worst famine of 1770 did not affect the Paharias when entire region was facing acute shortage of food-grains, the hill-men survived on Makai (*maize*) and Bora (*beans*). They also gave shelter to hundreds of plains-men who opted for going to the hills.[87] With large scale deforestation and delegitimization of shifting cultivation, the table was turned against the Paharias and other primitive groups. The colonial officials, anxious to harness the large reserve of timber and land-revenue, always looked upon shifting cultivation with a pronounced animosity. They were determined to curb and eradicate the freedom to forest resources and the right of slash and burn cultivation.[88]

The British rulers and their sponsored tribe, the Santals were responsible for the destruction of fauna as well. Captain Sherwill writes—".... The wild beasts that had been the terror of these hitherto unexplored wild were soon destroyed by the arrows of omnivorous Santhal…."[89] The wild elephants of the region were destroyed by the Paharias due to the reward announced by the Collector of Bhagalpur. The collector of Bhagalpur had announced a reward of fifty rupees (a handsome amount in those days) for killing one elephant.[90] Captain Sherwill narrates with disgust that "the last elephant destroyed in these parts is supposed to have perished about twenty years ago" (i. e. in about 1831 A.D.). Francis Buchanan has mentioned about elephants in different localities e.g. near Karharia, near Dumka, between Nalhatti and Birkheti, and in the hills near Bilahari (to the west of Farakka) near Rajmahal and to the south of Pirpainti. However, they became rare by the middle of 19th century.

Rhinoceros were also quite numerous according to the statement of Buchanan. During the period of his survey, they were becoming rare due to disturbances caused to them by "sports men" (Hunters particulary[91] Europeans)

O' Malley's statement is quite candid and straight regarding the extinction of fauna. "The Santal, moreover, is as destructive to the game as he is to jungle, and the result has been as extirpation of the smaller game, on which the larger carnivores prey, and the migration of the latter to other districts, where food is more plentiful. Not only do the Santals kill any small game they can knock down when alone, but occasionally they[92] organise large drives." As a result, tigers, leopards, bears, chital (spotted deers), barking deers, wild pigs and various birds became extinct in the region.[93]

This large scale deforestation, the loss of flora and fauna created a deep sense of anguish among the hill-men or Paharias. Folk-songs affirm the deep sense of loss felt by the victims. One of the forlk-songs of the Paharias is quoted below: *Jago Jago Jungle Raja Deen Daku Bolain chhini Laibon Jungle Raj,*

Jaan dibon Jiwan dibon nahain dibo jungle Raj Ghorai-Pirai nahin Chharibo jungle Raj.

"जागो जागो जंगल राजा दिन डाकू बोलय छिनी लैबों जंगल राज।
जान दिबों जीवन दिबो नहाँय दिबो जंगल राज घोड़ाय बीड़ाय नहीं छाड़िबों जंगल राज।।"

The large scale deforestation and depletion of natural resources created the problem of survival for the Paharia. In 1832, a band of thirty normadic Mal Paharias were arrested in connection with recurring clashes with the Santals, who were active in reclamation of land (cutting of jungles) in Birbhum, Bankura and Jungle Terai. The Paharias straightly stated "The articles produced from the jungle had become scarce and they had some difficulty in getting a livelihood."[94]

The condition of primitive tribes such as Paharias, Agarias, Baigas or Chenchus have been discussed by various anthropologists. However, the factor of ecology has not been given the importance it deserves.[95] A well preserved and robust environment imparts to a community a special quality issuing from the strength of resources and habitat. Conversely, a community, which seeks nourishment from "an impoverished[96] environment" languishes. Such tribes are unable to make both ends meet and its socio- economic milieu continues to slide[97] down. The Paharias of Jungle-Terai Santal Parganas are one such notable tribe[98] which faces the danger of being wiped out from the surface of the earth. The Birjias of Palamu the Bharias of Patalkot (Madhya Pradesh), the Paharias of our region and the Birhors of Singhbhum (Jharkhand) and northern Orissa exemplify this risk of extinction.

The noted anthropogist, Surjit Sinha, observed this regression minutely and he describes it as "secondary primitivisation" He postulates that extensive deforestation resulted in the loss of resources for them and they, who had been shifting cultivatiors, were forced to become hunter-gatherers.[99]

The worst effect of deforestation was on the cultivation. Ecologists inform us that deforestation leads to soil erosion. The trees not only increase rainfall of an area but also conserve water which falls on ground as rain.[100] Plants also reduce evaporation thus allowing water to remain in soil for a long time. With increased soil erosion there is the danger of desertification[101] and growing infertility of the soil making them barren.

We have concrete evidence to substantiate the above statement. The evidence is given by an acknowledged apologist of colonial rule and the compiler of district Gazetteers, O'Malley. He quotes in his Birbhum Gazetteer the statement of a gentleman (native) which has been recorded by Lt. Col. J. E. Gastrell in his Report on Bankura district in 1863[102].

According to the statement recorded by Lt. Col G. E. Gastrell and quoted by O'Malley, it is clear that by the year C. 1823 A. D. there was large scale deforestation in Birbhum. Let me quote him verbatim[103]—"the unrestricted clearing of the jungles has had great influence in decreasing the annual amount of rain and impoverishing the country. What about a half century ago was thick jungle and waving plains of grass, is now almost a sterile and barren waste. Wherever the land was fit for cultivation, it was ploughed up. The successive rains have washed away the soil of uplands, and have left only a bed of kunkury earth on which[104] nothing will grow."

He further narrates that only lowland in the valleys are worth-cultivating, thanks to *Paddy Kheti* owing to which "the soil of valleys had not been[105] carried away into rivers." It is apparent that it was not only deforestation rather the extinction of vegetative woods as well which was patronized by the company rulers and their collaborators, the Zamindars. It was the replica of *Greed par excellence* and a heinous crime against Nature and at the same time an unpardonable sin against the creator. In stead of the maxim of "the remorse of the west" expressed by Levi-strauss[106] for the Indian tribes, we would like to register our deep sense of anguish, and heart-felt sense of victimization of the East. We would also like to fix the responsibility for the annihilation of such marginal tribes as Paharias of Jungle-Terai or Birhors of Chotanagpur and Orissa on the shoulders of the merchant rulers.

However, it is interesting to see the other side of the Colonial policy, which was dictated, again, by imperial needs and not due to ecological concerns. The same British government who managed the *fierce onslaught*[107] on the forest as narrated above became *pious* in its intentions and initiated a policy of conservation of forests. With the depletion of oak forests in England and Ireland[108] and the growing demand for timber for the expansion of railways (From 7,678 Kms of railway line in 1870 to 51,658 Kms in 1910), the British rulers became anxious for protecting the forests. In 1862, Dalhousie had emphasized the need for the establishment of a Forest Department that could meet the enormous requirements of the railway companies (nearly one million sleepers annually). Impending shortages, observed Dalhousie, had made the subject of forest conservancy an important administrative[109] question."

This important administrative question of forest conservancy was started with the help of German Foresters in 1864. However, the "task of reversing the deforestation of past decades required the forging of legal mechanisms to curtail the exercise of use rights by village communities."[110] Thus came into existence the Indian Forest Act of 1878 with stringent provisions. This was a comprehensive piece of legislation which, by one stroke of pen, attempted to obliterate centuries of customary use of the forest by rural populations all over India.

Furthermore, this Act of 1878 was double-edged. It aimed to maintain strict control over forest utilization from the perspectives of imperial needs, and at the same time, envisaged the working of compact blocks of forests for commercial timber production in a "scientific" manner. As a result, sharp restrictions were exercised on customary rights.[111]

The agricultural expert of the colonial government advocated the creation of fuel and fodder[112] reserves for the improvement of agriculture but the government decided otherwise. The pace of exploitation of forest resources was escalated and intensified. Thus state forestry undermined the ecological basis of subsistence cultivation, hunting and gathering.[113] It must be pointed out here that there had been invasions on the forest resources in pre-colonial periods as well. Clearly the forest communities had for several centuries been subject to the pressures of agrarian civilizations of the plains. However, this colonial onslaught was different in nature. Prior to the British period, extraction of forest produce was restricted to such commodities as honey, Ghee, pepper, cardamom, ivory, turmeric herbs etc. which did not alter the ecological balance, or customary forest rights. It was the emergence of timber as the major commercial commodity that led to a qualitative change in the patterns of resource-utilization.

The first and foremost casualty in our region was the Paharia tribe. Several restrictions were put on *kurao or Jhoom* cultivation. The Paharias resisted at every step and put obstacles in the settlement. The officer deputed for settlement, McPherson writes: "... The one and only objection which was persistently urged was that their forest rights would be invaded."[114] Even before the passage of the Forest Act of 1878, the government got demarcated the forests, with an estimated area of forty square miles, south to the Bansloi river, and a "reserved" forest—block was created. This proposal involved the transplantation of 48 Paharia villages and was vigorously opposed by the local Paharias.[115] But in spite of all protests, villages were uprooted and the hill-men were deprived of their livelihood.

In the newly settled Paharia villages, jhoom or kurao was restricted within a limited and well demarcated area. In older many villages were deprived of the right to shifting cultivation. Out of 444 villages, jhoom cultivation was allowed on a limited scale in 239 villages only and in the rest villages, it was denied[116] totally.

All this bred discontent and led to disputes between Paharias and government foresters on the one hand and between Paharias and the Santals on the other. The Santals continued pushing the Paharias back and encroaching on their jhoom patches.

The poor Paharias had to face the two opponents of their way of life—The British government and the Santals. During McPherson's settlement, (1898-1807) an attempt was made to confine jhoom or Kurao rights in each hill but the Paharias always violated it.[117] In the next *Settlement of Gantzer* (1922-35), all wastelands in *Damin-i-Koh* were divided into two classes and placed in separate Khatians with the status '*Gair Mazrua laik jungle*' and "Gair Mazrua Digar"[118] i.e. wasteland suitable for afforestation and wasteland of other kinds. This was done with the object of checking village forests and forest rights. Cairns were erected by the forest department to prevent further cultivation by extension/ encroachment and also to check Kurao or jhoom.

The progressive tightening of state control over forest areas was the most deeply felt grievance of the tribe, particularly the Paharias.[119] The ban on shifting cultivation (Jhoom in Jharkhand and podu in Andhra Pradesh) was disastrous for tribals and poor peasants in forest. For unlike plough-cultivation, it did not require cattle or manure. For millennia virgin forests had provided a variety of free good for the rural poor–timber for fuel, dwelling and tools, grazing facilities, edible roots and plants, fish and game. D. D. Kosambi has emphasized the prodigality of sub-tropical nature as one of the important causes of the survival in our[120] country of primitive food-gathering side by side with settled agriculture and urban culture. After sponsoring the deforestation in this region (1770-1860), and then the sudden clamping down of the restriction on the use or even entry into 'reserved' forests rudely disrupted the deep rooted cultural and ecological norms. This resulted in pauperization of the Paharias and their ultimate conversion to Social banditry and other crimes. We do not agree with Hobsbawm[121] who has easily accepted the colonial theory of self-contained "criminal tribes and castes" as representing the Indian variant of social banditry. Arnold has mentioned the tribals of Gudem region in Andhra Pradesh among whom dacoity spread as shifting cultivation was banned in the forest.[122] We find a similar case with the Paharias.

Thus, the Paharias were forced to give up their age tested harmless means of livelihood and they were reduced to abject poverty. The post-primitive and cultivating tribe, the Santals also pushed them back to the hills. It has resulted in a deep-rooted psychological depression among the whole tribe of the Paharias. To borrow the well-known phrase of Verrier Elwin; it resulted in a *loss of nerve* and led them to extinction. The declining population of the Paharias presents the risk of their being wiped out from the surface of the earth. The post primitive and adventurous tribe, the Santals reacted in a different way.

The efforts of British authorities to prevent the Santals from cutting the forests met with little success and in 1880 they were found to be cutting down more than the permitted amount of timber.[123] The Santals also continued to clear the jungles for reclamation. The migration of the Santals continued and they cleared forests for new settlements to a greater extent than the Mundas and Oraons. This often resulted in Paharias-Santal clashes and also disputes between the forest officials and the Santals.[124]

Such pressures, combined with a loss of faith in traditional chiefs due to failure of the first phase of primary resistance movement (*the Santal rebellion of 1855*) led to the growth of revitalization movements of a millenia r/messianic nature among the Santals (*Sapha Hor Movement or Kharwar movement*). This movement 'revitalized' the Santals and nourished them with zeal required for survival. Thus, the Santals are surviving in spite of colonial onslaught which; the Paharias are continuously languishing and are on the verge of extinction.

This reminds us compulsively to the theory of Challenge and Response, as propagated by Arnold Toynbee.[125]

Toynbee conceives the obstacles put by Nature as the 'Challenge' and the concerned race's efforts to meet them as 'response.' However, in this case, we find the obstacles deliberately created by men before primitive tribes; making their lives and sustenance difficult.

We have a declining demographic profile of the Paharias and the reasons for this are not far to seek. It is true that in Pre-Colonial days, their livelihood was hard and the thing they could consume and own very few. But the basic sustenance was assured, even famines did not disturb the hill men. The vital clue of their survival and sustenance was the unfettered access to Nature. This was also the reason of their survival as distinct entities having a special kind of social cohesion; despite a long and not always peaceful history of interaction with pre-colonial political powers. However, with the gradual consolidation of the colonial state, we find definitive shifts and changes in the pattern of interaction between tribal societies and political authority. As the effective reach of the colonial state began to extend deeper into the hinterland, access to nature was progressively restricted. British land settlement meticulously, specified the plots encircled by settled cultivation but it simply took no notice of shifting cultivation[126] Land revenue settlements also initiated the process of appropriating vast stretches of land as 'reserved forests' and 'government lands.'[127] Its consequences have been simply annihilating for more than 90% of the Paharias. Their survival and livelihood depended on these lands from where they gathered forest produce, razed their cattle and practiced Jhoom. Under the colonial dispensation this mode of livelihood ceased to have legitimate existence.

To add fuel to the fire of annihilation, the penetration of market forces into rural-tribal hinterlands diminished the bargaining power of rural workers and artisan communities. A wide range of skills and crafts, vital to the earlier economy of the region were smothered out leading to deindustrialization[128] in Jungle—Terai—Santal Parganas Local manufactures were displaced gradually from the market by colonial goods. For most people the only choice was to enter the new industrial world as "unskilled workers. Bands of homeless destitutes, the Paharias and the Santals, began to migrate.[129]

To sum up, we find that an entire rhythm of life was torn by colonial forest policy. Folk songs affirm the deep sense of loss felt by the victims. Suffering and injustice can never be measured. The tragedy, unfolded in this region, needs to be understood. The process initiated by colonial intervention so defined the situation that our modern cognition is predisposed to overlook the well-being and livelihood of the tribals of this region. The destruction of their livelihood is represented as almost akin to an unavoidable natural calamity,[130] such a view is prejudiced and tries to absolve "the perpetrators of such horrendous destruction"[131] of any sense of guilt. However, no amount of "remorse" expressed by Levi-Strauss or no logic advanced by colonial historians can absolve the British rulers of the heinous sin committed against humanity. Cultural sensibilities and modes of livelihood are closely interwoven. Destruction of modes of livelihood (the forests) are moments of deep anguish. The sense of one's self and the world are traumatically shaken. It is high time the modern sensibility learnt to accept the destructive consequences inherent in modern process. Ecological devastation in Indian context, unlike Europe, has also to be comprehended as a question of life-style and survival.

REFERENCES

1. Ramchandra Guha, State Foresty and Social Conflict in British India: *Past and Present*, Oxford University Press, No. 123, p. 142.
2. To begin with, this humanist quest was directed, albeit in an oblique way, against theological fetters imposed by the church and Christian dogma. Jules Michelet gave to this sensibility and process a name that swiftly acquired universal currency—*Renaissance or Re-birth.* Jacob Burckhardt's *The Civilization of the Renaissance in Italy,* 2 Vols; Harper, 1975, remains even after a lapse of a hundred years, its classic conceptual reference cf Suresh Sharma—*Tribal Identity and the modern world,* Sage Publications New Delhi, 1994.
3. The second volume of the *Cambridge Economic History of India,* a well acclaimed and authentic account of colonial agrarian history has no section devoted to the management and utilization of the forests (Dharma Kumar (Ed) Cambridge-1983) Two premier review symposia appeared in two premier journals in the field: *Modern Asian studies* XIX, 1985 and *Indian Economic and Social History Review* XXI, 1984. However, this obvious deficiency has not been pointed out by any of the reviewers.
4. Ramchandra Guha, *State Foresty and Social conflict in British India,* op. cit., p. 142.
5. Ibid.

6. For details see, Leela Prasad, (1984): *Opposition to British Supremacy in Bihar,* Janaki Parakashan, Patna Also. O'Malley—*Santal Parganas Gazetteers*, Calcutta, 1910 Reprint Logos Press Delhi, pp. 33-39.
7. Sutherland's Report, Sutherland was the magistrate who was appointed to enquire into the maladministration in Jungle-Terai He submitted his report to W.B. Bayby, Secretary to the Government in the Judicial Department, Fort William on 8th of June, 1819. A Xeroxed copy is with the author. Paras 27th and 28th Loc. Cit.
8. Browne's *India Tracts of—Sutherland's Report.* Loc.Cit. Paras 30-31
9. Ibid.
10. Ibid.
11. Ibid.
12. Rajatkant Ray, *Colonial penetration and the initial resistance,* Indian Historical Review, Vol. XII, No. 2, pp. 20-25.
13. Nikhil Sur, *The Bihar famine of 1770, Indian Economic and social History Review*, Vol. XIII, No. 4. The conditions in Bhagalpur had worsened due to military depredations, p. 526.
14. O'Malley, (1984): *Santal Parganas Gazetteer,* Calcutta 1910, Reprint Logos Press New Delhi, p. 35.
15. O' Malley, *S. P. Gazetteers* op. cit., p. 35.
16. Jungle—Terai was a military collectorship under the direct supervision of the Governor. It contained the whole of the present Santal Parganas and Kharagpur hills, some parts of Ramgarh hills, and Hazaribagh.
17. K. S. Singh, *Presidential Address Modern India section,* Indian History Congress, Bhubneshwar, p. 376.
18. Ibid.
19. Suresh Sharma, op. cit., p. 68.
20. Levi, Strauss, (1984): *Tristes Tropiques*, Penguin, p. 48 ff.
21. K.S. Singh, (1971): *State, formation in tribal society* Journal of Anthropological Society of India Vol. 6, No. 2.
22. Sir Henry Maine, (1890): *Early law and custom*, Johu Murray, p. 131.
23. Text of Report of Robert Brooke vide Revenue Board of the whole council, original consultation, 6th September, 1773, No. 32 cf *Bengal, Past and Present,* Vol. 73, Part. I, 1954, pp. 57-58.
24. O' Malley, S.P. Gazetteers, op. cit., p. 36.
25. Ibid.
26. James Browne, *India Tracts*, pp. 73-88 cf Oldham (ed.), *Journal of Francis Buchanan of the district of Bhagalpur (1810-11),* Superintendent Government Printing Press Appendix 3, p. 240.
27. O' Malley, S.P. Gazetteer op. cit., p. 39.
28. Letter of Cleveland to Governor-General-in Council from

Sakrigali dtd. 21st August 1780 of Sutherland's Report, loc. cit., Para 38.

29. Suresh Sharma, *Tribal identity and the modern world*, op. cit., p. 185.
30. For the general tenor of relationships between the Mughal Emperors and chiefs in the outlying region see A.R. Khan, *Chieftains in the Mughal Empire during the reign of Akbar*, I.I.A.S., Simla 1977.
31. Sutherland Report, loc. cit., Para 49.
32. For Baigas and Agarias see Verrier Elwin, (1949): *The Baigas*, Oxford University Press, London 1934, The Agaria, Oxford University Press Bombay.
33. See Sardindu Bose (ed.), *Shifting cultivation in India*, 1991, Anthropological Survey of India.
34. In fact, shifting cultivation nurtures the soil of hill slopes see the exceedingly well considered argument in D. C. Kaith, *Shifting cultivation practices in India*, Indian Council of Agricultural Research, New Delhi, Review series, No. 24, 1958.
35. The only exception concerns certain parts of Finland. See *Journal of Finnish Anthropological Society*, 4/1987 Vol. IX.
36. For details see, Sardindu Bose (ed.), (1991): *Shifting cultivation in India*, Anthropological Survey of India.
37. Suresh Sharma, *Tribal Identity in the Modern World*, op. cit., p. 151.
38. See the remark of W. B. Oldham, once Deputy Commissioner of Dumka, and the views of John Petty Ward, demarcator of *Damin-i-Koh*. "He (Mr. Ward) had no sympathy with Cleveland's measure (which, through a succession of accidents continued to this day, were only intended as provisional by Cleveland himself and he (Mr. Ward) wrote without hesitation about "Perposterous claims of the Paharias." W. B. Oldham, I.C.S., *Some historical and ethnical Aspects of Burdwan district* (1894) A copy of this rare book is in the National library, Calcutta. The copy of Record Room Dumka was burnt during the fire in 1962. I have cited from P.C. Roychoudhry's *Santal Parganas Gazetteers*, Patna, 1965.
39. S. N. Mishra (ed.), (1998): *Antiquity to modernity in Tribal India*, Vol. III See the article of A. K. Danda on *Shifting cultivation*, p. 163, Inter India Publication Delhi.
40. See Baden Powell's remark's in the *Report of the Forest Conference*, Year 1873-1874.
41. The permanent settlement (1793) was the attempt by the colonial rules to transform hitherto 'Stagnant' countryside by fixing revenue demand in perpetuity. It was also conceived as a measure to regulate accumulation of surplus in the hands of a 'dynamic' class of landowners (likely to be collaborators of the colonial rule). For a meticulous exploration of 'intellectual ancestry' of

this idea; see Ranjit Guha—*A Rule of Property for Bengal,* Orient Longmans, 1982.

42. Sutherland's Report, Para 60, loc. cit.
43. For a detailed analysis of colonial forestry see Ramchandra Guha, "*Forestry in British and post-British India:A historical analysis*" 2 parts in Economic and Political Weekly 29 October, 1983 and 5-12 Nov. 1983. Also W. Fernandes and S. Kulkarni (ed.), *Towards a new forest policy* (New Delhi, 1983).
44. E.A. Smythies, (1925): *India's Forest wealth,* London, p. 6.
45. Sutherland's Report, Para 72, loc. cit.
46. Ibid, Para 84.
47. Ibid, Para 89.
48. Ibid.
49. Sutherland's Report, Para 134, loc. cit.
50. See for example, O'Malley, (1909): *Santal Parganas Gazetteer* op. cit., p. 44. Mc Pherson's *Settlement Report of Santal Parganas,* Calcutta, 1909, p. 32.
51. Ibid.
52. K. K. Datta etc.
53. Sutherland's Reports, Para 112, loc. cit.
54. Ibid, Para 125, Sub Para seven.
55. Sherwill, p. 547, loc. cit., Capt. Sherwill was the Revenue surveryor who made a tour through Rajmahal Hills in 1851. He has left a detailed note of his tour.
56. Ibid, p. 547.
57. Mc Pherson's Settlement Report, op. cit., p. 30.
58. Ibid, p. 34.
59. Ibid, p. 34-36.
60. Sherwill, loc. cit., p. 548.
61. Ibid.
62. cf. Mc Pherson's Settlement Report, op. cit., p. 30.
63. Ranjan Gupta—The aboriginal world of Birbhum from Ghatwal Revolt to the Santal Insurrection of 1855-56, in Bengal Past and Present, Vol. CXIII, Jan-April 1974.
64. The region lying in the western portion of Birbhum and region lying to the west of Birbhum has been described as *'Aranyaka'* in Digvijay-Prakash' (See Report of Surendra Jha on the temples of Malooti in the library of Ministry of Culture, Government of Jharkand, Ranchi), p. 31; The area around the Kharagpur hills and the region upto Birbhum and Santal Parganas was known as *Bara Jungle* or extensive and terrifying woods, see, Munshi Muhammad Kazim, *Alamgirnama*, Calcutta 1808, p. 493-95.
65. Martin, Eastern India, Vol. II, p. 152.
66. Ibid., pp. 152-164.

67. O' Malley, *S.P. Gazetteers*, op. cit., pp. 17-20.
68. Ibid.
69. Captain Sherwill's Report (1851), p. 558.
70. Ibid, p. 555.
71. B.B. Mohanty, *Shifting cultivation in Orrissa with a case study among the Juang*, Adivasi, (Journal), Vol. 26, No. 4, pp. 17-26.
72. Geeta Menon, *Tribal dependence on Forest Produce in Antiquity to Modernity in Tribal India*, Vol. III, op. cit., p. 174.
73. For motivations behind permanent settlement see Ranjit Guha—*A rule for property in Bengal*. op. cit.
74. See Madhav Gadgil, (1983): "*Forestry with a social Purpose*" in Walter Fernandes and Sharad Kulkarni (ed.). *Towards a new forest policy: People's Rights and Environmental Needs*, New Delhi, Indian Social Institute.
75. For details see O' Malley, *Santal Parganas Gazetteer*, op. cit., pp. 89-101.
76. For the concept of post-primitive tribes who were being peasantized, see the article of B.K. Roy Burman "*Challenges and responses in tribal India*" in Social Movements in India Vol. II (Ed) M. S. A. Rao, Manohar Publications, Delhi, 1979, pp. 101-105. About the Santals, he writes, "The case of the Santals was somewhat different. Traditional Santal society was not stratified in the same way as the Oraon. Munda or Ho were. They had effected an innovation in their social organization by which the primacy of the original settler's lineage was replaced by the supremacy of tribal Council; this in turn facilitated their fanning out since the later part of 18th century, all over uplands in the borders of Bengal, Bihar and Orissa which were being rapidly cleared up to serve the various needs of the colonial and mercantile establishments. Their settlement in these areas, in the face of opposition from the original settlers like the Sauria Paharias and Mal Paharias was possible largely because of the support that they received from colonial administration" ...

    See also, B. K. Roy Burman, (1975): *Population and Social process among the tribes of India*, Plural Societies, winter.
77. Mc Pherson's Settlement Report, op. cit., p. 31.
78. Sherwill's Report, loc. cit., p. 565.
79. Ibid, p. 577.
80. Ibid, p. 587.
81. Ibid, p. 589.
82. Ibid, p. 590.
83. Ibid, p. 590.
84. Ibid.
85. S.C. Dube (ed.), (1998): *Antiquity to modernity in Tribal India*, Vol.

I, Inter India Publications, Delhi, ch.4. The article of Bhupinder Singh.

86. Antiquity to Modernity, Vol. I See the article of Sachdidanand – "*Survival strategies of Indian tribals,*" p. 61.
87. Upendra Narayan Singh, (1980): *Some aspects of rural life in Bihar,* Janaki Prakashan, Patna, p. 12.
88. See Baden-Powell's remarks in the Report of the Proceedings of the first forest conference in the year 1873-1874, pp. 3-7. The British government claimed absolute rights over natural resources. and waste lands. See also *Explanatory notes on Forest Law,* Government of India Calcutta, 1926, pp. 10ff.
89. Captain Sherwill's Report, loc. cit., p. 565.
90. Ibid, p. 585
91. C.E.A.W. Oldham (ed.), (1930): *Journal of Francis Buchanan of the district of Bhagalpur (1810-11),* Patna, Appendix-7.
92. O' Malley, *Santal Parganas Gazetteers,* op. cit., pp. 17-20.
93. Ibid.
94. Dharma Kumar (ed.), *The Cambridge economic history of India*, Vol. II, op. cit., p. 305.
95. See for example—Robin Clarke and Geoffrey Hindley, (1975): *The Challenge of the primitives,* Mc.Grew Hill, New York, Sachchidanand-*Study of primitive Tribes*—Certain conceptual issues in L. P. Vidyarthi (ed.), (1981): *The profiles of the marginal and pre-farming Tribes of Central-Eastern India*, Government of West Bengal Publication Calcutta.
96. Bhupinder Singh, '*Primitive Tribal Groups*' in S.C. Dube (ed.), *Antiquity to modernity in Tribal India,* Vol. I., op. cit., p. 80.
97. Ibid.
98. Ibid, p. 77.
99. S.C. Sinha, "Urgent Problems of research in social and cultural anthropology in India—Perspectives and suggestions" in B. L. Abbi and S. Saberwal (eds.), (1969): *Urgent Research in Social Anthropology,* Indian Institute of Advanced Study Simla. See also S.C. Sinha and B.D. Sharma (eds.), (1977): "*Primitive Tribes: The first step*" Ministry of Home Affairs, New Delhi.
100. P. D. Sharma, (2003): *Ecology and environment,* Rastogi Publications. Delhi, p. 326.
101. Ibid, p. 327.
102. O' Malley, *Santal Parganas Gazetteer,* Calcutta, p. 4.
103. Lt. Col. J.E. Gastrell, *Report on the district of Bankura* (1863), p. 5 cf. O' Malley, *Birbhum District Gazetteers,* p. 4.
104. Ibid.
105. Ibid.
106. Levi, Strauss, (1984): *Tristes Tropiques,* Penguin, p. 48ff.

107. E.A. Smythies, (1925): *India's Forest Wealth*, London, p. 6.
108. R.G. Albion, (1926): *Forests and sea power*, Cambridge, pp. 35-36, 363-368.
109. C.G. Trevor and E.A. Smythies, (1923): *Practical Forest Management*, Allahabad, p. 5. The railways were built to facilitate both troop movements and trade.
110. Ramchandra Guha, State forestry and conflict in British India, op. cit., p. 145.
111. Ibid, p. 146.
112. Ibid.
113. See the views of Jyoti Rao Phule, Shetkary Asud: *The Whipchord of the Farmer* (1882-83). Reprinted in Marathi in the Collected works of Mahatma Phule (ed.), D. Keer and S. G. Malshe, Pune, 1969.
114. McPherson's settlement Report, op-cit., p. 181.
115. O' Malley, *S.P. Gazetteer*, op. cit., p. 178.
116. McPherson's settlement Report, p. 181.
117. Ibid, p. 182.
118. Gantzer's settlement Report, Superintendent Bihar Government Printing Press, Patna 1936, p. 32.
119. Sumit Sarkar, (1980): *Popular movements and middle class leadership in late Colonial India Perspectives and problems of a History from Below;* Centre. For Studies in Social Sciences, Calcutta, p. 11.
120. D.D. Kosambi, (1965): *Culture and civilization of Ancient India in Historical Outline,* London, p. 34.
121. Hobsbawm, *Bandits,* Pelican, 1972.
122. Arnold, *Dacoity and rural crime in Madras,* (1860-1940) 'Journal of Peasant Studies,' Jan-1979.
123. O' Malley, *S. P. Gazetteer*, op. cit., ch. 7.
124. John Mac Dougall, (1985): *Land or religion? The Sardar and Kharwar Movement in Bihar,* (1858-1895), Manohar, New Delhi, pp. 116-121.
125. Toynbee, Arnold, (1972): *A Study of History*, (Abridged one volume edition) Thames and Hudson, Oxford University Press, p. 97.
126. Explanatory notes on Forest Law, Government of India, Nagpur 1926, pp. 18-32.
127. McPherson, *Settlement Report of Santal Parganas*, op. cit.
128. Surendra Jha, (2004): *De-industrialization in 19th C. Bihar, A case study of Jungle-Terai Santal Parganas*, (1757-1947), *Journal of University Department of History*, Ranchi.
129. Chot Rai Desmanghi, *Reak Katha.*
130. Suresh Sharma, *Tribal Identity and the modern world,* op. cit., p. 201.
131. Ibid.

12. MORAL DIMENSIONS OF MAN-NATURE RELATIONSHIP

Pratima Ganguli &
Mritunjay Kumar

In the field of Environmental Ethics the philosophy of 'Land Ethic' given by Aldo Leopold is very important. As evident from the name itself the ethics is related to the earth (land) and its total ecosystem. Aldo Leopold felt that we need a 'new ethic,' an 'ethic' to deal with man's relation to land, animals and plants. 'Land ethic' is large enough to include soils, waters, plants, animals or collectively the land.[1] Leopold summed up the basis of his new land ethic in the following manner:

"A thing is right when it tends to preserve the integrity, stability and beauty of the biotic community. It is wrong when it tends otherwise."

In fact, the work 'Land Ethic' by Leopold is considered an important milestone in the history of the development of Environmental Ethics. It clearly reflects the interdisciplinary approach to comprehend environment and its ethical import. First we will have to understand the intricacies of environment only then its moral values can be deduced and analyzed.

Let us now have a brief survey of the fundamentals of Environment. The first question is:

(a) What is environment ?

'Environment' generally means 'surroundings' around the organisms which have a direct influence on their activities.[2] More specifically the sum total of physical and biotic conditions affecting the responses of organism constitute environment. In other words, all of the external, physical and biological factors that directly influence the survival, growth, development and reproduction of organisms depict environment. It comprises the biotic or living environment which refers to the relationship between different organisms and a-biotic environment (non-living organism) being controlled by the physical soil, light and electric potentials. Thus environment is multifactoral as it consists of many external factors acting in concert to affect organisms.

'Environment' necessarily involves the technical terms like 'ecology' and 'ecosystem.' 'Ecology' is concerned with the relationship between plants and animals (including man) and the environment in which they live.

'Ecosystem,' is another technical term. It is made up of two terms—'eco' and 'system.' 'Eco' means environment and 'system' implies an interacting inter-dependent complex. Thus ecosystem may be defined as any unit which includes all the organisms in a given area which interact with the environment resulting in the flow of energy and biotic diversity as well as material cycle.

The total physical environment of any living organism is called biosphere. Biosphere consists of the sumtotal of hydrosphere, lithosphere and atmosphere into which life penetrates.

The above description of environmental will help us a lot in comprehending the 'land ethic.' Infact, the entire ecosystem containing plants, animals birds, men and physical conditions exist on land. Thus 'land ethic' presents a wholistic view to understand the values of species or the ecosystem. The wholistic view takes a comprehensive look of ecosystem of the earth. According to it, if small organ of ecosystem is upset, it will disturb the entire ecology. Unfortunately, man, so far, has ruthlessly damaged the ecosystem by removing wilderness, killing animals, birds and other eco-destructive practices. In this way, he has contributed to the global warming and other ecological catasrophies. What is required is the review of human conduct with regard to nature within the framework of Environmental Ethics. We can consider the following questions in this regard:

(A) Is it morally justified to exploit nature ruthlessly and, kill birds and animals for human use ?

(B) Whether animals, birds and plants (or other sentient

beings) have any inherent virtues which may merit them to be treated at par with mankind ?

(C) What sort of techniques should we adopt in our conduct in the best interest of ecosystem of this planet?

Regarding the first question we can advance argument that it is highly immoral to kill animals and exploit nature ruthlessly since it goes against the basic moral doctrine of *respect for all forms of life* on this only living planet. If human life is precious, why not other forms of life are equally precious? Animals are slaughtered for human food and other commercial and scientific purposes. If man is given the similar treatment, will it be morally justified? Unfortunately nature sometimes in the form of various calamities like tsunami, floods etc. play havoc with human life, then we begin to criticize that nature's hands are full of blood. Sometimes terrorists' onslaught results into huge loss of humanlife and property. In such cases, man kills man. Don't we feel pain for such unfortunate incidents? But, the same humanbeings sometimes behave ruthlessly with other animals for their self interest and we remain silent. This act of humanbeings can never be justified, as moral.

It is to be noted that thousands of animals and birds are killed daily in various labs and slaughter houses across the globe. Some beautiful species of wildanimals and birds have either become extinct or endangered due to excessive hunting and killing. For example, Asiatic lion, black buck, the great Indian bastard, leopard, panda, crocodile, whales, dolphins are in endangered list.

Let us now view the thing from utilitarian stand point which advocates in this case *maximum happiness for maximum numbers.*

If we put this theory, in the context of environment then there is no way other than considering the happiness of the whole of the ecosystem, which includes not only humanbeings, but also animals, birds, plants and every form of energy. But the case is not so in reality, meaning thereby, humanbeings take least care for the happiness of all other lives and energy of this planet.

Now let us have a glance of this gloomy picture. On the international front, too, the situation is quite grim. Tropical rain forests are fast disappearing from our earth which may accelerate the process of global warming. We are aware of the fact that forests (particularly rain forests) are storehouse of medicinal plants having anti-cancerous properties and lots of scientific knowledge about biodiversity. So by removing rain forest man is destroying the possibility of scientific knowledge. Not only this, forests control the hydrological cycle and keep the climate soothing and pleasant by releasing oxygen and lots of humidity into the atmosphere. It also attracts the rain-cloud. It has been found that the land having rich vegetation has good store of underground water. But once greenery is removed the water table begins to slide down and down causing deficiency of drinking water for man.

Thus we see that for shorter interests, humanbeings are indirectly causing harm to the maximum numbers of living organisms which is totally against the theory of utilitarianism. Here also lies a paradox. Despite all the advantages man procures from the nature, he is not miser in destroying it. He forgets that while doing this, he simply commits suicide.

The pertinent moral question which can be raised here is: *Whether humanbeing has any right to disturb the ecological balance as a result of which survival of all lives on the earth becomes difficult?* The answer can easily be given in negative form. We know very well that due to destruction of forest area, the wildanimals and birds lose their suitable habitats. Also they die of hunger due to non-availability of sufficient food as a result of destruction of natural forests. Hence many species of different animals and birds are on the verge of extinction. The time has now come to review and re-examine human conduct with regard to man-nature relationship.

It seems that we certainly need a code of conduct to behave with wild nature, flora and fauna. Humanbeings will have to do a lot of soul-searching activities. Whether he has got any moral right to destroy wildlife and alter the course of nature which may ignite natural calamities. Since he can't give life, he has no right to take it.

If we discuss the whole problem we will see that neither human-centred ethics nor deontological ethics encourage ruthless humanbehaviour with animals and exploitation of nature.[3] Human centred ethics tells us to preserve wild flora and fauna at least in the best interest of mankind. The value of conservation has a key role here. On the other, hand deontological ethics inspires us to honour wildlife and conserve wildnature for the sake of values itself inherent in them, irrespective of human benefit or loss. Human beings are not to impose values to animal world and wild nature.

The values are intrinsic into them irrespective of human recognition. It is for this intrinsic values that evoke a prima-facie duty on our part to honour their life and allow them to flourish with pleasure of living.

Regarding the second question whether animals or plants have any virtues which put them at par with man for moral consideration, our reply may be positive based on the following arguments.

A group of philosophers are of the opinion that certain animals do have rational elements, hence they fit to our moral realm. The heart of the matter is that in western tradition 'rationality' is considered the criteria of moral consideration. From this angle humanbeings do have rationality, so only their actions have moral worth. If at all 'rationality' is the only criteria for moral consideration, then certain species of primates having fair degree of intelligence deserve moral consideration.

Here the objection of philosophers is that many mentally derailed persons, newly born baby, mentally handicapped children etc. have no rationality, yet their, lives are honoured and safeguarded. On the other hand, some of the apes and other animals must have better intelligence than those of mentally derailed persons but they are ill-treated by men and their actions are not considered moral—such attitude and conduct of humanbeings (so called moral agents) are totally unjustified.[4]

However, some other group of thinkers have given ·their opinion that the best way to extend traditional moral philosophy is to fix 'sentientism' as criteria for moral consideration in place of 'rationally.' The sentient beings having future interest may deserve moral consideration. Peter Singer fully endorses the interest theory. He is of the opinion that many living beings do have interest to survive for a long time. They live with pleasure and multiply their offsprings. But owing to irresponsible human conduct animals future-prospect is broken. Let us see, how ?

Suppose in order to built a dam we drown a big forest. By so doing we not only kill animals and destroy vegetation, we also drown the future of animals.[5] Had the forest been intact, wildanimals and their coming generations would have continued to enjoy the pleasure of living for millions of years. Also the forest canopy would have facilitated the growth of millions of rare varieties of medicinal plants. Here it should be mentioned that virgin forests have been standing on the planet since millions of years. Its canopy gives shelter to many animals and plants, but once the forest is cut and it regrows, the forest canopy will never be the same, and the soil under it will never support the similar vegetation. Of course, the lost wild life will never be back, and in this way, the old forest never returns. The loss of virgin forest means breaking link with past and ancient values: it is also a great loss to coming generations, nature-lovers, poets and philosophers. We have no right to deprive coming generations of the beauty of forest and possible pleasure of roaming amidst wild nature and animals.

The scientists say that forest canopy is millions of years old. Several trees in rain forest are standing since thousands of years. They experience pain and pleasure, since they also have life and capacity to feel. If 'sentient' being means creature capable of feeling, then trees are also sentient beings and thus, they are entitled to the same moral consideration which humanbeings do have.

It appears that from moral point of view it is wrong to destroy trees and plants. In different religions and cultures too, plants and trees are worshipped and respected. Different religions of the world give due consideration to vegetable life and animals. For instance, the Hindu religion advocates its followers to worship trees, plants animals, birds and rivers. In India the river Ganga is considered holy and worshipped. As per Hindu tradition, we should not defile the holy Ganga. Among the trees *Peepal, Nim, Banyan and Tulsi* are worshipped. Destruction of grown up green trees in Hindu tradition are regarded a sin as equivalent to killing one's own son. We can trace the similar elements pertaining to Nature-worship in other religions of the world also. We hear about tribal prople who worship nature and her various aspects.

Regarding various arguments of preserving wilderness or flora the one very important argument is *Deep Ecology*. It is considered as milestone in the history of Environmental Philosophy.[6]

Deep Ecology was born in Scandinavia, the result of discussions between Naess and his colleagues Sigmund Kvaloy and Nils Faarlund. All three shared a passion for the great mountains. On a visit to the Himalayas, they became impressed with aspects of 'Sherpa culture' particularly when they found that their Sherpa guides regarded certain mountains as sacred and accordingly would not venture onto them. Naess extended this ideas into the larger perspective of nature.

Now *Deep Ecology* views all living things alike in having values in their own right, independent of their usefulness to human purposes. The deep ecologist respects this intrinsic value, taking care for example, not to cause unnecessary damage to the plants while walking on the mountainside. Naess says a very remarkable thing in this regard that we derive deep satisfaction from our association with other forms of life in nature which also contributes significantly to our life quality.

Naess also lays focus on the concept of 'Shallow Ecology' which like *Deep Ecology* honours conservation of nature but on a different ground. For example, it denounces pollution and resource depletion which, if not checked, may endanger human survival with immediate effect. It is said that central objective of 'Shallow Ecology' is the health and affluence of people in the developed countries. In this way, it views nature within the framework of human interest. But *Deep Ecology* looks upon nature from the perspective of nature itself. It takes the stand that values are inherent in living nature and hence they deserve protection and respect on our part and also moral consideration at par with humanbeings.

Now the question is that if we go on regarding and worshipping nature only, how can we survive since our survival depends on plant-produce. The solution to the problem probably lies in the philosophy of sustainable development.

The third question regarding *ethics in the interest of eco-system* is interesting and quite thought-provoking. It inspires us to develop certain code of conducts to deal with natural resources. The code of conduct may vary from place to place considering the availability to natural resources for human use and the demographic pressure. It is true that certain nations have massive population pressure upon their natural resources. In that case, certain measures will have to be taken to control and check the rising trend of population. In addition to this, the doctrine of Sustainable development will have to be strictly followed. The philosophy of sustainable development lies in judicious and curtailed use of natural resources along with maintaining ecological balance.

It means development and balance in nature should go side by side. We should take from nature whatsoever is urgently required for our survival and wiseful economic development. Here we are reminded of Gandhi who once told that nature is kind and liberal.

she has enough for man's needs but little for his avarice. It is only the human temptation which is responsible for the ruthless exploitation of nature.

Apart from sustainable measures we can contemplate upon other steps to be taken in the interest of Environmental Ethics. Such steps may range from using eco-friendly technology to saving and recycling resources, besides many other things.

Our most of the technologies are based on using fossil fuels and burning coals to ply vehicles and run various industrial plants. It is well-known fact that NTPC fires coals to produce electricity which causes tremendous pollution. We also know that vehicular pollution is the most dangerous one. Firing coals or woods for power is considered the outdated technology. Therefore, we need to have eco-friendly technologies like using air, sun and water to produce power. Hydrogen power is the latest one and hydrogen can be derived from air and water both. Through hydrogen power we can ply our vehicles and run industries besides supplying it to household use.

Air turbine can be put to use to produce electricity. Solar energy may be quite effective and cheap source of power with zero pollution. Thus electricity derived from air, sun and water causes least pollution.

Hence, we are required to make huge investment in energy and transport sectors to make these totally eco-friendly. Using CNG gases to run our buses is good. But we need hydrogen cell to power our entire transport system.

Simultaneously, cycling should be encouraged and made popular among students and Government employees. In Denmark and Netherland people mostly use bicycles propelled by battery or cell. In China office-goers necessarily use bicycles. However, in India the Government is yet to pay attention to cheap means of transportation in which fossil-fuel is not at all used. Our students and Government employees still have craze for motar bikes and four-wheelers which consume fossil-fuel and cause horrible atmospheric pollution.

Besides eco-friendly technologies, we should shift our attention to make least use of natural resources. Some viable alternatives of woods have long been invented. For example, steel, fiber, plastic etc. can replace wood. Therefore, use of wood in furniture and construction industries should be totally banned in order to protect the remaining forests on this planet.

Recycling resources is another effective way to save forest. For example, used papers can be recycled to save natural resources. Carelessly to throw our material that can be recycled is a form of vandalism or the theft of our common property in the resources of the world. In this way, Environmental Ethics finds virtue in saving and recycling resources, and vice in extravagance and unnecessary consumption.

The other measures as objectives of Environmental Ethics may include also bringing awareness in masses for conservation value and resorting to simple way of life. Simple way to lead a good and healthy life lies also in adopting *vegetarian diet* and *practices of frugality.*

The most important thing in this regard is that we should teach our kids and youngsters about environmental values and inspire them to inculcate a culture in which environmental concern finds its due place. This may be called 'Eco-culture' or 'Environmental culture' which inspires us to learn and imbibe various ecological virtues for the well-being of planetary system, nature and mankind. The most important virtue in this regard is 'holistic attitude' or 'holistic thinking' towards nature which is the *Mother* of the rest of the virtues. Let us now reflect upon these virtues.

Holistic thinking, reverence, eros, compassion, attunement, humility, acceptance of finitude, earthiness, asceticism, creativity, inclusivity, are the virtues that each and every human being should cultivate in the best interest of environment. These virtues may provide a window to witness a coherent ecological virtue ethic. Let us put each virtue in a larger conceptual framework, paying attention to connections as well as tensions between the various virtues.[7]

Holistic thinking is a mental disposition, an intellectual virtue, requiring left-brain as well as right-brain activity. It implies the ability and willingness to see connections among various strands of nature. It advocates to appreciate both totality and particularity of ecosystems.

The second ecological virtue is *respect*. The term respect has become somewhat of a buzzword in the environmental movement. Rather than connoting politeness to superiors it refers to the attention and consideration humans must give to the non-human world. It is an attitude with practical implications. Yet at the core lies a propensity to halt at the mystery of the other and to "proceed with care" at every encounter. At the root of respect there lies reverence which is a sense of marveling at the existence of the other.

Respect and reverence lead the way to *eros, a desire to commune*. This is a desire to commune with the Earth and animals. Nature is always beautiful and blissful which gives subtle message to all forms of life to co-exist in harmony.

Eros can be treated as virtues for two reasons. First of all eros is a desire combined with efforts. This means that for modern people to rekindle such a desire requires real effort, involving self-examination, overcoming past habits and inhibitions, and courage to tread unfamiliar ground. One grows in many traditional virtue. The cultivation of eros has come to resemble the process by which one grows in many traditional virtues.

Secondly, in an environmentally sensitive world view, communing is a way of flourishing (for all involved). Eros thus is a virtue which aims at *ecological good*.

The desire to commune leads to *sharing of joys as well as suffering*; eros *leads* to ecstasy as well as compassion (co-suffering), the next in this list of virtue. Compassion is an important ecological virtue since it lays the groundwork for responding to the brokenness of the world. According to Rosemary Ruether, establishing a new social practice requires "a new sense of urgency about the tenability of present patterns of life and compassionate solidarity with those who are its victims."

Attunement, the fifth virtue supplements compassion. Compassion can become pompous if it is not accompanied by a continuous attuning to the changing situation, needs, moods and energy levels of the other. To a certain extent, attunement is "receptivity of the mind." Attunement implies harmonizing with a changing reality, whether it be a changing melody or harmonizing with the dynamics of change in the natural world.

The sixth ecological virtue is *humility*. Christians have traditionally understood humility as a relational virtue, connoting human acceptance of inferiority and indebtedness in relation to God, the Creator and king. Environmentalists have recast the virtue of humility to connote human acceptance of their "properplace" in relation to the non-human world. This "properplace" is not one of moral inferiority or superiority. Rather, it is a place like any other place in the complex web of creation: a place that is unique and yet nothing special (since humans are dependent on the rest of the web, like other creatures). The most important function of the virtue of humility is to deflate an inflated ego that gets in the way of relationship. As an ecological virtue, it is part of a cluster of attitudes. The term 'humility' stems from the Latin term *humilis*, which means 'lowly,' or 'close to the ground.' 'Humilis' is in turn derived from 'humus' which means 'earth.' The grounding becomes the basis for a renewal of relationships. Albert Fritsch, for example, sees humility as a model for growth in 'eco-identification' with the earth.

Acceptance of finitude is another important virtue in the sequence. Death of living beings is accepted as a regular part of the cyclical renewal of nature. Death occurs to give life. The whole old generations give way to new one. So man must understand his limit and do away with the attitude of amassing wealth by exploiting the bounty of nature. We may find that we can do with the small resources at hands instead of destroying the ecosystem. *Acceptance of finitude, then, is an attitude that can greatly enhance the flourishing of the environment*. But so far as virtue is its own reward, the individual is benefited with inner peace and bliss for having made peace with outer limits (not upsetting natural system).

An attitude of earthiness arises in the experience of the earth as one's home, with all its beauty and messiness. People endowed with this virtue work best as down-to-earth people, practical enough to know that all undertakings are imperfect. Earthy persons fully taste the joys of their home—a sunset, the taste of chocolate, the hug of a child. Yet they are not romantic dreamers. They will get their hands dirty to do what needs to be done if the house needs cleaning. In order to balance their great love of life with the constant messiness of life, earthy people need a sense of humour. By tea-parlor standards, earthy humour may seem coarse; by environmentalist standards, it simply represents healthy laughter.

Asceticism, the ninth virtue, is associated by Albert Fritsch with the objective of "strengthening willpower." Fritsch gives the example of abstaining from meat as a way to strengthen oneself for future action. This example shows clearly how environmentalists tend to reappropriate ascetic traditions. *The vision of asceticism leads to vegetarianism which is essential for purifying oneself and sparing the lives of other animals.* The vision of ascetic practice clearly diverts from traditions that associate asceticism with a desire to be freed from material bonds.

Constructive solutions to environmental problems require *creativity*, the tenth virtue creativity requires reintegration of man and nature.

The final virtue is inclusivity. Environmentalists tend to be acutely aware of the extent and necessity of the world's diversity. Since diversity can give rise to destructive conflict, however, environmentalists also regularly call for tolerance and inclusivity. They advocate for peaceful co-existence with nature. They stress not merely on peaceful coexistence but in benevolent symbiosis with nature. Thus inclusivity is an ideal virtue in an ecological framework.

The environmental virtues should not be forced upon anyone rather people be inspired to understand and cherish these virtues for the good of ecology. In fact such virtues may still be amended and replaced by another one, since quest for eco-virtues is a continuous process and Environmental Ethics has to keep pace with changing high-tech socio-economic values. But we should always keep in mind that emerging ecological virtues have much to do with 'Nature' which is regarded as *Mother Nature* in different religions and cultures. *Mother Nature* is regarded as one of the tremendous sources of moral inspiration. She, in fact, is friend, philosopher and guide to the mankind towards leading a prosperous and blissful life in the harmony of natural system. Perceived as an active influence because of her moral claim, Nature teaches holistic thinking (through the structures of ecosystems); halts and awes one into respect and reverence; pulls one into communion (eros); awakens one's compassion; captures one's attuning sensibilities; grounds one; guides one into discipline (e.g. through rules of health); inspires and nourishes one's creativity; and models the way of inclusivity. Let us adore, worship and preserve the *Mother Nature* who nourishes all lives on this planet and teaches lots of moral lessons to mankind to save the Earth from the possible eco-catastrophes.

Overall, the emergence of an ecological virtue ethic, with all its diversity, is a development of great significance. This is not an artificially contrived ethic designed as a programme for moral improvement. Such attempts are bound to fail. Rather, this is an ethic emerging from an existing practice; namely, the practice of committed environmentalism. The virtues such as holistic thinking, respect for nature, creativity, and inclusivity mentioned here already guide the lives of many. They signal the breakthrough of a new, cross-cultural empowerment, providing realistic prospects for ecological hope.

REFERENCES

1. Leopold's (1949): Proposal for a 'land ethic' can be found in his? *A sand county Almanc, with essays on conservation from Round River*, New York,
2. Srivastava, K.P., (2002): *An Introduction to Environmental Study*, Kalyani Publishers Noida (U.P.), p. 47.
3. Thiroux, J., (1998): *Ethics: Theory and Practice*, Prentice Hall NJ, p. 55.
4. Ibid, p. 424.
5. Singer, Peter, (2000): *Practical Ethics*, Cambridge University Press, p. 264.
6. Ibid, p. 268
7. Siker, L.V.W., (1995): *Review and Prospects*, (article contributed to the Book 'Ecological Prospects' edited by C.K. Chapple), Sri Satguru Publication, Indian Books centre, Delhi, p. 211-213.

Others

S. Subbaro (2001): *Ethics of Ecology and Environment*, Rajat Publication, New Delhi.

The Monist, Journal, Vol. 75, No. 2, 1992, La Salle, Illinois Hegler Institute publication.

13. TECHNOLOGY, SCIENTIFIC PROGRESS AND HUMAN INTERVENTIONS IN A MUDDLED WORLD

Debashis Guha

Technology and scientific progresses have become utterly notorious twins of modern man, they should behave, and for that we should behave as we should. But how should we behave in the face of the terrible muddle in the world as created by our Frankenstein twins? We need to intervene positively to save our faces perhaps but how can it be possible when the mute things and beings are laughing at us by remaining so awfully mute? Well, for that let us first look at human beings for their nature and dispositions. Let us further weigh the ethic of technological and scientific progresses in the context of our ethical concern about environment. It is undeniable that human beings are qualitatively different from many other beings in nature. Don't read here 'supremacy' of our race as we realize it very well that amoebas and molluscs are unique and different, too. We mean to say that human beings have certain features which we now cannot help as not having them lest some factors playing in evolution does not take away something from us, which would amount to regress and not progress. The stark truth is that we now cannot help that we think about our good and good of other human beings and for that reason invent means available in and around us. There is no way that we shall continue using natural things and beings for our good such as vegetations, water bodies, air, space, animals and even human beings. Yet, we shall take about many things and beings whom we use for their good. Truly, we shall also continue not to care much for these things and beings. There is really no going back on our general progress for we are such beings who prefers progress and not regress. Equally true is that we cannot become hermits who live alone, does not need any thing or any being for him or her. The nature has been usually used by us and we shall continue using them for our existence. Still, in the midst of what we 'are' we continue to deliberate on what we 'should,' and this marks our unique feature though not less unique is that we are dual-thinking and masked people often not caring to do something we thought we 'should.' If we look around us, we do not find our parallel in the way we usually live in nature for we have extensively created or made 'a world within the world,' that is, our created environment. Our creation has been huge, quantitatively numerous and qualitatively either gorgeous or ugly. We talk much about ant-colonies, beehives, nests of birds and so on but are they comparable to ours? Certainly not, because among other things, we have created an environment which needs not merely natural things but such things in plenty. Still, we are concerned about "judiciousness" of such needs which ants and bees might not care for they are believed to be judicious in their need and use by their standards. Our talk of 'proper" and "improper" needs and uses of natural things and beings make us believe that something is wrong. It may well be that we were not "judicious," something is running out of our control and we may be gradually slipping through a slope of calamity. Our optimism did lull us to danger while our pessimism may be now at best a warning but not a solution—we have to face it.

The enormous structural progress that human beings have made and the intricate patterns of living they have meshed were possible owing to the advents of science and technology. However, much talk about "judiciousness" hovers around such advents because they have been riding mainly for their success, on the waves of needs of people on the one hand and the extensive use of natural things and being on the other hand. It has been imagined that science and technology are the means for massive exploitation of our environment though we did create another one for us. Developments are prominent as well because science and technology were made scapegoats to cover up human follies. They were needed for noble purposes, not only for human beings but for the welfare of animals and even natural things. Hence, much blame is on people who have much need and greed but do not have balance and lack sense of rights of natural existential. They are thus charged as "injudicious" people, who are for many reasons, unethical (fools!), for among other things they were busy cutting the branch on which they were comfortably seated.

A glimpse of all this amounts to an ethical concern about scientific and technological progress man has made particularly in view of the states of environment, natural and artificial and our renewed ethical interests in the environment, the natural and the artificial. Weighing scientific and technological progress is a complex matter but here we have selected one parameter that is how far the said progress is ethically desirable or good particularly when an open eye could see what direct and indirect environmental impacts the progress had, which is already under our ethical scanner. Hence, any contemporary ethical analysis of environmental matters should include a correlative ethical analysis of scientific and technological progress man has made. If we look at this discussion starting from the seventeenth century, the advent of modern science, it has been a "man centered" because the crux of it was to find out whether or not the "happiness" of man and his general "well-being" has been cared for. Hence, weighing the "progress" ethically was pivoted on utilitarianism and the anthropocentric welfare. Though it has been accepted that humans should be happy any way at the cost of using his powers in nature. There is perhaps no question of unethicality or undesirability here as human beings should show what they are capable of doing in nature and with nature. It would be also a kind of "disgrace" as Leibniz said to human nature which had ability to make discoveries for need, satisfaction and happiness and yet, could not do all that. Perhaps it is due to this that we are so many but do so little for human folks. The ethic of scientific progresses we have made thus depends much on anthropocentric welfare and happiness maximization, which involves without any doubt, some degree of intervention in nature or even using up nature. However, by the nineteenth century the happiness balloon was punctured by several things. First was the endless rise of the need graph of man, among which was (though jokingly), use of our power to have birthdays throughout twelve months of a year. Second, with the need, we increased inventions, and with it we increased the use of nature's potentials. In any case 'human centeredness' did not shift its grip in ethicality. The scientific and technological progresses were thoroughly dominated by gross hedonism; utilitarianism soon went this way and welfarism was constricted to the zone of economics. It was really looking like a brainchild of economics which had no ethics of "other centeredness" owing to the growing capitalist cultures or in the cultures where colonies were made to exploit new resources, natural and human. The exploitation of man by man, growth of classes of the exploiters and the exploited and the battered environment really punctured the happiness ideal we constructed so dearly. Hence, what was the basis of the ethic of progress was itself under an ethical scanner when environmental well-being came to the fore. We were pressed further for our moral extension. Malthus and Darwin must have been particularly responsible for a moral extension in one way as renewed interests in ecology; stiff competition in nature and the moral ideal laid down by the evolutionary thesis were remarkable. Not only this, we came to realize that now as we move in a hedonic paradox, man must be against man for they have rivalry for the control of nature. The idea that scientific and technological progress enhances our happiness and well-being were questioned for ethical validity. This was noticed by many conscious philosophers as did Lotze who remarked that "each step of progress with the increase of strength it brings, brings also a corresponding increase of pressure."[1]

Nevertheless, the point is that we cannot easily trash scientific-technological progress as unethical just on the basis of anthropocentrism because "happiness" and "well-being" themselves did not have much to be blamed nor does human happiness and well-being have anything inherently evil. We are concerned about two things: maximization of happiness irrespective of minimization of the same of other beings and things. As such, even if the ethical basis of scientific progress is human happiness, we have to weigh this basis on its positive and the negative aspects, we cannot simply trust it. There is hardly anyone who doubts about human well-being being positively contributed by modern science and technology. The 'positive' contribution is not a vague term, it means, some definite good, produced over some not so good or evil conditions prevailing erstwhile. Further such contributions are good or valuable in their own right and not for any other reason. Best instances come from the fields of medicine and information and communication technologies. Certainly we would not prefer deadly viruses killing innocent lives (or, shall we for the sake of rights of viruses?). Yet, some 'negative' aspects are clear as well, which aspects are producers of evil over good and they are on their own rights, disvalues. It is here that we may consider the case of using innocent monkeys for cosmetic tests and the case of using means of mass communication for ulterior political exploitations. In fact, most of the times science and technology comes out as admixtures of positive values in so far as human happiness is concerned and negative values only in so far as maximization of the ideal has been overplayed at the cost of larger well-being. In any case, it is our ways of using science and technology which comes under ethical scanner because it stands out as means to some end in life. Per se, science and technology is neither moral nor immoral but the inventions and its users are moral or immoral in so far their goals might be intrinsically good or bad. The ethic of science and technology thus refers to humans because their positive and negative intentions are weighed by us. Hence, it is we who should either encourage or discourage some technologies which are either good or evil. Potentially, certain scientific and technological discoveries, when they are made, does not necessarily unfold fully their inherent capacities (on their own right), to be called positive or negative or both. It may well be that though discoveries are for human well-being, which is good-itself, turns out to be negative as well as positive to some extent. For this, we may have to wait for some time. The point is that once its negative repercussions come out, should we still deliberately use them for the sake of yet another goal to be achieved? These negative repercussions, whether or not they outweigh the positive aspects, is not very important rather, most important is to know whether or not they contribute negatively to the happiness and well-being of humans only or they are so when we consider well-being of a larger whole. It is here that our moral extension is made possible and the ethic of science and technology could be weighed properly. Equally true is that while we consider the positive aspects of the same things, a moral extension is possible because we have every reason to find out whether or not these things enhances human happiness and well-being but does little or nothing for the well-being of many existential. Both points made above make any sense if some scientific and technological discoveries are in reality capable of positive and negative contributions towards a larger ecological community and therefore, not restricted to human beings. It is clear those complex ethical considerations about science and technology does not remain restricted to human centered talk rather, they should be extended when they are pertinent enough to cover other-centered talk. It is also clear that any talk about goodness of technologies as means towards an end, which is good and not bad, cannot be solely human-centered because such values are not restricted to things like 'human happiness' and 'human well-being.' We have also to understand that science and technology per se cannot be weighed as ethically good or bad by mere reference to what their inner capacities are but with reference to their use. Truly, these things cannot be valued overnight as good though they contributed negatively by inflicting much pain on human beings and others. It is due to this that though modern medicines have alleviated human miseries, we ask about the ethic of pain relieving drugs being tested on animals for their effectiveness. It is here that we tend to think broader in terms of ethic of science and technology because we feel that a human-centered-happiness-oriented-talk is too narrow. It is exactly due to our renewed weighing of the moral value of scientific and technological progress on the broader environmental or ecological contexts that we are seriously considering the obvious counter productiveness of science. This counter productiveness is too many for us now and they should be weighed not on non-ethical terms only because it is not only a matter of pragmatics and prudence rather, depends on what amount of evil it produces in the ecological community as such. However, such resolution of ethical impasse regarding science and technology is a matter of moral dialogue.

Another point is that we have to weigh science and technology on ethical terms when not merely human well-being is kept in mind rather, when for that well-being many human beings are deprived or not. Most important is that many human beings on earth are deprived of scientific, technological and economic progresses. A large population is poor and needy. We should consider the ethic of reaching benefits of science and technology to a class of people at the cost of depriving the poor class. Often science and technology becomes sources of mass exploitation as we did see after the spread of British colonialism in today's Commonwealth nations. Or, even today it may be seen in glorious democracies where a spurt of progress as planned by great people reach a class, not mass. Interestingly, many contemporary world organizations of great humanitarian repute make great environmental hullabaloo after they have licked top cream of technological progress because they now find the ideal of happiness to be reached by curbing science and technology for world disaster and preach ethics for the poor nations. Aptly Fidel Castro remarks: "The solution cannot be that which burn the development of those who need it the most; the fact is that everything that contributes to underdevelopment and poverty is an open violation of ecology."[2] An extreme view may be like this as well: "If I were a Brazilian without land or money or the means to feed my children, I would be burning the rainforest too."[3] Why should we wonder about such reactions? Are they grossly unethical? Granted that remaining poor is not an ethical ideal as is the ideal of remaining unhappy but being affluent by mass exploitation may be ethically still worse. Science and technology should be thus evaluated for ethical value if they have capacity to alleviate poverty and satisfy the neediest. It is here we have tough question to face when ethical concern in environment are posed, which we thought is a remarkable basis for our moral extension while evaluating the values of science and technology. The second quote projects this tough question. Is it proper to burn our rainforests to exist? Is it proper to cry over tiger projects when men are starving? Is it desirable to say that we must risk some green house effect to alleviate poverty? The last question is more pertinent here when we are considering the ethic of scientific and technological progress. The problem is that though human well-being and well-being of the poor and the needy are great ethical ideals, is it feasible if the means are slowly but surely counter productive to people and to environment? Does it not amount to some kind of childish idea of allowing poor nations to use nature's bounties with the help of technologies available today in so far as they are not developed (if not rich), though they are sure to suffer in the longer run for their ruins? Is it not true that this opinion is extreme and anthropocentric welfarism? In fact, what the moral opinion stated here wants to stress is not that ecology is not worth caring about, what it stresses is that if poor do not exist, there is no status of an ecological hue and cry. It wants to say that an environmental ethic and an ethic of science and technology should not be unethically imposed on us who want to exist decently first for we have all right to enjoy such existence when others did long ago. Still, they might not stress that we shall go on exploiting nature at whims for maximization of our goods in so far as rest of the cream has not been licked by none other than 'our' class. The poor and the developing are not unethical people who use technology for using up what has been left in nature and then cry over it. They know it well that this is a capitalist-mercantile ideal of happiness much touted in the name of gross utilitarianism. It is perhaps due to this ethical vision of science and technology in developing and underdeveloped countries (in the broader context of environment), that weighing the ethic of technological progress is possible, not merely on the basis of what are our preferences 'now' but what should be our preferences in the 'future' because we are not worried about the poor and the needy 'now' but for others as well who might still live under the oppression of economic exploitation. It is this ethical concern that enable them to weigh why some pseudo-scientific progress in the name of poverty alleviation are also ecologically (and thus humanly disastrous). Much of this point was focused in our discussions about multipurpose projects and ruthless urbanization owing to heavy industrialization. In reality, the poor and the needy are ecologically conscious for they fight against exploitative technologies which do not aim at poverty alleviation. The ethic of scientific and technological progress is thus closely related to our ethical concerns in environment and its ethical value should be weighed by keeping in mind several factors not any one.

Let us now switch over to consider weighing 'human interventions' in nature so that what has been maligned is at least patched up or substantially recovered. This is needed for no one would certainly like to live in a mucked nature, not even the poor and the needy, but what 'should' we do now as several things are gone out of control? More worse, a huge chunk of population holds the right to live decently and other natural things and human beings too does enjoy rights to exist not really as they were but in a manner so that something we called "nature" is well recognized for days to come.

This last assertion is not liked by many ethicists particularly those of the Heideggerian tradition because according to them we should not interfere with natural system in any case or change them according to our wish or exploit them for our needs. Hence, the ethical basis of ecological management is "Let Being Be," which is the guiding force for the deep ecologists of our times but not for the Leolpoldian naturalists. What I want to maintain about this should be preceded by weighing 'human non-intervention or non-inference' first and then by weighing 'human interference' in ecological management. Again the ethics-talk is predominantly "human" as it is we who likely interfere in nature though undeniably we rely heavily on the natural things and beings. And from our earlier discussion, we need not remain poor and needy.

First thing about the non-interference theory of ecological management is that we cannot swing the clock backwards to find nature as it was, completely non-interfered because always forces within nature changed its face slowly or rapidly. The problem is when in addition to it, "we" interfere? "We" are in plenty, not only humans because other animals do interfere in the vast natural setting because they have their own needs and thus own environment to be built for living. It is also true that when we speak of the natural systems on the whole, we do conceive humans and animals within the system and not out of it. Hence, we cannot curse humans for using several natural existential for their need and their living. Moreover, as other animals, we too, owing to the queerness of our "nature," do "use" nature and even create an environment for us. This is so natural within nature that there is hardly anything to be branded as "unethical." Yet, what the proponents of "non-interference" holds is that we do not have any ethical right to manipulate and change natural systems so much so for not merely our need but the greed of maximization of pleasures and happiness so that the Beings are unrecognizable for their identity or they simply fizzle out of existence. Strangely, we do not realize that proactive interference ruins the whole system, including man, so the message is not to become hermits or go for mass hara-kiri but do not tease natural systems for greed. Another point is the ethics of non-interference is that though it is foolish talking about swinging the clock back or to restore the nature as it were even in a small locality, we may nevertheless; seriously consider some kind of "nihilism" *now* in so far as any further ecological disturbances are concerned. This may amount to either complete nihilism in *extracting* something out of the natural systems any further or complete nihilism in *extracting as well as restoring* parts of the systems methodically or nihilism in *changing and manipulating* natural systems any further or nihilism regarding considerable positive changes and manipulation from external outputs by man like *artificial settings* to make–up for the loss. In any case, natural systems 'now' do not need any *therapy* to cope up with the various losses. The ethic of such "therapeutic nihilism" is supported by some of the Heideggerian supporters mostly championing deep ecology which is well explained by E.C. Hargrove (1989).[4] These people build their ethic of nihilism on ontological basis as it is common with deep ecologists to hold that the *fundamental structure* of nature is much beyond our creation, manipulation, change and artificialities. Man cannot put any amount of effort to replace this structure and therefore, should not enjoy any right to do so. At best they should put their hands off the natural systems to at least preserve the structure which has still not crumbled completely. Hence, the ethical upshot of the argument is that therapeutic nihilism is a desirable *ethical management* of environment as it restored the basic form of natural systems which is desirable in itself. Hargrove confuses such "nihilistic ethic" as environmental "management," which is perhaps owing to medical nihilistic management. This is a confusion because not doing anything or hands-off from environment cannot really "restore" or "heal" the mucked nature, it is really not "management." The idea may be at best nature "taking care of itself" and man has to do nothing at all. This may be an old fashioned idea as if wounds will heal as it does at times needing no medical intervention. To wait for some catastrophic change or disaster by virtue of natural forces as if nature "follows its own course" to fill up deeply dug coal quarries, may be the inherent idea. This in fact, rules out our systematic and scientific efforts to facilitate *restoration* works in nature.

Well it is nothing unethical to nurture an ideal structure of nature but doing nothing now may be still unethical for different reasons. One is that active interference might result into stopping of nature's plunder as well to help its restoration. The other is that we cannot stop fulfilling our urge to develop and needs. Those people who are equally vulnerable and nearly extinct also fight for basic subsistence. Hence, it is but natural for us to extract and also restore otherwise living in an ideal state of inaction does not count much. Moreover, when we are well-placed intellectually to understand the ways in which nature recovers its losses, we may go for some such means which may happily go along with it or help the healing up process to some extent. If our ethical basis is to care for the whole of the ecological community, including ourselves, why should inaction be good, is not known to us. At least 'inaction' is not ecological management.

Our discussion has revealed that though we cannot go back to an original natural system we can do something now for the recovery of and prevention of several losses. Equally true is that we have to use something for our existence. How can both things go together? The ethical basis of environmental management which calls for some action at least involving natural systems cannot be thus nihilistic because no ethical ideal remains valuable in inaction. Ideals are valuable or are known to be of worth if we try to achieve them. Truly, we cannot achieve well-being of the whole system immediately and fully but we can keep trying. Keeping these things in mind many ethicists criticize the severe *environmental pillage* including short-term 'using-up-to-satisfaction' and 'leaving-the-area-used for mercy.' These people are against the anthropocentric hedonists because it is grossly against ecological well-being, which we did not favor in our earlier discussion. There are also criticisms on ethical lines about environmental 'long-term-using-up' such as in agriculture or settlement, particularly when that is not backed up by restoration projects. It would be a bad idea to think that nothing in nature belonged to us and we have grabbed everything for our good. Hence, cleaning land for agriculture and using it up are said unethical practices. The grave error lies in thinking that one who is part and parcel of a natural system is unethical in using something he possesses. However, the reality is that we do not grab anything when we depend so much on those things for our existence. Naturally, we use natural things and beings for our basic needs. Similarly, we clear places for our settlement. We can ask the critics of use-theory that what should be done if we do not use what we already have. In fact, in an attempt to answer this we are further pushed to the ethical basis of restoration or ethical environmental management, but not inaction. Another criticism on ethical lines is about using up followed by filling the gaps or a combination of extraction and restoration because what has been used up is too substantial and too many or too much which can never be 'filled up' by 'us' in anyway causing mounting losses. There is suggestion about not using anything therefore and inaction as well. The problem is one of realizing the 'using up' dogma which has been misconceived for its meaning. Why should we think that using up is to unjustly grab natural things in its totality or to a maximum extent? Undoubtedly we have not stopped at extracting something where we should have done so, but that calls for action, some management on the part of human population, the evaluation of needs and the follow up judicious use. Further, granted that certain things cannot be 'filled up' now for their huge losses but we can still try to do so to some extent at least when it is physically possible. Or, we should leave no alternative left but to evaluate methods using nothing any more and wait for nature to heal its pains. If natural systems need an overall care for its well-being, doing something is a must. Environmental management thus calls or human interference to a certain degree. We have to understand that much useless criticism declaring using up thesis unethical is due to a misconceptions about what I call 'mercantile-capitalist' using-up goals and correlate management vis-à-vis 'environmental conscious and people friendly' using up goals and correlate management. The former sets a goal of "class welfare," whereas the latter that of "mass welfare." The first thus takes up class-management or we may call it "covenantal management" whereas the latter calls for "people's management." When we go for a de-classed people's management of environmental losses most balanced, we get results because people's management is essentially "feminine"—it is *caring and sharing*. What I feel is that the idea of nature taking care of itself is well understood when apart from the natural laws and movements, people as sons of nature support it as well. It is due to this that human interference in environmental management is ethical.

Many ethicists feel that a feminine people's management of natural systems is neither saving the system nor restoring the system, nor is it *rehabilitating* the system. It is nothing but "faking" the natural system, which is unethical because after incurring many losses for human good, nature is caricatured causing more bad than good. Such efforts amount to modern technological support, significant manipulations and replacing the natural with the artificial as well as dwarfing, constructing and narrowing down the natural things and set ups. R. Elliot[5] suggests "though these people pretend to be with the environmentalists camouflaging arguments but certainly they trash environmental active management because they say that what the environmental engineers are propounding is that we accept a fake or a forgery instead of the real thing."[6] The problem with people like Elliot is that he or we or anyone else did not ever see the whole of the natural system in *originality* or more in its *basic form*. Given that impossibility, a 'fake' is really so-called when in relation to the 'original,' it aims at taking the place of the 'original' but turns out to be laughing or inadequate or even bluffing. However, the wrongly called 'faking' is in reality *restoration* because the original has not been referred to or could not at all be referred to fake it. Isn't it possible that we very well know or have seen an original state of a part of the natural system which after much use has been abandoned by us? When we actively manage for recovery of that part by trees, lakes, brooks whatever were there, is it not "faking" and thus "joking" with nature? Is it proper to do such things? Elliot and others forget that there is little or no chance of a picture-perfect restoration of even a part of a natural system as if a great master's work of art has been replicated by someone for a great bluff. Moreover, unethicality of faking may be largely owing to wrong financial or other gains. Sometimes faking involves some sort of aesthetic end. In the case of environmental restoration none of these may happen. Greatest problem with Elliot's argument is that faking does not amount to restoration rather, replicating an original. When a work of art is restored, it is different. In any case, if environmental management amounts to not restoration but deliberate artificial manipulations of the states of nature as if the "now original" has been restored in totality, it is certainly unethical as that does not aim at nature's well-being rather well-being of some planners who invest hefty sums on such bogus things.

Some ethicists like Richard Sylvan thinks that even the "restoration" program in management may not be so desirable because it always follows in modern times after lot of extortion for what a class-needs. Hence, whatever steps are taken later on by that exploitative class or their henchmen, are at best *present value* assumptions involving unethical practice of *skimping* many relevant considerations. This practice is comparable to 'skimping' in ethical theories as well, particularly when we are obsessed with one moral theory for the resolution of environmental issues. Sylvan thus ends up saying that "even where some serious attempts were made at restoration, environmental value is significantly reduced."[7] This amounts to the acceptance of the truth that gross hedonic extraction or plunder of nature's wealth can never be 'restored' for the topsoil is lost, which is among other things, impossible to restore. Moreover, several losses of local species flora, fauna in more or less same number (eye estimated) cannot be restored. In fact, the concept of "eco-sustainable development" also faces great challenge in so far as the sense of development is not made clear. If the type of development envisioned is class-based and present-time-based maximization of human pleasures, eco-sustainability hardly makes any sense.

Sylvan[8] is of the opinion that the ethically desirable alternative in environmental loss management is rehabilitation and not restoration. This is because successful rehabilitation programme show us that rather than restoring what was extracted, it is possible to increase the *natural value* of the damaged place. Hence, 'rehabilitation' is one way to manage damaged nature by increased value-inputs at different locales. It is due to this that a dead swamp may be cleaned, a pool of bad water may be thrown, dug afresh deeper, fresh water stored and so on. Such practices may be of limited nature and needs some technological interventions as well, but it does contribute to loss-make-up in most eco-friendly ways. The people of a locality may be often seen in such successful practices, most of the time not needing much capital investment. However, Sylvan reminds us that not all rehabilitation management be feminine or ethical. Some are very optimistic, involving huge technological inputs, money, manpower etc. These are vehemently opposed by E. Katz[9] who says that nature can never be wholly rehabilitated because any ultramodern technology and any amount of investment is to satisfy a class interest but not the interest of the mucked nature. But Sylvan thinks that though Katz may be partly right, he is not entirely right in bashing rehabilitation. Katz thinks wrongly that rehabilitation is an "artifactual enterprise," which it is not. In rehabilitating nature not necessarily we act as artifacts rather, we put some labor to give back some lost value so far as it is practicable. In fact, as Katz thinks, we do not create or recreate anything; we just help in regaining something lost.

Sylvan thinks that a nature-emphatic enterprise as this one at small scales may have many hurdles. Some are practical and some are about lack of information and lack of technology. To this I may add, lack of interest on part of our politicians and policy makers for they might form more domineering rehabilitation because they involve large investments. Sylvan rightly says that "Rehabilitation can be viewed as a cooperative venture, between the rehabilitators and Nature."[10] I would like to add that a lot of 'talking' about 'what ought to be done' among the restorers should go on continually, for which, not exploiters but empathesizers, who may be scientists, technologists and thinkers may be included. Equally true is that rehabilitation needs a lot of practical effort after thinking. Most important is to ward off dangerous exploiters if some chance of ecological management is there for us, any further.

REFERENCES

1. Rescher, Nicholas, *Unpopular Essays on Technological Progress,* University of Pittsburgh Press, p. 5.
2. Rajagopalan, R. (2005): *Environmental Studies: From Crises to Cure,* O.U.P., Delhi, p. 287.
3. Ibid, p. 287.
4. Hargrove, E.C., (1989): *Foundation of Environmental Ethics,* Englewood Cliffs, N. J.
5. Elliot, R., (1982): "Faking Nature," *Inquiry*, Vol. 25, pp. 81-95
6. Ibid, p. 144.
7. Sylvan, R., (1998): "Mucking with Nature" in Edgar Morcher ET. Al (eds.), *Applied Ethics in Troubled World*, Kluwer, London.
8. Ibid, p. 71.
9. Katz, E., "The Big Lie: Human Restoration of Nature," *Research in Philosophy and Technology*, Vol. 12, pp. 231-241.
10. Sylvan, R., op. cit., p. 79.

14. A BRIEF STUDY OF PLANTS AND ANIMALS OF THE RAJMAHAL HILLS IN THE 19TH CENTURY

V. N. Dinesh

The Rajmahal Hills occupy the eastern portion of the Santal Pargana Division in Jharkhand. These hills stretch from Sahibganj to Nagalbanga. There is a succession of hills, plateaus, valleys and ravines.[1] Before the study and observation of the famous Geologist *V. Ball*, the hills have been regarded as a continuation of the Vindhyan range of Central India. But after detailed examination of these hills, Mr. Ball revealed that the Rajmahal Hills form an isolated group. He explained that the north eastern extremity of the Rajmahal Hills constitutes the turning-point of the Ganges and came to the conclusion that they are physically quite detached from the Vindhyan range.[2]

These Hills, its adjoining villages, autochthons, other natives, flora and fauna etc. have been the central theme of study by officials and scholars, *Captain James Browne* wrote *India Tract* containing a broad description of Jungle Terai District.[3] Lt. T. Shaw published an account of "*Inhabitants of the Hills Near Rajmahal*" in Asiatic Researches.[4]

During 1810-1811, Francis Buchanan surveyed the entire region and described his findings and observation in detail.[5] In 1818 Sutherland, Joint Magistrate of Bhagalpur investigated the state of landed tenure of the Hill People and submitted his report[6] in 1819. In 1827 Bishop Reginald Heber published[7] his "Narrative of a Journey Through the Upper Provinces of India: From Calcutta to Bombay 1824-1825."

Robert Mont-gomery Martin wrote *Eastern India*[8] on Geography, Topography, History and Ethnology of the region. Captain Walter Stanhope Sherwoll toured through the Rajmahal Hills in 1851 and wrote "*Notes upon a Tour through the Rajmahal Hills*."[9]

Sherwill was a revenue surveyor who gave a vivid and broad portrayal of the Rajmahal Hills. With various aspects of the Ethnology. Sherwill broadly wrote on flora and fauna of the Rajmahal Hills. Thus his "*Notes*" is very significant for ecological study of the Rajmahal Hills in the 19th century.

Sherwill at first wrote on the Paharias and the Santals and described them as "the original inhabitants" and "interlopers" respectively.[10] His "*Notes*" contain an interesting description of socio-economic and cultural aspects of these "two distinct races."[11] Apart from these aspects, we also find a detailed account of ecological treasure of the Rajmahal Hills. His tour through the Rajmahal Hills started[12] on 16th January, 1851 and continued[13] up to 15th February, 1851. In course of his tour, Sherwill passed through various Hills and Forests and visited a number of villages of the Paharias and the Santals. It appears that he was very much interested in ecological wealth of the Rajmahal Hills as he broadly recorded various kinds of flora and fauna grew on and found in the vicinity of the Rajmahal Hills. The ecological description of the Hills as narrated in this paper is percolated from his "*Notes*."

Flora

During his tour through the hills, Sherwill saw "soondree trees" and from it , he observed, "is obtained a bright red dye chiefly used in dying wools and silk."[14] He spent much time across country at the base of the Belplatta Hills. Here he found large quantity of Mahua trees that occupied the stony and gravel ridges.[15] It seem that the Mahua trees fill the most of the area and gave "a park like appearance."[16]

From the "*Notes*" we know about the principal trees grown in the vicinity of jungels in Santal Parganas. Sherwill mentioned, "*asun, agye, dhamin and dhow*" as the principal trees. He "observed some very fine sal and semul trees."[17] On the Tatukpara hill, Sherwill found "a fine collection of trees of a very large growth," the principal were "mango, fan-leaf palm, tamarind, kuru, pipal al or moringa, asan and cheronji."[18] As it is observed by Sherwill, the Santals greatly favoured "Sohajana tree" also.[19]

As stated above, Sherwill visited a number of villages and broadly wrote on what he saw and witnessed in course of his observation. The hill village of Jola "surrounded by fine mango and fan-leaf palm tree, much jungle has been cleared away from all the hill-sides for the cultivation of junera and Indian corn."[20]

On 27th January, 1851, Sherwill visited from the high Sunjori hills to Telki village where he found "two trees situate in a jungle on the banks of a nullah."[21] "...one of which was of great beauty had a tall straight stem sixty or seventy feet in height, surmounted by an umbrella-shaped arrangement of branches, which projected from the main stem at right angles, half way the main stem was a similar arrangement of branches; from all the smaller branches and twigs an infinite number of the delicate green pods a one foot in the length, but not thicker than a quill, hung in festoons, forming an elegant fringe to the lower outline of the foliage. All parts of the tree yield large quantity of a thin white milk, which falls in large drops in quick succession when any pod, leaf or twig is broken. The leaves grow round the branches in circlets of eight leaves, from amongst which spring four delicate stems which in their turn are again surmounted by eight leaves; the leaves are three or four inches in length, narrow and pointed, smooth and very milky; the native or Santhal name for the tree is *Chutmi*, and the milk is used in hydrocele;... none of my up country recognized the tree. I have, since writing the above seen two stunted specimens of the same tree growing near Sooree; they were also called Chutmi by the villagers."[22]

In course of his tour Sherwill ascended the Mori hill supposed to be the highest hill in the whole of the Rajmahal range and went to Busko village situated "in fine forest of large trees principally asun, kurum, mango, tamarind and dhow above which is situate the village Mori."[23] Sherwill visited Mori village also and observed, "The summit of Mori, which is almost two thousand feet above the sea is covered with a fine forest principally Kurm, some of which have attained an enormous size, one in particular is well known all over the country, and has been of great use to me during the progress of the survey of the hills as it stands, a prominent landmark visible from most parts of the northern hills. From this tree there is an extensive view of the greater part of the hills as well as a great portion of the plains of Bhagalpur."[24]

Thus from the *Notes*, it is obviously clear that upon every peak in the hills, there were villages "surrounded by mango and palm trees etc, Sherwill reported that *Mr. Pontet* has planted a garden at *Meghee* in which are flourishing coffee trees, lemon, casuriama; pine-apples, peas, cauliflower, beet, mint, carrots and plantain."[25]

From the "*Notes*" we know about the love of Paharias for their trees. On Simuria hills, "some missionaries had felled a quantity of the finest trees for the purpose of erecting a house; the spot had, however, been deserted and the missionaries had never returned, old Kesoo (Kesoo Sirdar) mourned over his trees remarking that although they had been felled in one day, they had taken fifty years to grow."[26]

The forests on the northern hills were fine and contained much fine timber. Sherwill observed, "the principal trees are Cassia fistula and a tree much resembling in, bearing the same long pod, but the tree yields a thick white milk when bruised; the Grislea or Dhow; the Bijeesaul or Dalbergia also called Sitsaul, Pahsar, and Sisoo, the name depending upon the part of the timber mentioned, the color of the wood, and age of the tree, Dhow or Grislea; Asun or Urjoon, both Treminalias, and Sakua, which I take to be a Shorea. The Saul forests in the northern hill are fast disappearing."[27] The forests around Banjhi (near Sahibganj), according to Sherwill, were composed of the same kind of trees as noticed by him in the forests of the northern hills "except that a few Saul trees appear, also a dense underwood of bamboo-grass, reeds, grass and numerous shrubs, amongst which the wild Jasmine spreads its branches laden with sweet smelling flowers."[28] In one field of mustard near Nargunja, a twelve month old Santal village, Sherwill "saw upwards of fifty-five timber trees standing in this naked condition offering melancholy and curious contrast to the neighbouring green and luxuriant forest, with which the field was entirly enclosed."[29] Sherwill further observed. "In a few years not a tree will be left in these now timber crowded valleys, almost the whole of the large Sal forests have already perished under the operation of girdling for the production of the resin known as Damuter or Dhooma."[30] Both the outer and inner forests around Boril Bazar, according to Sherwill, "Forests are over-run with jungle, palm-trees, fine forest trees, bamboos, grass and marsh weeds."[31]

Through a very heavy forest of sal, sakua, a sun and dhow,

Sherwill visited Gowpara, the largest village in the hills. According to Sherwill, "The village is surrounded by heat hurdle fences enclosing tobacco, mustard, plantains, date and palmtrees, and in the centre of the village and around the houses are numerous fine palm-treees, tamarind, peepul, mango, jack, eleumps of bamboos and platains..."[32]

Fauna

The "*Notes*" also contains a broad account of animals found and bred by the people of the region. Now most of them, specially wild beasts, are not found in the hills, but in the 19th century, various kinds of animals infested the entire hills. From the "*Notes*" we also know about the menace of wild animals specially of elephants and tigers. Now-a-days tigers are not found, but a herd of elephants are still found in the hills and the reports on their menace and destruction frequently appear in various dailies. From the "Notes" also, we know about the presence and menace of wild elephants in the hills in the 19th century. He wrote about "a small herd of wild elephants" which consisted of "one male, several females and their young ones" in the jungles of kulang hills.[33] According to Sherwill, "These animals create much alarm in the villages lying along their beat, many of which have been lately deserted on account of the total destruction of the rice fields and in some instances of the huts of the Sonthals, which being probably covered with leguminous or cucurbitaccus creepers have tempted the elephants to tear down and devour their tempting and verdant covering.[34] But inspite of their menace and damage done by them, the Santhal women used to pay high respect to the elephants. Sherwill observed, "The Sonthal women, whenever they have an opportunity, pay great respect to the elephant; I have seen them place their young children on the foosteps of the animal whilst they themselves bowed down to the ground touching the earth with their foreheads. At a village I passed yesterday the women in a large body stopped a very fine and large male elephant that was carrying my tents, and insisted upon rendering him all due honour which they did with much noise and laughter, smearing his noble forehead with vermillion and oil."[35] But after admission of the Santhals "before whose axes the forest disapeared in a few years; the wild beasts that had been the terror of these hitherto unexplored wilds were soon destroyed by the arrows of the omnivorous Sonthal...."[36]

Sherwill passed through several Santhal villages and in each of which, as he observed, "were a profusion of poultry, pigs, buffaloes, cattle and pigeons; small patches of tobacco, and large fields of mustard. Tall castor oil plants surrounded the log huts which are thached with rice straw."[37] Sherwill pointed out that "Buffaloes for their superior strength, are preferred by the Sonthals, both for agricultural purposes as well as for draught, to the common grey cattle, which latter animals are readily exchanged with the Hindus from the plains, who import buffaloes for that purpose, all the solid wheeled carts if possible are drawn by buffaloes."[38]

At Mori villages, Sherwill saw several skulls of barking deer and two skulls of the four-horned antelope in the house of Manjhi (Chief) of the village. At Chapri village also Sherwill saw "a tree covered with skulls" and he "could recognize only one that of a neelghye." (Nil-cow). Then Sherwill passed through hill villages (Sathbera, Damlee etc.) and saw "large troops of Sungoor monkey"[39] while at the Hill village Hurra, he saw "numerous skulls of the spotted deer, wild hog, porcupine, hare and barking deer."[40] "Some of the pigs at this village," according to Sherwill, "were of an enormous size. and of a different breed from the ugly long legged pig of the plains."[41]

Sherwill wrote that in the north of Murroro village was a new cleared country "which three years ago was a dangerous jungle on account of tiger," while the jungle at the foot of Balto, a few years ago, was the resort of wild elephants which have been exterminated by the hill-men. Their mode of destroying these animals was by placing in their track Indian corn that had been poisoned with DAKRAN root; the Collector of Bhagalpur rewarding their success with fifty rupees for each elephant poisoned. The last elephant destroyed in these parts is supposed to have perished about twenty years ago."[42]

Apart from elephants, tigers, four-horned antelope, barking deer, Sungoor monkey, wild hod, spotted deer, porcupine, hare, long legged pig etc., there were leopards and bears also as Sherwill saw "tracers of leopards and bears in the jungles."

Sherwill took much interest in resounding echoes of birds and observed, "The woods (around Banjhi) resounded on all sides with the cries of jungle fowl and peacocks. Boa-constrictors, mouse deer, leopards and various kinds of deer, are found in the secluded nooks of these hills."[43]

Thus the "*Notes*" of Sherwill is very significant and informative as it contains a broad account of ecological repository, with various aspects of socio-economic-cultural history, of the Rajmahal Hills. His account can not be doubted as Sherwill wrote what he saw and witnessed himself. He narrated his findings and observations honestly and suffered much in moving through the hills and visiting villages of the paharias and the Santals. Facing the problems of road communication in those days of the 19th century, Sherwill vastly collected the facts, what he looked himself that he mentioned in his "*Notes*." In fact, his "*Notes*" is an invaluable historical note and for this Sherwill deserves our respect and praise. It is to be noted that he was a revenue surveyor and did his work brilliantly, but as an annalist he was matchless.

REFERENCES

1. Alok Kumar, (1986): *Tribal Culture and Economy*, New Delhi, p. 37.
2. W. W. Hunter, (ed.) (1975): *A Statistical Account of Bengal,* Vol. 14, *Bhagalpur and the Santhal Parganas* (London, 1877) Reprint, New Delhi, pp. 266-267.
3. *Black Fraires,* England, 1788.
4. *Asiatic Society of Bengal,* Vol. IV, Calcutta, 1795.
5. *An Account of District of Bhagalpur*, Patna, 1939.
6. *Report on the Management of the Rajmahal Hills,* 8 June, 1819. Deputy Commissioner Record Room, Dumka.
7. In Vol. 3, Vol. I, London, 1827.
8. London, 1838.
9. *Journal of Asiatic Society of Bengal,* Vol. 20, III, 1851, Calcutta pp. 544-606.
10. Ibid, p. 545.
11. Ibid, pp. 544-562.
12. Ibid, p. 562.
13. Ibid, p. 602.
14. Ibid, p. 602.
15. Ibid, p. 563.
16. Ibid, p. 564.
17. Ibid, p. 567.
18. Ibid, pp. 569-570.
19. Ibid, p. 570.
20. Ibid, p. 572.
21. Ibid, p 580.
22. Ibid, pp. 580-581.

23. Ibid, p. 581.
24. Ibid, p. 581.
25. Ibid, p. 584.
26. Ibid, p. 587.
27. Ibid, p. 588.
28. Ibid, p. 588.
29. Ibid, p. 590.
30. Ibid, p. 590.
31. Ibid, p. 591.
32. Ibid, p. 593.
33. Ibid, p. 563.
34. Ibid, p. 564.
35. Ibid, p. 564.
36. Ibid, p. 565.
37. Ibid, p. 564.
38. Ibid, p. 579.
39. Ibid, p. 582.
40. Ibid, p. 583.
41. Ibid, p. 583.
42. Ibid, p. 585.
43. Ibid, p. 588.

15. MEDICAL SCIENCE IN INDIA

Bhavesh Chandra Pandey

Struggle against diseases has been one of the earliest concerns of man. Even when man was a helpless creature living amidst the wild animals, and exposed to the forces of nature he was constantly busy in the quest of herbs and hybrids that could cure his ailments. However like most other sciences the early approach to diseases and medicines was highly irrational. Most diseases were ascribed to previous sins. 'पापेन जायते व्याधि'[1] or 'पूर्व जन्म कृतन् पापं व्याधिरूपेण बाधते' shows the early approach to diseases. The body was treated as an abode of diseases (शरीरं व्याधि मंदिरम्).[2]

However, health enjoyed a very special status for the Indian people right from the vedic ages. Ayurveda treated health as the root of the four '*Purusharthas*' of man and disease was treated as an abductor of '*arogya*' or health:

धर्मार्थ काममोक्षाणामारोग्यं मूलम् उत्तमम् ।
रोगास्तस्यापहर्तारं श्रेयसो जीवितस्यच ।।

Human body was accorded much value and significance and achieving longevity was one of the primary desires of man. Thus the *Yajurveda* expresses the heartfelt desire of man 'जीवेम शरदः शतम्'[4]

The history of early Indian Medical Science dates back to the vedic age. The *Atharvaveda* is said to be consisting of as many as seven hundred hymns related to medicines. *Ayurveda*, the science of longevity is said to have been received by the divine physician *Dhanvantari* from Brahma. The motto of Ayurveda was the prevention and cure of diseases:

'प्रयोजनं चास्य स्वस्थस्य स्वास्थ्य रक्षणमातुरस्य विकार प्रशमनं च।' ।[5]

Even in the later vedic (Post vedic) period medicine continued to enjoy high esteem. Lord shiva—one god from the trinity of Brahma, Vishnu and Mahesh was called *Baidyanath*. A *Vaidya* was held in high esteem as he was compared to God himself. 'वैद्यनारायणो हरिः' goes the popular Sanskrit saying.

Talking about the mythology sage *Chyavan* is said to have regained youth by taking a special medicine. Similarly the unconsciousness of Lakshaman in *The Ramayana* caused due to his being wounded in the war could be cured only when Hanuman brought the herbal medicine '*Sanjivani Buti*' prescribed by *Susen vaidya*. In *The Mahabharata* also king Pandu was suffering from jaundice.

The evolution of Indian Medical Science can be roughly divided in three parts—ancient, medieval and modern. The ancient period ranges from the earliest period to 1000 AD, the medieval period last still the establishment of the British colony and the modern period starts from the time of the establishment of British rule over India. The ancient period has been divided into vedic and post-vedic period.

The vedic period of medicine lasted till 800 BC. The early Indian Medical Science was highly religious. Diseases were supposed to be caused by demons or godly displeasure. '*Jalodara*' for example was said to be caused by 'Varma' and fever by demons entering the body. The concept of health was based on the precise balancing of three chief elements spirit (air), phlegm and bile. Most diseases were attributed to disturbed relationship between them: 'रोगस्तु दोष वैषम्यं, दोषसाम्यममरोगता.'[6] Diseases wre classified under several groups like fever, cough, consumption, diarrhoea, dropsy, siezure, tumour etc.[7]

The post-vedic period ranging from 800 BC to about 1000 AD. is considered the golden period of Indian Medicine. Varanasi and Taksasila became the centres of medical learning. The teachings in these books were compiled into great books of medicine. '*Susruta Samhita*' is a compendium of teachings of Susruta at Varanasi. The teachings of Atreya at Taksasila was collected by his pupil Agnivera. This was compiled by Charak as *Charak Samhita*. Vagbhatta also wrote two books on the principles of medicine. Besides, Jivaka earned his fame as a great doctor during the Buddhist period.

Ayurveda had eight organs: (i) Surgery ('*Salya*') (ii) Ophthalmology, otology (*Salakya*), (iii) Medicine (*Kayachikitsa*), (iv) Taxicology, medical Jurisprudence (*Agada Tantra*), (v) Psychiatry, Microbiology (*Bhuta Vidya*), (vi) Paediatrics (*Kaumarbhritya*), (vii) Science of Aphrodisiac (*Vajikaran*).[8] The diseases were supposed to be caused by the imbalance of phlegm, bile and spirit. This '*trivikara*' concept was similar to the Greek concept of 'humours' blood, phlegm, bile and spirit. Besides the 'trivikars' some other elements also influenced health. These secondary elements were chycle, blood, flesh, fat, bone, marrow and semen.[9]

The treatment was both dietic and medicinal. It involved five procedures—emetics, puragatives, enemata, oil enemata, and sneezing. Besides these teachings, cupping and bleeding were also applied.[10] The thrust of medical advancement was very high on developing medicines of longevity and reproductive and sexual power or '*Vajikaran*.' Hygenic rules were emphasized and cleanliness was given high priority. Bathings, ointment, cleaning of teeth and eye-washes were routines. There were elaborate methodologies for these regular activities different mantras were recorded for each one of them, in '*Nityakarma paddhati*' fasting was part of the religious practice and there were occasions for fasting in each month. Fasting has high hygenic value in controlling digestive disorders. A salt free diet was prescribed for nephritis and fat and fleshy foods for tuberculosis.[11]

Religious intervention apart, ancient Indian Medical wisdom enjoyed the systematicality of sciene too. The *materia medica* was very extensive and well researched. For example the *Susruta Samhita* mentions as many as 760 plants. There were some very common medicines used as household remedies. These are cinnamon, sesame pepper, cardamom, ginger and garlic. Besides some chemical elements like oxides, chlorides, sulphates of tin, iron, copper, silver, gold and mercury were used. Moreover inorganic substances like arsenic, sulpher, potash, common salt alum, and salt-ammoniac were also employed.[12]

The highest division of healing arts was surgery. The vedic surgeons are said to have accompanied armies to the battlefield. Besides this operations like taking factus out of womb, treatment of fistula, removal of gall bladder, and plastic surgery of nose cut was also known.[13] Medicines were both herbal as well as chemical.

The flower, root, fruit, leaf and bark of trees and plants were used as medicines. Three types of medicines were in use—rasa (*liquid juice*), 'bhasma' (*ashes*) and bati (*pills*). Iron and gold were used in some medicines. Milk, butter and honey were used as medicines and sometimes they were prescribed to be taken with some medicines for better result 'Gomutra' (*Urine of Cow*) was also applied in some ailments.

During the medieval period Indian Medicine received elements from the Greek and Persian medical system. There was difference of opinion regarding the action of drug. *'Tuhfal-ul-Muminin'* by Muhammad Mimin Hasami Tunkabuni discusses in detail the differences of opinion. There were specific treatises on particular parts of a body. 'Nur-ul-Uyun' by Zarrin Dast (AD 1087) is a book related to eye diseases. There are treatises on anatomy of human body describing in detail the bones, nerves, veins, arteries and various organs, such as *'Mukhtasar-dar-lim-tasrih'* (13th BC) by Al Baidawi, Riyadh-I-Alamgiri (17thC) by Muhammad Rida, and Khula sat-ulTashrih by Abdur Razzaq. The Sanskrit sources also influenced the Persian texts and there was a mutual transaction of expertise in the field of medicine. *Bhuwabin Khwas Khan's Madan-u-sh-shifa's-i-Shikandar Sahi* (AD 512) is based on Sanskrit sources.[14]

Some very important Sanskrit texts were written during the medieval period. Among those Tisata's *'Chikitsa Kalika'* (14th C), Bhavamishra's *'Bhava Prakash,'* Lolimbraja's *'Vaidyajivan'* were most famous. The first important book on plant diseases is *'Vrikshayurved'* by Parasar. Besides these two books on pharmacology the two famous book *Yogasutra* by Patanjali and 'Kamasutra' by Vatsayan were also great treatises on complementary disciplines. The *'Yogasutra'* gave elaborate description of *'asanas'* and *'pranayam'* for physical fitness and mental acumen and peace.

The modern age of Indian Medical Science set in with the establishment of British rule over India. The British people criticised the Indian medical wisdom on two grounds. According to Whitela Ansli the ancient Indian medical science was inter fused with religion and it was seen as a gift of god and it was viewed with high honour. Secondly, the ancient medical knowledge of surgery has been forgotten and the Ayurvedic doctors were complete unaware of the internal mechanism of body[15] Some British writers went straight forward to outrighly reject all medical texts of ancient

India. Sir William Jones, for example, claimed that there was not a single book on medicine in any Asian Language that can be categorized as science.[16]

However, there were also some words of appreciation for the Indian Medical Science. The Court of Directors in 1814 underlined that the Sanskrit texts contained some very good information regarding the nature and qualities of medicines and the European doctors ought to know them.

One very remarkable fact about the medical history of India before the Britishers is that the state did not make much organized effort to control widespread diseases. Besides this no regular and systematic efforts were made to update the medical knowledge with new experiments. Chemotherapy and pathology were not much developed. Surgery was not painless and the use of local, spinal or epidural surgery was unknown or rarely practised. The administration of enaesthetics was introduced some 140 years ago with the use of other in 1846 by Morton. There was thrust on permanent relief rather than instant relief. The knowledge of anti-bacterial and antiviral medicines was unavailable.The over all nature of medical wisdom was religious rather than scientific.

The British era of medical science in India began on a very subdued note of adoption of the existing Indian Medical Wisdom. But gradually the British people made some very significant inroads in introducing their own skills in the study of the diseases and their remedies. Early medical interventions came in military and missionary fields. European surgeons accompanied the British military during wars. On the other hand the missionary people used their medicines to prove their superiority in some tribal and backkward areas. David Arnold says that the Indian Medical services came up as a result of military need of the early colonial rule.[17] After the Battle of Plassey the Bengal Medical Service was established in 1763. By 1858 the governmental obligation was limited to the Indian Army. But by the end of the 19th century it was extended to civil areas and the Indians were allowed to enter it for routine purposes.

In 1824 the Calcutta Native Medical Institution was set up to produce 'native doctors' trained in Ayurvedic as well as the paralled medicine. However, this age of mutual co-operation soon ended with the closure of the institution.William Bentink ordered the opening of a new college in its place in 1835 and ordered to teach entirely western medical science. Ronald Martin treated this decision of Bentink as more important than Sati eradication in 1829 as the spread of medical knowledge will prove the superiority of European knowledge before the native Indians very clearly and effectively.[18]

The average reaction of the English people regarding the indigenous Indian medical practice was that of contempt. They regarded it as highly irrational and superstitious. However there were also some examples of mutual acceptance. The use of quinine as a cure of malaria was one such case. It was used by the Begali '*Kavirajas*' and Panjabi '*Hakims*' for treatment of malaria. It found full scale use in curbing the menace of *Vardwan fever* in 1860.[19]

The superiority of Europeon medicines was proved beyond doubt in respect of curbing the menace of smallpox, malaria, Bubonic plague and cholera. In 1883 Robert Koch, the German physician, while in (Calcutta) Kolkata as the head of the Cholera Commission, discovered the cholera germs. He defined the criteria for attributing an organism as the cause of specific disease, referred to as Koch's postulates.[20] A few years later Ronal Ross in 1890 discovered at Secunderabad the role of anopheline mosquitoes in the transmission of Malaria. Vaccination against smallpox was started by the company in 1802. It replaced the variolation popular in India as a check against smallpox.The company was very serious in curing smallpox. It was compared to '*sati*' and infanticide and the Smallpox Commission termed it as a bloody business. The Indians treated it as associated with Goddess '*Sitla*' and look recourse to religious rites and recitations. Early response of Indians towards vaccination was restrained. But gradually vaccination was opted for and by 1827 the entire India was divided in four vaccination jones. By 1886 vaccination was made necessary by law in some areas by the government. By the end of the first world war there was a considerable check on death rate due to smallpox.

The British people were more organized and systematic in respect of dealing with the problem of diseases. They worked on specific diseases with a definite action-plan. They applied a rational approach in studying the causes and remedies of diseases. They prepared a medical topography. The experiences of other hot and tropical climates like the West Indies were worked out with. Reference may be made of the book of James Johnson. The Influence of Tropical climates, more specially the climate of India, on the European constitution, published in 1813. With the help of topographical survey and collection of statics of diseases it was possible to make some preventive arrangements. Some of the statistics collected during that period are horrible. For example the Health Commissioner of Bengal declared in 1890 that about 10 Lakh people died of Malaria that year.[20] There was a continuous efford to find out the solution to this menace. Even before Ronald Ross, T.E. Dempster had succeeded in finding the link between malaria and spread of canal irrigation. He had prepared a '*Spleen Index*' which was a dependable guide of the spread and intensity of the disease.

Cholera was yet another epidemic disease that caused mass casualties. It is believed that it killed 15 million people between 1817 and 1865.[21] The cause of this disease was ascribed to the local topography or monsoon or famine. The Health Commissioner J.M. Kanningham, however, agreed to meteorological and social causes. According to him the possible cause of cholera was the poisonous air wapour. In 1868 T.R. Lewis and Kanningham were appointed to study the eteology of cholera and after a long study they concluded that like malaria the cause of cholera was also topographical. Later on Robert Koch discoverd the cholera virus in 1884.

The European medical system flourished during the British rule due to state patronage and conservation. The indigenous medical system suffered a setback. Its pharmacology was more and more herbal and it lacked scientific precision. The state neglect of this system hampered its natural growth and evolution. Nevertheless, it is quite unjust to outrightly reject the entire treasury of Indian medical wisdom. In fact there is an urgent need to popularize some of the faiths and beliefs regarding hygiene, food habits, cleanliness and preventions. Much of the Ayurvedic medical wisdom is of immense help in dealing with some routine health ailments. However, the old Indian medical knowledge needs to update itself with the help of new instruments and pathological skills. The Ayurvedic medicines need to incorporate the innovative skills in the fields of anti-bacterial, anti-viral, surgical and pathological fields. There is a need to promote research in the field of bio-technology and to utilize the rich treasure of bio-resources in India. President *A.P.J. Abdul Kalam* has expressed the need to capture the global herbal market. He says that India is rich in herbs, germplasms, and micro-organisms. It must add its own technology for conversion of such resources to value-added products for use in domestic requirements as well as for export of the global herbal product market of 61 million dollar.[22]

This is an established fact that most common diseases are caused due to reckless living. A break can be put on them if the ayurvedic principles of '*Vrata,*' '*Upavas,*' '*Pranayam,*' '*Ahar,*' *Vihar* etc. are followed. The traditional medicines can be cost effective and easy available. These mediciens will, however, need to prove their utility in curing diseases and providing instant relief. There is a need to develop scientific precision and sceintific approach as well. Fortunately, a need for the revival of traditional medical wisdom is being felt. The legal battle for securing the patent of turmeric and neem between India and the U.S.A. is a testimony of the growing Indian concern for the preservation of traditional medical wisdom.

In the recent past India has evolved as a popular medical destination. The health facilities have improved considerably. But much remains to be done. There have been organized efforts to wipe out diseases like polio and small pox. Due to growing awareness of health the birth rate and death rate have gone down significantly. Many fatal diseases have been curbed successfully. However, it is quite sad to know that even today people die of malaria. Besides this the number of AIDS patients in India has grownup quite significantly. Thus there are challanges ahead to fight. There is a need to combine tradition and modernity in order to make medicines patient friendly and cost-effective.

'A brief survey of the evolution of Indian medical system convinces us of the fact that the modern age has been more systematic, precise, rational and organized than the earlier stages. However it is not justified to outrightly reject the traditional Indian medical wisdom. The harsh criticism of traditional medicines by the British scholars is an example of a colonial prejudice.

REFERENCES

1. ब्रह्मखंड 16/51-53.
2. चरक संहिता सूत्र.

3. Ibid 1/5-16.
4. *यजुर्वेद,* 16/28.
5. *चरक संहिता सूत्र,* 30-26.
6. *अष्टांगहृदय सूत्र,* 1/20.
7. *Gazetteer of India* Vol 11 (1973) pp 208-10.
8. Dr. Jaisawal. S. *Kalyan Arogyank* Jan-Feb. 2001, pp. 173.
9. *Gazetteer of India* pp. 208-10.
10. Ibid.
11. Ibid.
12. Ibid.
13. Ibid.
14. Ibid 468-69.
15. Ansli. W. *Materia Medica* II, London, 1826, pp. V-VII.
16. Mukhopadhyay. G. *History of Indian Medicines from Earliest Ages to Present Time*.I, Calcutta 1923, pp. 4-5.
17. डेविड आर्नल्ड, *औपनिवेशिक भारत में विज्ञान, प्रौद्योगिकी एवं आयुर्वेद,* वाणी प्रकाशन (2004), पृ. 84.
18. Martin, *Notes on the Medical Topography of Calcutta,* 1837, pp. 89.
19. आर्नल्ड, पृ. 89.
20. Greg. W.H. *Malarial fever in Bengal CR 88* (1889) pp. 384.
21. आर्नल्ड, वही, पृ. 108.
22. A.P.J. Abdul Kalam, *Vision for 2020 in Prism,* Macmillan, 2005.

16. TREES, TRADITIONS AND TRENDS

Ranjan Kumar Sinha

Every culture has narratives or beliefs which answer in different ways the fundamental questions about how we came to be, how and where people originated, collective transformations undergone by the community, and how people should behave towards one another and their environment. Forests are the subject of a great deal of myth, legend and lore. Societies most closely entwined with forests tend to regard them with a healthy respect, an awe at their splendour and majesty, sometimes dread and fear of the powerful spirits that lurk within them. Trees are universal powerful symbols, a physical expression of life, growth and vigour to urban, rural and forest dwellers alike. They symbolize historical continuity and human society. They are often of frightening magnitude, linking earth and heavens, arbiters of life and death, and home to both good and bad spirits. Ancestors often find their resting places in forests, many wandering in various states of unease and spitefulness.

There exists an intimate relationship of man to forests that combines fearful respect and awe at the beauty and mystical source of life. The tradition of conservation of trees in the form of Sacred Groves is prevalent through out the world and in one way or the other they share many similar features. These sacred groves are segments of landscape containing vegetation and other forms of life and geographical features that are delimited and protected by human societies as a symbol of relationship of human with the divine or the nature (Huges & Chandran, 1998). These are specific forest areas imbued with powers beyond those of humans; they are home to mighty spirits that can take or give life; they originate from a range of roots, and include: sites linked to specific events; sites surrounding temples; burial grounds or cemeteries housing the spirits of ancestors; the homes of protective spirits; the homes of deities from which priests derive their healing powers; homes to a powerful animal or plant species; forest areas that surround natural sacred features such as rivers, rocks, caves and 'bottomless' water holes; and sites of initiation or ritual (Gadgil and Vartak 1981).

Sacred Groves and Traditions

The Dai people of China, believe that the forest is the cradle of human life, and that forests are at one with the supernatural realm. They believe that the interrelationship of human beings with their physical environment consists of five major elements: forest, water, land, food and humanity (Pei Shengji, Posey 1999). In his reference to the four hundred 'dragon hills' Pei Shengji mentions: "...sacred grove is a kind of natural conservation area... a forested hill where the gods reside. All the plants and animals that inhabit the Holy Hills are either companions of the gods or sacred living things in the gods' gardens. .... the spirits of great and revered chieftains go to the Holy Hills to live following their departure from the world of the living." In Ghana, beliefs about forests include the belief that they are the home of dwarfs, and the domain of the mythical Sasabonsam—a legendary figure responsible for all the woes of mankind and to which mishaps and everything evil are attributable. Ties to nature manifest themselves most notably in Turkish culture through attitudes to plants in general, and trees in particular. After conversion to Islam, the importance of trees grew in local culture because Mohammed compared a good Muslim to a palm tree and declared that planting a tree would be accepted as a substitute for alms. Trees are planted after children are born, when a son is drafted into military service, after a wedding, and as a memorial to the dead. The oak tree was worshipped by Romans as the home of deities. In Europe, fairies were said to make their homes in old oak trees, departing through holes where branches had fallen; it was considered healing to touch the fairy doors with diseased parts. In India, as elsewhere in many parts of the world, a number of communities practice different forms of nature worship providing protection to patches of forests dedicated to the deities or ancestral spirits. These vegetation patches, as protected by local communities, through social taboos and sanction reflects the spiritual and ecological ethos of the community. Such beliefs and convictions are prevalent all other parts of the world in one form or the other but the reverence to this natural bounty is unquestionable.

Access to most sacred forests is restricted by taboos, codes and custom to particular activities and members of a community. Gathering, hunting, wood-chopping and cultivation are strictly prohibited in these groves. The Dai people believe that these activities would make the gods angry and bring misfortune and disaster upon the community. In Maharashtra, regulations and religious customs are set down by priests with a knowledge of the forest deities, their ties to the surrounding landscape, and their influence on the daily lives of the community. Ancient folklore and stories are told which include fairly specific detail on the supernatural penalties that will result should the groves be desecrated, especially by felling trees. However, control over extractive activities in sacred groves varies from region to region, and in many places a complete ban is not in place, and limited collection of fallen wood, fruit from the forest floor, medicinal plant collection, honey collection, and other activities are permitted, if strictly controlled. The newly formed state Jharkhand is extensively dotted with sacred groves. Various anthropological studies report the tradition from this region (Vidyarthi and Rai,1997).The tradition is popularly known as *Sarana* or *Jaherthan*. In Chotanagpur there are various types of Sarana like Sarhul Sarana, Duvaria Sarana etc (Troisi,1978). In such groves annual rituals and ceremonies are performed to propitiate the deity for the well being of the people, animals, crops etc The presiding deities are believed to look after the well being of the people and also protect the groves by administering punishment (mostly death) to the offenders. The practice of oath/vow taking in the groves is fairly widespread in the region. Hembram (1983) states that *sarana dharma* brought together discrete ethnic groups of Chotaṇagpur into a common platform for asserting their rights to self-determination. The sarana dharma, in fact, helped them in consolidating their common identity and solidarity between the Christian and non-Christian tribes of the region.

Sacred Groves as Conservation model

Sacred groves have survived for many hundreds of years and today act as reservoirs of much local biodiversity. Its significance to local denizens or forest dwellers touches life in various ways like:

Religious: Propitiation of deity/spirits, propitiation of ancestral spirit, propitiation of totems;

Cultural: Providing cultural space to the community as a common property resource, well-being of individual/ family/ community;

Political: Assertion of group identity and group solidarity, Establishing new alliances;

Health: Fertility and Paternity;

Economic: Good rainfall, good agricultural production, Well being of crops and animals, Success in haunting;

Psychological: Moral support and guidance;

Biological: Soil conservation, nutrient release and recycling. Rapid litter decomposition rate, folk medicine, safe refuge for threatened species.

Biologically SG plays a crucial role in soil conservation and nutrient recycling. With a rapid litter decomposition rate, nutrient release in the soil of these groves is very high. Many sacred groves constitute pristine vegetation and are particularly rich in trees and associate groups of organisms like epiphytes, amphibia, reptiles, birds, butterflies etc.

A number of studies have revealed that many SGs are climax forests and probably constitute the only representative of near-natural vegetation in many parts of India (Godbole et al, 1998). Sacred groves in general, act as nursery and storehouse of many ayurvedic, tribal and folk medicines. Sacred forests are of great forestry interest as indicators of the natural productivity of the region. Ecologically valuable species like *Albizia lebbeck* and *Ficus glomerata* which conserve high amount of N, P, Mg & Ca in their leaves are found in several SGs. Many animal species including birds that are otherwise threatened and becoming rare find a safe refuge in many sacred groves linked to the survival of many other species. Many groves hold water resource in the form of springs, ponds, lakes, streams or rivers. They act like a sponge during wet periods and release water slowly in times of drought. The ponds and streams adjoining the groves are often perennial and in some cases act as the last resort to many animals and birds during dry seasons.

As a result of the high conservation and biodiversity values held in sacred groves, increasing attention is being paid to their potential as a tool and model for biodiversity conservation. In Paris summit UNESCO(1996) while highlighting the significance of sacred sites as a reservoir of cultural integrity and biological diversity mentions that *'Sacred groves have served as important reservoirs of biodiversity, preserving unique species of plants, insects, and animals. Sacred and taboo associations attached to particular species of trees, forest groves, mountains, rivers, caves, and temple sites should therefore continue to play an important role in the protection of particular ecosystems by local people. Particular plant species are often used by traditional healers and priests who have a strong interest in the preservation of such sites and ecosystems. In some regions of the world, beliefs that spirits inhabit relict areas have served to quickly regenerate abandoned swidden plots into mature forest. In other areas, sacred places play a major part in safeguarding critical sites in the hydrological cycle of watershed areas. Furthermore, in a number of instances sacred sites have also been instrumental in preserving the ecological integrity of entire landscapes. For these reasons, sacred sites can help in assessing the potential natural vegetation of degraded ecosystems or ecosystems modified by humans.'*

Threats to Sacred Groves

All the above facts indicate that the conservation of sacred groves is essential for maintaining local/regional biodiversity, the comprehensive health of a landscape and preserving the socio-cultural integrity of local communities. The socio-cultural edifice of many endogamous tribes of the country basically rests on sacred groves. However, this ancient and widespread institution shows signs of weakening in terms of both cultural and biological integrity in many parts of the country. The nature and extent of threats and pressure are often region and even grove-specific.

Sacred groves have survived in many regions despite tremendous economic pressure on forest resources. With the continuing destruction of forest all around, these groves have become fragmented habitats of genetic pools and have become the last refuge for many threatened, endangered and endemic plant and animal species. As per reports, so far about 13,000 sacred groves have been identified all over the country whereas the figure may round about 1,00,000 to 1,50,000 (Malhotra,1998). In some parts of India, sacred groves have retained high levels of biodiversity and remain largely intact, while government-controlled forest reserves are often in poor condition. Local level control has been vital to the protection of these areas, but economic pressures are mounting, and changing land-use patterns have contributed to a serious depletion of resources and a phenomenal rise in the price of land. This in turn has provided an irresistible incentive for some local people to sell the groves, irrespective of the sentiment that at one time it was life line for their survival. Even in cases where local communities are determined to retain sacred groves, they are often as vulnerable to outside political and economic forces as other forest areas. The government or the private agencies promise in return to encourage 'community participation,' 'the development of sustainable forest management,' and 'income generating schemes,' which are considered 'empty and pointless' offers for a priceless ancestral forest that cannot be equated with monetary and material conditions.

Although sacred groves undoubtedly contribute to the conservation of biodiversity, it is questionable whether the complex history and traditions that have created and maintain these areas can be operationalized as a tool or model for further conservation efforts. Conservation is often a side-effect of customs that associate or dedicate forest resources to the deities. In the Western Ghats of India, rather than managing resources for future use, communities are instead attempting to benefit from the protection and good-will afforded by the deity in return for not disturbing the sanctity of the sacred grove. This would be a difficult dynamic to reproduce in a conservation programme.

REFERENCES

Gadgil, M. and Vartak, V.D., (1981): Sacred groves in Maharashtra—An inventory. In: S.K. Jain (ed.), *Glimpses of Indian Ethnobotany*, Oxford & IBH Publishers, New Delhi, pp. 279-294.

Godbole, A., Watve, A., Prabhu, S. and Sarnaik, J., (1998): Role of sacred groves in biodiversity conservation with local people's participation: A case study from Ratnagiri district, Maharashtra, In: Ramakrishnan, P.S.,Saxena, K.G, and Chandrashekara, U M. (eds.) *Conserving the Sacred for Biodiversity Management*, Oxford and IBH Publishing Co., New Delhi, pp. 233-46.

Hughes, J.D. and Subash Chandran, M.D., (1998): Sacred groves around the earth: An overview, In: Ramakrishnan, P.S. Saxena, KG. and Chandrashekara, U.M. (eds.) *Conserving the Sacred for Biodiversity Management*,Oxford and IBH Publishing Co., New Delhi, pp.69-46.

Malhotra, K.C., (1998): Anthropological Dimensions of Sacred Groves in India: An overview, In: Ramakrishnan, P.S. Saxena, K.G. and Chandrashekara, U.M. (eds.) *Conserving the Sacred for Biodiversity Management*, Oxford and IBH Publishing Co., New Delhi, pp. 423-38.

Troisi, J., (1978): *Tribal Religion: Religion and Practice among the Santhals*, Manohar Publishers, New Delhi.

Vidyarthi, L.P. and Rai, B.K., (1977): *Tribal Culture of India*, Concept Publishers, Delhi. Viji, C. 1995. The sacred groves, The Hindu, 5 September.

17. HISTORY OF TRIBAL ART AND CULTURE FOR MAINTAINING THE ECOLOGICAL BALANCE

S.P. Roy

Modern civilization, from its very inception, has been homocentric in general and ethnocentric in particular. All discoveries and inventions have been oriented towards human welfare. The non human element of the creation has been ruthlessly exploited to provide comforts, real as well as imaginary, to human beings. Consequently more than half the known animal extinctions have occurred just since 1900 A.D. Currently, estimates of the International Union for Conservation of Nature and Natural Resources, an average of one animal species is lost every year; and about one thousand birds and mammals are now thought to be in jeopardy. This alarming reduction of the creation would not, possibly, have stirred the conscience of the homocentric man, had this impoverishment of the non-humans been in his favour. To our utter dismay we have suddenly realized that an untimely death of even an 'insignificant' plant or animal pushes man a step forward, however, small it may be, towards doom. Thus, the fear of his own ignominious end forced the 21st century 'civilized' man to be sympathetic towards his non-human environment.[1]

Whatever be the motives of this sympathy, the common man is led to think that concern for the environment to maintain a balance among its various components is an attribute of the civilization.

State of Environment and Forest Dweller Economy

Forest are among the most depleted natural resources and deforestation has great impact on the weaker sections. It is estimated that in eleven countries of the world low land forests have disappeared and the existing forests will not last for more than 10 years if the present pace of deforestation continues. The depletion of forests in India has been massive as seen in the fact that not more than 11% of the total geographical area of India is under at 33% by the National Forest Policy, 1952 and the National Commission on Agriculture, 1976. Regarding the pace of deforestation it is estimated that the annual loss of forest area is 1.61 lakh hectares of 441 hectares per day.[2]

History of Ecological Balance

The objective of this paper is to show that the concept of *ecological balance* is far older than civilization; and that it was vigorously practiced by those whom the 'modern man' calls 'uncivilized,' 'barbarian,' 'savage,' 'tribal,' 'forest dwellers,' 'animistic' and the like: and their way of life is described in such terms that would connote an antithesis of what the 'civilization' stands for. In our arrogance, we have exhausted our vocabulary in calling names to these people for the depletion of our forest, this is evident in almost all forest policies of our Governments.

Tribal Thought

Neverthless, these tribal people practiced/practise a way of life that clearly recognized/recognize the importance of the non-human component of the creation. They have developed such cultural devices which automatically guaranteed a reasonable safety to the flora and fauna of their environment; and maintained the ecological balance to a reasonable extent.[3]

Social Aggregates of Tribals

Universally tribal people group themselves into defined social aggregates. Such groups are more often named after animals, and plants; and less often after the inanimate object of their surroundings. This object is the totem, (originally a North American Indian word adopted to the anthropological literature).

All over the world people who are totemistic take care of

their totem objects; and have devised elaborate social taboos for their protection.[4]

Totems and Taboos

A number of totems and taboos are prevalent among tribes of Bihar State like that of tribes of Madhya Pradesh and Orissa State. These totems and taboos are helpful in protection of wild-wealth. Majority of tribals do not kill cow as it is a sin to kill it, since they worship them as Goddess. Some tribal communities do not kill squirrels and tortoise due to their religious taboos. Peacock is also worshiped by some tribes due to their religious sentiments.

Examples of totems and taboos

The *Birhor*, classified as one of the most primitive tribes in India consider eating, killing, or destroying the totem as equivalent to killing a human member of the tribe. They also believe that a diminution in the totem animals, plants and other objects caused by their destruction and killing will bring about a corresponding decrease in size of the tribe. Violation of this taboo entails payment of a fine to provide a feast to the community members.

The *Asur*, another primitive tribe of Central India, not refrain from harming the totem object, but also stricken with grief when they see the animal lying wounded or dead. At one time in their tradition they used to give such dead ones a burial. It is observed that they change their totems periodically. Such a practice may be taken to mean an adjustment with the changing environment; whenever such changes occur.

The *Munda*, one of the most ancient tribes of India is divided into a large number of groups, called, killi. Each killi has a totem. Dalton, one of the earliest ethnographers, recorded 142 kills with animal or bird totems, and 83 with plants. Another record of the Munda totems enumerates 11 birds, 3 fish, 2 reptiles, 2 insects 4 trees yielding edible fruits, 4 trees of which nothing is eaten, 3 food grains, 1 pulse, 2 herbs, 2 edible tubers, 1 edible oil plant, 1 condiment plant, 1 plant from which a drink is extracted, and 4 inanimate objects.

The Bhumij have 11 animal totems and 4 plant totems. The Korwa has 36 totems of plants and animals. The Juangs of Dhenkanal have six totems, namely, the Fig. Tree, the Satinwood tree, the Semur tree, the squirrel and the wood-pigeon. Their counterparts in pallahara and Keonjhar have 20 totems of which 12 are trees, 5 animals, 2 grains, and the last is the river Baitarani.

The Gonds of Chattisgarh have divided themselves into 5 groups. Each called a got. The gots are: Tekam (Teak), Netam (Dog), Kariam (Cock), Singram (a variety of Fish), Marai (a Tree). The Bastar Gonds have the Bakra (Goat). Kachchim (Tortoise), Nag (Cobra) Sodi (Tiger) Bheinsa (Buffalo), Netam (Dog) Chamchadai (Bat), Markam (Mango Tree), Tekam (Teak Tree), lrpachi (Mahua Tree), Tumrachi (kendu Tree) and Warkara (Wild Cat) as their Totems. The Adilabad Gonds have totems, such as, the tortoise, the crocodile, the iguana, the porcupine, the tiger, the sanas, the cobra, etc. For the Gond as a whole 56 totems are reported. Among these there are 18 beasts, 7 birds, 5 reptiles, 9 fish and other acquentic creatures, and 17 plants.

Community structure of Santhals

The Santhal has 12 totems viz. Hansda, Murmu, Kisku, Hembram, Marandi, Soren, Tudu, Baski, Pauria, Choure and Bedea. Each totem is further divided into various taboos, which are named after the plants and animals of their area. It was found that "Gua Hembram"—a taboo of Hembram feels that they might have originated from "Gua" (Santhali) meaning supari *(Areca catechu Linn)*. Santhals having surname "Gua Hembram" neither cut the trees of supari nor eat supari instead worship it. The cutting, destroying and killing of such plants/animals means the killing of their own clan. Thus, these tribes conserve the plants and animals.

Religious beliefs

Santhal culture is directly associated with local plants and animals. On the occasion of birth ceremony grinded margosa leaves mixed with rice are served as food to guests. A hen is buried along the dead body of Santhal. Santhals worship mahua and mango tree. The presence of mahua tree in the marriage place shows richness of the family. They have no temples, nor any shed for worship but they have a place known as "Jahisthan" where religious ceremonies of the village are performed. The "Jahisthan" is generally under the trees of sal, mahua, mango, neem etc.

Folklore

Santhals lead a semi-nomadic life, in which they move in search of food. They have elaborate song cycles for festive occasions and for various stage of agricultural cycles.

Recreation

Santhals are jolly, cheerful and contented people. Mass hunting of wild animals, fighting of livestocks specially sheeps and hens are the main recreational activities of Santhal. They are musical people. They make their own favourite instruments such as flute from bamboo stick and a special musical instrument utilizing a hollow pumpkin covered with a piece of skin of snakes or other animals.

Festivals

There is a succession of festivals throughout the year, nearly all connected with agricultural operations. The principal Santhal events of the year starting with the festivals of the "Sohrai" and "Maghsin" in the month of January. The "Jahra" and "Baha" are celebrated between the falling of the mahua flowers and the gathering of the fruits then great annual hunts are held.

In fact, their social life, philosophy, thinking and their rituals practically all are centered on different agricultural activities. In the lean period of agriculture they used to lead a semi-nomadic life, always on the move in search of food. In this period they depend upon hunting, fishing, food gathering from the forests. Thus, agriculture is the principal occupation of Santhal but fishing and food gathering are still considered important source of their sustenance.

Thus, Santhals have 12 totems and each totem has been further divided into taboos which has been named after the local flora and fauna. The cutting/killing of these biodiversity is just similar to destroying their own clan. Thus, the concept, myth, folklore and philosophy of these tribals help in the conservation of the environment.[5]

Considering such importance of the tribals United Nations had celebrated from January 1994 to December 2004 as "International decade for Indigenous People" throughout the world.

The scope of this paper does not permit us to compile the information that ethnography has its disposal. In fine, it can be said with emphasis that tribal people all over the world lives or are living in close kinship with nature. Through this kinship real or fictitious, they have come to look upon every aspect of the creation with reasonable respect which imperceptibly maintained what we now term as 'the ecological balance.'

Conclusion

My submission is that restoration of the ecological balance can never be achieved through seminars and workshops by the 'intellectuals.' The key to such a restoration lies in sheding our arrogance and learn from our 'Jangali' neighbour the art of respecting our environment—human as well as non human.

REFERENCES

1. Gadgil, Madhav, Narendra Prasad and Rauf Ali, (1983): *Forest Management and Forest Policy in India: A Critical Review*, in Walter Fernandes (ed.) Forests, Environment and People, New Delhi: India Social Institute.
2. Govt. of India, (1976): *Report of National Commission on Agriculture,* Part IX Forestry, New Delhi: Ministry of Agriculture and Irrigation, Government of India.
3. Govt. of India, (1982): *Report of the Committee on Forests and Tribals in India,* New Delhi: Ministry of Home Affairs, Tribal Development Division, Government of India.
4. Joshi, Gopa, (1983): "Forest policy and Tribal Development: Problems of Implementation, Ecology and Exploitation," In Walter Fernandes and Sharad Kulkarni (eds.), *Towards a New Forest Policy: People's Rights and Environmental Needs,* New Delhi: India Social Institute.
5. Roy, S.P., (2006): 'Sustainable Development: A Case Study of Santhal Pargana (Jharkhand)', *Vikramshila Journal of Social Sciences* (In Press).

18. ENVIRONMENTAL HISTORY OF MODERN INDIA

Raman Sinha

The History of Environment in India is very old. In Hindu Philosophy, it is believed that the human body is composed of five elements *(Panch Tatva)* viz; *Air, Water, Ether, Earth and Fire*. In this way nature creats human body. Nature possesses an inherent quality of purging pollution by itself. After the birth of mankind, the environmental pollution started growing. The protection and clearing up of environment was the essence of Vedic culture. In Hindu theology forests, trees and wildlife protection held a place of special reverence.

Environmental Management in India is as old as its history, its social and cultural milieu. Our forefathers used to worship the mountains, the rivers, pipal tree etc. since time immemorial. Elephants (GAJRAAJ) and Cows are worshipped even today. The concept of bio-diversity and the green cover is age-old in India. The social and religious fabric was woven round the concept of Environment Protection and Promotion.[1]

Nature reserves immense potential to maintain ecological balance. Once upon a time there was a perfect ecological balance of nature. With the growth of economic power and unplanned industrial development the pressure on natural resources has increased considerably. In his lust for comfortable life, man has miserably built up a high degree of pressure on natural resources causing thereby a danger to human well-being and health. Perhaps man has forgotten that the depletion of natural resources may lead to the destruction of human race itself; that his duty is to add something to the natural wealth in consideration for what he receives from nature. All this has resulted in an eco-catastrophe. Due to man's increased interference with nature, the problem of environmental pollution has assumed international dimensions. The continued degradation of human environment is the gift of modern living, technological advancement and industrialisation.

The economic and industrial development results in environmental pollution. It may be added that introduction of large amount of pollutants affects the environment adversely—the air pollution, water pollution, soil and nuclear pollution is increasing every day. The desertification, deforestation and soil erosion have caused ecological imbalance. The huge industrialisation has resulted in water and air pollution. Whereas all the water resources including seas, rivers, canals and drains have been contaminated due to the rapid growth of industrialisation, the air pollution has affected all the major cities and towns of the country. Water pollution gives rise to soil pollution which contaminates all our eatables. The increased use of fertilizers and pesticides in agricultural fields has also caused environmental pollution.

The establishment of *British Rule in India* ushered in an era of the plunder of natural resources. At the same time, this regime saw the beginning of organised forest management. It was the forestry, wild life and water pollution which attracted the attention of the rulers. Today's seriousness was not attached with the environmental problem, nevertheless, some enactments pertaining to the environmetal protection were done, no doubt, with the sole purpose of serving the ends of British empire. To glance through some of the legislations passed during British rule is necessary for drawing out a clear picture of historical aspects of environmental protection.[2]

However, during the nineteenth century (19th Century), attempts were made to regulate water pollution, wild life and land use by enacting laws by the British Government. These laws, however, had a narrow purpose and limited territorial approach. The Shore Nuisance (Bombay and Kolaba) Act 1853, Oriental Gas Company Act 1857, The Forests Act 1865, Indian Fisheries Act 1897 were the relevant legislations containing provisions thereof. Similarly Bengal Smoke Nuisance Act 1905, Bombay Smoke Nuisance Act 1912 and the Boilers Act of 1923 were the earlier laws, enacted during the British rule, aimed at controlling air pollution. Forests Act 1927 was passed with a view to providing teeth to the Forest Policy of 1894 of State monopoly over the forests. Further, in the field of wildlife protection early legislations were limited to specific areas and species. In 1873 Madras enacted first wild life statute for the protection of wild elephants. The Elephant Preservation Act 1879, The Forest Act 1878, and Wild Birds and Animals Protection Act 1912 were other legislations which introduced the practice of closed hunting seasons, bag limits and permits. The Britishers also established wild life preserves in Kajiranga in the year 1926 and Hailey (Now Corbete) National Park in the year 1936. As regards the land utilization policy, land was not properly utilized because of inadequate water resource management during the British rule. However, the British Government took initiative to consolidate land holding in the year 1920 with the help of Co-operative consolidation societies and through enactment of consolidation of Holding Act 1929.[3]

The 1920s and then of 1930s movements (*The Forest Satyagrahas*) were against the British over the exploitation and commercialisation of forest land and pastors as protected areas or King's Forests. The pre-World War-II scenario in India betrays lack of governmental concern for environmetal issues as is evident from environmental regulations in force during the colonial rule. It has been observed that scattered provisions were to be found in certain statutes e.g., The Indian Penal Code 1860, The Code of Criminal Procedure 1898 (now repealed by Code of Criminal Procedure 1973). The Forests Act 1927, The Fisheries Act 1897, etc. but their thrust was peripheral and limited to prevention of air and water pollution, preservation of forests and wild life. The Indian Penal Code penalised a person who voluntarily fouled the water of any public spring or reservoir whereas the Factories Act required the owners to make effective arrangements for waste disposals. Similarly, the Fisheries Act imposed a penalty for killing of fish by poisoning of water. Provisions were also made for preserving the fauna and flora as well as the wild life. However, the effort was piecemeal and fragmented and its implementation was tardy.[4]

The above said laws were made by the Britishers for their own interests and were of limited effects.

In Hindu philosophy it is believed that (*Vishnu Dharma Sutra* Says) if you plant a tree it will be your son in the next generation.

The plantation of trees was treated in Hindu culture not only a sacred ceremony or a religious activity but regular protection and patronage was also prescribed, cutting green trees was prohibited and punishment was prescribed for such acts.

On a single day in 1731, more than 350 persons—69 of them women—sacrificed their lives to protect their trees from being felled in Jalnadi village, near Jodhpur.[5]

"Following an extended drought and widespread deforestation, Jambhoji, the son of a village headman in Rajasthan, had a vision that the hard times were a result of the conflict with nature. In 1485, Jambhoji, who was now known as Swami Jambeshwar Maharaj and the founder of the Bishnoi sect, laid down 29 tenets for his followers, which included banning the killing of animals, cutting green trees and specially the the *Khejdi.*, and cremation to save firewood."

"Though on several occasions Bishnois have laid down their lives to protect trees, the sacrifice of Amrita Devi of Jalnadi village. 25 K.M. from Jodhpur, in 1731 is particularly memorable."

"Maharajah Abhay Singh of Jodhpur wanted to build a new palace and despatched an agent, Giridhar Das Bhandari, to fell the forest around Jalnadi. As Bhandari's axemen approached the site, Amrita Devi rushed to them, and pleaded in vain for the trees to be spared. In desperation, she then hugged the first tree that was to be cut and uttered the now-famous couplet of the Bishnois. —*'A chopped head is cheaper than a felled tree.'* Then she fell to an axesblow, but her three daughters stepped forward to take her place. They, too, met the same fate."

"Bhandari sent for reinforcements and, in turn, the Bishnois sounded the alarm in 84 villages. Volunteers responded from 83 villages. By the end of the day, 290 men and 69 women from 49 villages were felled by the axemen. When Abhay Singh was told the tale of Bishnoi's bravery, he was filled with remorse. He stopped work on the palace, visited the Bishnois to apologise and promised them that they would never again be asked to provide timber, no *Khejdi* tree would ever be cut and hunting would not be permitted near a Bishnoi village."

"Jalnadi is now known as Khejarli and a concrete tower there marks the spot where Amrita Devi fell."[6]

Water as commons because it is the ecological basis of all life and because its sustainability and equitable allocation depend on the co-operation between members of a community. Although water has been managed as a commons throughout human history, across diverse cultures, and although most communities manage water resources as common property or have access to water as a commonly shared public goods even today, privatization of water resources is gaining momentum.

Prior to the arrival of the British in South India, communities managed water system collectively through a system called *Kudimaramath*[7] (self repair). Before the advent of corporate rule by the East India Company in the 18th century, a peasant paid 300 out of 1,000 units of grains he or she earned to a public fund and 250 of those units stayed in the village for maintenance of commons and public works. By 1830, peasant payments rose to 650 units, out of which 590 units went straight to the East India Company. As a result of increased payments and lost maintenance revenue, the peasants and commons destroyed 300,000 water tanks built over centuries in pre-British India, affecting agricultural productivity and earnings.[8]

The East India Company was driven out by the first movement for independence in 1857. In 1857, the British passed the Madras Compulsory Labour Act of 1858 popularly known as the *Kudimaramath* Act mandating the peasants to provide labour for the maintenance of the water and irrigation system. Because *Kudimaramath* was based on self management and not coercion, the act failed to mobilize community participation and to rebuild the commons.[9]

In India, farmer's associations for the construction and maintenance of water systems were once widespread. In Karnataka and Maharashtra the associations were known as *Panchayats*. In Tamil Nadu they were called *Nattamai, Kavai Maniyam, Nir Maniyam, Oppidi Sangam or, Eri Variyam* (tank committee). Village water system required irrigation functionaries who looked after the day-to-day operation of irrigation system. In the Himalayas, where *Kuhls* serve community irrigation needs, irrigation managers are called *Kohlis*. In Maharashtra, they were known *Patkeris* and *havaldars* and *Jogalaya*. In Karnataka and Tamil Nadu, they were known as *Nirkatti, Nirganti, Nirpaychi, Niranikkans* and *Kamkukatti*.[10]

Community rights are necessary for both ecology and democracy. But the self-management systems suffered when the government took control over water resources during British rule. Community ownership was further eroded with the emergence of borewells and tubewells, which made individual farmers dependent on capital.[11]

India is a country of hundreds of thousands of villages where most cooking depends on non-commercial fuels like firewood, dung cakes and agricultural wastes. With the second largest population in the world it is not surprising that the country burns about one hundred and thirty three million tonnes of firewood, seventy three million tonnes of dung and forty one million tonnes of agricultural waste each year. Since the forest area is rapidly decreasing, ecologists are working to avoid possible environmental hazards in the future. Dung is bound to become the major source of rural energy. Since time immemorial this animal waste has been used in multiple ways in rural India. For the Hindus, cow dung is considered sacred and is used in most religious rituals. It is used extensively in the construction of mud houses, as a cure for tentanus wounds and as manure after composting. All this because we have the largest livestock population in the world. According to the *National Council of Applied Economic Research*, India produces one thousand three hundred and thirty five million tonnes of wet dung each year. It is a valuable resource. These dung cakes are unfortunately burnt in open *Chullahs* or stoves which are not only inefficient but also create hazardous micro-environments in kitchens. The Fuelwood Study Committee has also stressed the need for replacing conventional *chullahs*. Also, it has been suggested that agricultural and organic wastes should be converted into secondary fuels by briquetting. Those pellets give more energy and less pollution.[12]

Often it has been said that British rule gave us the Railways, Post and Telegraphs, the concept of nationalism in India and indeed the corner stone of our political existence, parliamentary democracy. But, there is one more aspect of British rule which has not been realised by most.

Appreciation of nature in India is as old as nature itself. Yet more than anything else it were the British who gave its study an empirical, analytical approach. British administrators, boxwallahs and travellers began writing on the subject of nature in this new genre. Zoological and Botanical surveys were a logical consequence and quite naturally was born, in 1883, the *Bombay Natural History Society*.[13]

The society today justly lays claim to eminence on the solid foundation of acclaimed works on mammals, birds, butterflies, trees and shrubs. It has in its collection 25,000 bird and 20,000 animal skin, 3,000 reptile and 50,000 insect specimens, truly an enviable horde of research material. These achievements are the result of selfless service by the society's members and well wishers most of whom were British till 1947. In fact, the society very nearly departed with the empire but managed to survive our independence only because Jawaharlal Nehru stepped in to help at the instance of Dr. Salim Ali. Today it is respected the world over and remains one of the few private institutions to attain the heights of achievement it has. By far the greatest contribution of the society is its scientific journal which has been published regularly. The Journal is a portrait par excellence of the Indian Sub-continent's living beings and a panorama of changing human attitudes from *Shikar* to conservation towards nature.[14]

The value of *A Century of Natural History* is an authentic and unparalleled portrait of nature's bounty in the Indian sub-continent, speedily desecrated and destroyed in the very same eventful hundred years of our and the society's existence. It is quite proper to include it in a time capsule.

KAVI GURU RABINDRANATH TAGORE was an eminent environmentalist. He started an educational institution, under the *'Jamun Tree,'* Santiniketan on 22nd December 1901, under the name of Bolepur Brahmacharya Ashram.[15] He presumed that he could give the children of the nation much better and healthier education on much more improved methods than the education was imparted in other institutions in those days.[16]

The index of education was broadened and Santiniketan developed into *Viswabharati* (where the whole world finds home in one nest). The word 'Viswabharati' was invented by the poet himself (kavi Guru). 'Viswa' in Sanskrit means the world in its universal aspect; *Bharati* means wisdom and culture.[17] His ideas on education were derived mainly from his own experience. He had realised that restricted city life under the supervision of servants made the children suffer badly making them timid and far from self-relient hence he derived the conclusion that they should be given freedom of space. 'Freedom' and 'Cultured' environment as has been seen were the master keys to the poet's world of education. Santiniketan's extra-curricular activities have unquestionably played an important role in 'humanity.' Tagore says:—"My view is that we should follow the ancient Indian principles of education. Students and teachers should live together and in national surroundings and the students should complete their education by practising bramacharya.... In favourable whether the classes should be held in the shade of big trees. Part of the teaching should be in the form of discussion between teacher and student while they are walking between the rows of trees. In the evening recess the students should read the stars, cultivate music and listen to legendary and historical tales."[18]

GANDHIJI's economic ideas were closely linked to the protection of environment and the livelihood of weaker sections. In view of the disruption faced by environment and the livelihood of weaker sections, these views are highly relevant today. Mahatma Gandhi tells us that while the basic needs of all people should be met, there should also be consciousness regarding placing a limit on consumption. Although the pressures on nature had not become so acute in Gandhi's lifetime and there were no scares either of ozone depletion or climate change, this wise man had the foresight to see that our planet's capacity is not infinite and some restraint will have to be placed on how much pressure we can place on its air, water, forests and minerals. Ghandhi said—*Nature has enough to satisfy the needs of everyone but nothing to satisfy the greed of even a few.*[19]

The relevance of Gandhian ideas as such in the environmental history remains unexplored. Gandhi was predominantly concerned with the moral issues which are termed as internal environment of man. Gandhi's concern for environment is expressed in the guise of many issues like non-violence, animal rights, vaishnavism, food habits, medicare, village communities and so forth. Here I take four areas that require for our special attention. They are *conservation, animal protection, rural reconstruction and opposition of industrialism.*

Gandhi's views on *conservation and tree planting* were expressed categorically in the wake of his visit to Kutch and Kathiawar in 1925. Two pieces identified in Volume 28 of *collected works* are concerned with this.[20] In the first place, even conservation here is related with a sense of 'religion.' Gandhi writes—"All religion is presumably in response to the human aspiration or need. Religion is some irresistible binding force. Digging of wells where water is scarce is a religion. It would be ludicrous to dig wells where the water supply is inexhaustible. Similarly whilst tree plantation would be superfluous in, say, Travancore, in some parts of India it is a religious necessity. Such a place is undoubtedly Kutch. It has a beautiful climate but some parts threaten to be a desolate waste unless there is a proper rainfall in them. Rainfall can by almost regulated by deforestation or afforestation. Kutch needs conservation of every tree and every shrub."[21]

Gandhi went there with a specific purpose of 'planting trees and protecting them.' He also inaugurated a tree plantation and protection society initiated by Jaykrishna Indrajit. Jaykrishna, the author of an important work on the flora and fauna of Barda Hills of Porbander State, convinced Gandhi that the regions which the wind ruined by turning them into the sand heaps could be converted to gardens if judicious plantation was introduced.[22] Gandhi continued. 'What is true to Kutch is equally true of Kathiawar.... The conservation of forests, systematic plantation of trees, irrigation and many other things cannot be properly done without a common policy.... Kathiawar is likely to suffer from water famine of such magnitude as to make life impossible. In Kutch, Kathiawar, Rajputana, Sind and such other places a study of practical Botany should be compulsory in all schools' [23] It is important to note here that the Gandhian views on conservation, however unique they might be during the pioneering days, were shared and influenced by others.[24]

Regarding *animal protection*, Gandhi was prolific and his arguments followed a more chequered and insightful course. We have been able to locate more than fifteen pieces which present the variety of his concern: *Cow protection, torture of bullocks, animal slaughter, animal rights, killing of ravaging monkeys and even consideration akin to euthanasia*.[25] Gandhi detected a dichotomy between violence amongst animals and violence towards animals and he found a solution—"I feel that the law of animals and of the lower order of creation is not the law of man" who "should himself refrain from participating in violence and prevent inferior creatures as also animals under his control from tormenting one another."[26] Gandhi's views on cow protection *(Goseva)* were more complex, partly because of their connection with a contemporary political issue.[27] In his Presidential Address at the Cow Protection Conference at Belgaum on December 28, 1924, Gandhi made certain points categorical. He began with the idea that "cow slaughter and man slaughter remained the two sides of the same coin." Gandhi believed, "in its finer or spiritual sense the term cow protection means the protection of every living creature."[28]

Gandhi's views on *rural reconstruction* can also be related to his *environmental awareness* in a broader sense of the terms. *Amalendu De* writes that "Gandhi dreamt of bringing about a tiny republic in each village inhabited by at least a thousand persons. There should be arrangements for providing food, dwelling-houses, basic necessities of living, man-power, manure, sufficient waste land and forestry to maintain the ecological balance, basic education etc. for all inhabitants residing in such a republic."[29] However, his ideas of rural developement with the village as a unit, along with decentralised and local governance, was pragmatic. For him, *Panchayati Raj* in the villages could become a major vehicle of social, economic and environmental change. He talked of perfect sanitation of the traditional kind, based on local recycling of human and animal manure. He developed an Eighteen Point Programme for village help, known as *Pallisri* in Ahmedabad region.[30]

The environmental significance of Gandhi's views on conservation, animal protection, rural reconstruction and industrialisation is manifold. Environmental ethics is an expanding discipline and Gandhi's relevance is deep and immediate. In deed, it has been claimed that—*"he is even more relevant today than he was in his life time."* Gandhian ideology seems to sustain many of the locally rooted environmental movements in contemporary India. Re-assessment of some other issues in the environment debate can also be made from the Gandhian viewpoint. Finally, the significance of Ghandhi in environmental history rests not merely in his person or in his individual thought, which itself was variegated and accommodating within Indian tradition. The Gandhian world view of environment should represent all of them, before it is placed in the short but chequered *history of Indian environmentalism* more analytically.[31]

K.M. MUNSHI (Dec., 30, 1887, Feb., 8, 1971), was also an environmentalist. He held charge of the Union Ministry of Food and Agriculture for a brief period from February, 1950 to May, 1952. He popularised—*Vana Mahotsava* or Tree-Planting has now become an annual festival in the country. He wished—"Ecological studies and the relation of our national existence to our land, water, rivers and forests is more closely studied."[32] It was Munshi's measures which paved the way for the *"Green Revolution"* to sweep the Indian Agricultural economy in later years, making it possible for this country to attain self-sufficiency in food.[33]

Post-Independence Era

With the dawn of Independence, India stood up to achieve the economic development in order to become self-dependent. Industrialisation became the main source of gaining the goal of economic development. The industrialisation has thus started growing rapidly and has consequently brought to the forefront the problem of urbanisation. Thus, the natural environment has been affected adversely.

The Constitution of India originally did not contain any provision for protection of environment but some indirect provisions have been found under Articles 39, 42, 47, 48 and 49 of the Constitution of India. Articles 246, 248, 252, and 253 of the Constitution of India empower the Parliament of India and State Legislature for providing terms for environmental protection. After signing the Stockholm declaration (June, 1972), Indian Parliament has inserted two new Articles i.e. 48A and 51A(g) by the 42nd.Constitutional (Amendment) Act, 1976.[34]

Relationship between man and his environment is undergoing profound changes in the wake of modern scientific and technological developments. These developments, while offering unprecedented opportunities to change and shape the environment of man to meet his needs and aspirations also involves great danger.[35]

Man is both creature and moulder of his environment which gives him physical sustenance and affords him the opportunity for intellectual, moral, social and spiritual growth in the long and tortuous evolution of the human race on this planet. A stage has been reached when through the rapid acceleration of science and technology, man has acquired the power to transform his environment, the natural and the man made, are essential to his well being and to the enjoyment of basic human rights even the right to life itself.[36]

India is a signatory to the Stockholm Declaration which provided—*"to defend and improve the human environment for present and future generations has become an imperative goal for mankind."*

Purusant to the Stockholm Declaration tremendous additions of wide import took place in the constitutional scheme concerning the environmental protection.[37] The Constitution (42nd Amendment) Act, 1976 has incorporated direct provisions for protection of environment and has made it a Fundamental Duty to protect and improve the environment. The new Articles 48A and 51A(g) have been inserted in the Constitution which runs as follows:—

Article—48A

> *"Protection and improvement of environment and safeguaarding of forests and wild life—The State shall endeavour to protect and improve the environment and to safeguard the forests and wild life of the country."*

—The Constitution of India
(As on the 1st September, 1991) Page No. 14, Part IV
Published By - Law Department
Rajbhasa Block, Govt. of India

Article—51A *Fundamental Duties:—*

It shall be the duty of every citizen of India:-

> *(G) To protect and improve the natural environment including forests, lakes, rivers and wild life, and to have compassion for living creatures;*

—The Constitution of India
Page No. 15, Part IVA

After independence, Factories Act 1948 was passed; the purpose of the Act is to provide safety of workers, discharge of pollutants and occupational health of workers. In the same manner Industries (Development and Regulation) Act 1951 which aimed at proper siting of the industries was of much importance from the environmental point of view. Siting of industries is an important factor in environmental protection strategy in today's context of rapid industrial growth. The Mines Act 1952 dealt with the safety of mining activities and the health and well being of the minors. Prevention of Food Adulteration endangering public health, the Insecticides Act 1968 was passed to regulate the manufacture, sale, transport and use of insecticides in agriculture which causes a formidable threat to the environment. Today, along with industrial pollution, agricultural pollution has assumed critical dimensions.[38]

The Parliament of India has also passed some special statutes or the environmental protection after signing the Stockholm Declaration in 1972. These Acts are:[39]

(A) Wild life (Protection) Act, 1972.
(B) Water (Prevention and Control of Pollution) Act, 1974.
(C) Water (Prevention and Control of Pollution) Cess Act, 1977.
(D) Forest (Conservation) Act, 1980.
(E) Air (Prevention and Control of Pollution) Act, 1981.
(F) Environment (Protection) Act, 1986.
(G) The Public Liability Insurance Act, 1991.
(H) The National Environment Tribunal Act, 1995.

Apart from these Acts, The Indian Forest Act, 1927 also operates in India. The Government has framed various rules under the aforementioned Acts to preserve and protect the environment.

The rate of enactment went up after Bhopal disaster (1985) which resulted in a comprehensive environmental legislation called Environment (Protection) Act, 1986. An Apex Ministry—the Ministry of Environment and Forest (MOEF) has been created. This Ministry is required to monitor and enforce the environmental quality standards in the country through the Pollution Control Boards and conduct environment assessment and surveys.[40]

Environment protection is not a pre-occupation of the educated and affluent. It has socio-political dimensions. The disposal and control of toxic waste and governmental regulation of polluting industries is public interest oriented. The effective implementation of environmental legislation is a social learning process, which could fundamentally change the character of public administration in the country. From a global perspective, the struggle to preserve a '*livable environment*' is a part of broader struggle to create a more just global society both within and between nations. The impact of the human dimensions on the economically and educationally disadvantaged who inhabit the developing areas cannot be underscored.[41]

Restoring nature to the natural state is a cause beyond party and beyond factions. It has become a common cause of all the people. It is a cause of particular concern to young Indians because, they, more than us, will reap the grim consequences of our failure to act on the programmes which are needed now if we are to prevent disaster later. An onerous obligation which we owe to posterity is clean air, clean water, greenery and open spaces. These ought to be elevated to the status of birth rights of every citizen.[42]

Unfortunately, the much needed bonding between people and nature cannot be taught or learned through a text book within the four walls of a classroom. Human beings must be taught the art of living "environmentally sustainable" lives, right from early childhood. Only then will they realise the role of human beings in natural resource depletion and, as adults incorporate environmentally sustainable habits into their daily personal lives and seek pragmatic, environmentally—sound developmental options in their professional lives. This alone can permanently change the course and pace of environmental degradation in the long run.[43]

In 1991, the Supreme Court of India realised that individuals were not living environmentally sustainable lifestyles, either because they did not have the knowledge, practical skills or tradition or community spirit. Recognising the importance of Environmental Education, the Apex Court ordered that the subject be incorporated into the curriculum. However, a majority of schools think that students only need to be empowered with data on environmental problems, which will sensitise them to Nature. Therefore "Environmental Education" is equated with the popularly known subject of "Environmental Science" or "Environmental studies." This focuses on providing students with scientific facts and figures on global environmental problems.[44]

Thirteen long years later, the Supreme Court in 2004 re-asserted that Environmental Education be made a mandatory, independent subject in all schools and colleges and that it must be an "action-oriented" subject. For example, practising energy conservatism, waste management, rainwater harvesting, edible landscaping and greening, service learning and other important socio-environmental issues.[45]

Tsunami and the Environment

But sometimes Nature and naural calamity apart from causing great disaster, offers us vast opportunity for archacologists and historians to explore further hidden treasures of history. Tsunami is one such calamity.

December 26, 2004 (Sunday), will not be forgotten for a long time. The devastation that the giant tsunami waves wreaked in countries stretching from Indonesia in the east to Somalia in the west will remain vivid in our memories. The land along these coasts will bear the scars, as will the people who were lucky to survive that day. But even as efforts are made to repair the land and rehabilitate the people, there is reason to ask whether there are lessons that can be drawn from this tragedy. A country like India. which has a 5, 422Km. long coastline,[46] needs to evolve developmental policies that incorporate the vulnerabilities of the coastal lands and of the people who live there. The tsunami tragedy has exposed the shortsightedness of policies that disregarded the importance of *natural environmental safeguards*, such as sandbanks and mangroves, which protect coasts. It has also brought into focus the needs of millions of people, like fisherfolk, who live in coastal areas. We need policies that protect these coastal lives and coastal eosystems. That is the only insurance against future disasters.

TSUNAMI IN SOUTH ASIA

	Date/Year		Place
1.	1524	—	Near Dabhol, Maharastra
2.	02 April, 1762	—	Arakan Coast, Myanmar
3.	16 June, 1819	—	Ran (Boundry) of Katch, Gujrat
4.	28 November, 1845	—	Makran Coast, Baluchistan
5.	31 October, 1847	—	Great Nicobar Island
6.	31 December, 1881	—	Kar Nicobar Island
7.	26 August, 1883	—	Kakatoao Volcuno Blast

Tsunami is a Japanese word. *"TSU"* stands for harbour and *"NAMI"*means sea waves. The word is current among those fishermen who find thier belongings spoiled after returning from the deep sea. Since they remain there in the deep sea they do not experience the intensity of the waves. Tsunami is referred as sea-waves but not in true technical sense. It is a series of waves that gets produced due to sudden jerk in water (sea). It rises like a high wall of water. It is mainly caused by the earthquake beneath the sea-water or land sliding or the burst of volcanoes or explosions or mete or impact i.e. the falling of stars (Ulka). Such waves are produced when the sea-floor gets raised or displaced or disturbed

LIST OF IMPORTANT EARTHQUAKE IN INDIA AND NEIGHBOURING COUNTRY

	Date/Year		Place
1.	16 June, 1819	—	Katch, Gujrat
2.	30 May, 1869	—	Soupar, Jammu - Kashmir
3.	10 June, 1869	—	Near Kachhar, Assam
4.	12, June, 1897	—	Shillong Plateau
5.	04, April, 1905	—	Kangra, Himachal Pradesh
6.	08 July, 1918	—	Srimanglam, Assam
7.	02 July, 1930	—	Dhubri, Assam
8.	15 January, 1934	—	Border of Bihar - Nepal
9.	26 June, 1941	—	Andman Island
10.	23 October, 1943	—	Assam
11.	15 August, 1950	—	Boarder of Arunachal Pradesh-China
12.	21 July, 1956	—	Anjar, Gujrat
13.	10 December, 1967	—	Koina, Maharastra
14.	19 January, 1975	—	Kinnor, Himachal Pradesh
15.	08 August, 1988	—	Border of Manipal-Myanmar
16.	21 August, 1988	—	Boader of Bihar - Nepal
17.	20 October, 1991	—	Uttarkashi, Uttranchal
18.	30 September, 1993	—	Latur, Usmanabad, Maharastra
19.	22 May, 1997	—	Jabalpur, M.P
20.	29 March, 1999	—	Chamoli, Uttaranchal
21.	26 January, 2001	—	Bhunj, Gujrat

(Compiled from YOJANA, Hindi—Year - 48, Issue - 11, February, 2005, Page No.-32,33 Published By Publication Division, Ministry of Information, Govt. of India, New Delhi)

and a huge amount of water is thrown out to the shore at a rapid speed. Also when dense oceanic plates get slipped beneath the continental plates, it results into an earth-quake-lead Tsunami.[47]

Tsunami caused great disaster, killing more than three lacs people and rendering several lacs homeless in South-East-Asia. However, Nature sometimes creates surprising opportunity even in calamity. Tsunami waves while returning, after causing great disaster, offered us remains of a few temples near Mahabalipuram town. In a way, it is the *gift of Tsunami* to the archacologists that would throw light on several historical monuments and impart informations.

Some fifty kilometres from Chennai, Mahabalipuram temple was constructed between 7 A.D and 8 A.D. Some archeologists have always been speculating about the possibility of some other temples besides the one that is known today. However, Tsunami, when it returned, unfolded many unknown structures, atleast three big *"Shilakhand"* (Sotnepillars). These *"Shilas"* (Pillars) were standing on large base and their upper part was like a *"shanku."* This goes on to prove that there are some improtant historical structures (Virasat) still submerged in distant sea. Some stone structures were present but not very prominent, because they were covered with sands. Now they have been unravelled by Tsunami. The temple unravelled by Tsunami is made of rocks. This is *"Rath-Temple"* Sketches of elephants, horses and lion have be drawn on the *Rath-Temple*. There were seven temples as per the historical myths.[48]

One T. Satyamurti, an officer of the archaceological department holds the view that there are several historical temples of the time of Pallavas. Some archaeological items found, indicate that they belong to 7. A.D. The technical survey has already been initiated. The Indian Navy has been co-operating with Archaeological Survey of India. The work has been started under the supervision of the archaeological expert Alok Tripathi since February, 2005. A.K. Sharma, the Commander of the Navigation team, has claimed that the structures discovered beneath the sea-water, resemble the structures of Seven Temples paintings that have so far been a myth only. His team has also found the remains of a temple and a long *"Praster Khand."*[49]

Lt. Commandant Satendra Vaidya holds the view that the place is very significant for archaeological survey. He also says that there has been a temple like structure discovered during the navigation survey. The Archaeological Survey of India and the Indian Navy combined together, have worked successfully. It is said that a wonderful town situated near the sea-bank of Mahabalipuram, has sub-merged much earlier in the sea.[50]

To the south of the existing temple near Mahabalipuram, another temple has been discovered where a small *"Puja - Sthal"* is there near *"Chaukor Garbhgrih."* There is a varandah like structure around it. Among the newly discovered things, a very beautiful *"Well"* made of baked soil is a prominent achievement.[51]

Only after 24 hours of Tsunami, on 27 December, 2004, some 15Km. from Mahabalipuram near *"Maipakkam"* village, fishermen found a basket of bamboo containing a heavy object. When this basket was opened after sometime, *a golden statue of Lord Budha of six inch height was found.* This statue has been sent to the museum of Chennai.[52]

Conclusion

Nature has been a great balancing agent, effecting ecological balance by providing gifts and creating surprising opportunity for makind apart from causing large scale devastation. It also warns us against the interference in the functioning of Nature.

India, like most other countries is fast losing its natural resource reserves to the mounting demands of an ever-increasing population and economic growth. Large stretches of forests are promptly clear—felled for developmetal schemes, vast tracts of mangroves are mindlessly destroyed for recreational schemes, unsustainable agricultural techniques are readily promoted with little foresight, seas and rivers are turning into cesspools of untreated waste, and, even protected areas like National Parks are under constant threat and have become battlefields of heated conflict. Human beings and the natural environment are on a collision course.

The problem lies in the fact that nations lack an environmentally literate citizenry. Generation upon generation of citizens do not realise how and why man and his processes are closely linked to nature nor do they feel connected to or a part of nature. Therefore, individuals do not view the environment as a *"Personal asset"* that needs to be conserved as a long-term investment to safeguard their own future. More importantly, they do not realise that it needs to be conserved not by a government or a legally appointed ministry but by themselves, their lifestyles and their own demands.

In order to understand, respect, conserve and collaborate with the environment, it is important to view it in the context of human influences, incorporating an examination of economics, culture, political structure, and social equity as well as natural processes and systems. For each environmental issue, there is not just one right answer or solution—there are many perspectives and much uncertainty.

On a long-term basis, the socio-economic health of a nation depends on and is directly proportional to the health of its environment. A nation unable to effectively conserve and manage its natural resources eventually pays a dearer price for short-sighted policies. However, the world is slowly acknowledging the close link between economy and environment and recognising that "Sustainability" is the most essential part of education. Therefore, The United Nations has declared this decade, 2005-2015, as a "Decade of Education for sustainable Development."[53]

•

NOTES AND REFERENCES

1. *Vikramshila Journal of Social Sciences*, published by Vikramshila Research Institute Adampur, Bhagalpur, Bihar Vol. 2, No. 1 (Jan.-June, 2005) p. 70, Article By Dr. A. Sahay. Prof. of Strategic Management, Management Development Institute, Gurgaon, Journal is financially support by I.C.H.R., New Delhi, Title—"Environmental Management in India: Its Social, Economic and Legal Aspects."
2. Vikas Vashishth, Advocate, Supreme Court of India, *Law & Practice of Environmental Laws in India*, 1999, p. 7. Published By Bharat Law House, New Delhi.
3. Ibid, p. 7.
4. Ibid. p. 7.
5. Down to Earth, (1993): *Science and Environment Fortnightly*, Vol. 2, No. 1, May 31, p. 44. Title of Article is—"Putting trees before human life" Published By Society for Environmental Communications, New Delhi.
6. Ibid, p. 44.
7. In South India, collective labour investment was the primary investment in the construction and maintenance of village water system known as *Kudi maramath*.
8. *Yojana* (A Development Monthly) Vol. 49, June, 2005, p. 6. Article—"The First and Last Commons" Published By Ministry of Infromation and Broodcasting Govt. of India Publications Division. Written by Vandana Shiva, Director, Research Foundation for Science, Technology and Ecology, New Delhi.
9. Ibid, p. 6
10. Ibid, p.7.
11. Ibid, p. 7.

12. T. Sampath Kumar (1984): *The India Magazine*, The Business India Groups of Publications, Bombay, Vol. IV, No. 12, November, pp. 31-36 Article BITODAS: "Energy Pyramids of Rural India."
13. J.C. Daniel (ed.), (1984): The India Magazine Vol. IV, No. 5, April, p. 83, Extract from Book Review of *A Century of Natural History,* Published By Bombaby Natural History Society.
14. Ibid, p. 83-84.
15. R. J. Paul, Tagore, *A Chronological Survey Tagore Centenary Souvenir,* p. 262, Calcutta.
16. V. Prakasanathan, *'Tagore's Mission',* Tagore Centenary Souvenir, Calcutta, p. 168, Appendix.
    Cited in
    Mrs. Bani Chatterjee, (1986): Unpublished Ph.D Thesis of Lucknow University. *Rabindranath Tagore and the Swadeshi Movement in Bengal (1903-1908),* p. 194.
17. Mrs. Bani Chatterjee, Ibid, p. 196-197.
18. Ibid, p. 195, 196, 208.
19. Bharat Dogra, (2003): *Yojana,* A Development Monthly, published by. The Ministry of Information and Broadcasting, New Delhi, Vol. 47, No. 10, October, p. 28, Title of Article "Gandhiji's Economics Ideas Remain Relevant."
20. M.K. Gandhi, Modern Histrical Studies, Journal of the Dept. of History, Rabindra Bharati University, , Kolkata, *Collected Works,* Vol. 28, pp. 447-58 and pp. 469-71, *Extract taken from* Vol. 1, No. 1, July-Dec, 1999, p. 67,
    Title of Article *"Ghandhi on Environment: An Interpretative Essay."* Written By Arun Bandopadhyay.
21. Gandhi, *Collected Works*, Vol-28, p. 457.
22. Ibid, p. 469, 458.
23. Ibid, 458.
24. *Modern Historical Studies* (Journal), op.cit., p. 68.
25. Ibid, p. 68-69.
26. Gandhi, *Modern Historical Studies*, *Collected Works*, Vol. 30, p. 324. *Cited in* Ibid, p. 69.
27. Gyanendra Pandey, (1990): *The Construction of Colonialism in Colonial North India*, New Delhi. *Cited in Modern Historical Studies,* p. 69.
28. *Modern Historical Studies*, op. cit., p. 69. See also.
    * Gandhi Collected works, Vol. 25, 515-522.
29. Amalendu De, (1997): 'Mahatma Ghandhi's Conception of Religion and Politics in *The Coming of Modern Age in India: Essays in Honour of Dr. Phulrenu Guha,* Calcutta, p. 94.
30. *Modern Historical Studies*, p. 71-72.
31. Ibid, p. 72-73.
32. V.B. Kulkarni, *Makers of Modern India: K. M. Munshi,* pp. 197-198.

Published By Publication Division, Ministry of Information and Broadcasting, Govt. of India, New Delhi.

33. Ibid, p. 200.
34. Vikas Vashishth, *Law & Practice of ENVIRONMENTAL LAWS in India,* 1999. P-Preface, Published By Bharat Law House, New Delhi.
35. United Nations General Assembly Resolution No. 2398 XXIII, dated: 03.12.1958
    Cited in
    Vikas Vashishth, Ibid, p. 11.
36. Proclamation made by United Nations Conference on Human Environment, held in Stockholm from 5th to 16th June, 1972.
    Cited in
    Vikas Vashishth, Ibid, p. 11
37. Vikash Vashishth, Ibid, p. 12, 13.
38. Ibid, p. 8
39. Ibid, Preface.
40. *Vikramshila Journal of Social Science.* Published Bi-annually By Vikramshila Research Institute, Swami Vivekanand Road, Adampur, Bhagalpur, Bihar, Vol. 2, No. 1, Jan-June-2005, p. 70, Article is "Environmental Management" in India: Its social, Economic and Legal Aspects." By Dr. A. Sahay Prof. of Stratagic Management, Gurgaon, Journal is financialiy supported Institute, Management Development by the I.C.H.R, New Delhi.
41. Vikash Vashishth, Op. cit, p. 105.
42. Ibid, p. 105.
43. *The Hindu*, SURVEY OF THE ENVIRONMENT—2005, (Yearly Magazine) Published By - N. Ram By Rakesh N. Pardiwala, Chennai, p. 145, 46. Article—*Environmental Education:Experience Nature,* by Rakesh N. Pardiwala.
44. Ibid, p. 146.
45. Ibid, p. 146, 147.
46. Ibid, p. 5.
47. *YOJANA*, (A Development Monthly Magazine) Year 48, Vol. 11, February, 2005. Article—"Tsunami Leharo ka Tandav" (in *Hindu*) Written By—Madhu R. Shekhar
48. *Kadambini*, Hindi Monthly Magazine, Published By H.T. Media Ltd., New Delhi, August-2005, p. 51-52 आलेख–'सूनामी ने वापस की समंदर में दबी विरासत" लेखक– राय अवधेश कुमार श्रीवास्तव
49. Ibid, p. 52-53.
50. Ibid, p. 53.
51. Ibid, p. 53-54.
52. Ibid, p. 54.
53. *The Hindu, SURVEY OF THE ENVIRONMENT—2005,* (Yearly Magazine), op. cit, p. 145.

PART III

19. जगदीश चंद्र और एनवायरनमेंट में दिए गए बंगला का क्रमवार हिंदी अनुवाद

विनय कुमार महाता

वृक्ष क्या कुछ कहता है? अनेक ने कहा, यह फिर कैसा प्रश्न है? वृक्ष क्या कभी बातें करता है? आदमी क्या कुछ प्रकट करता है? और जो प्रकट नहीं करता है, वह क्या बात नहीं है? हमारे एक नन्हा है, वह सब कुछ कर नहीं पाता है।

पहले जब अकेला मैदान या पहाड़ों में घूमने जाता था, सब उदास लगता था। बाद में वृक्ष, पक्षी, कीड़े-मकौड़ों को प्यार करना सीखा, तब से उन लोगों की बहुत सी बातें समझ सकता हूं, पहले जो मेरे बस के बाहर था। ये जो वृक्ष कुछ भी नहीं बोल पाते हैं, इनका भी एक जीवन है, हमारी ही तरह भोजन लेते हैं, दिन-ब-दिन बढ़ते हैं, पहले ये सबकुछ नहीं जानता था। अब समझ पाया हूं। अब इनके अंदर भी हमारे जैसा अभाव, दुख-दर्द देख पाता हूं। जीने के लिए इन को भी सदा व्यस्त रहना पड़ता है।[1/3]

सांस लेने के बाद जब हम सांस छोड़ते हैं तो सांस के साथ एक प्रकार का जहरीली वायु निकलती है, उसे अंगारक वायु कहते हैं। अगर वह धरती पर जमती रही तो चंद दिनों में सभी जीव-जंतु का सफाया हो जा सकता है। विधाता की करुणा की बातें सोचो। जीव-जंतु के लिए जो जहर है, वृक्ष उसी को भोजन कर वायु को साफ करता है। पत्तों पर जब सूर्य किरण पड़ती है तब पत्ते सूर्य के तेज की सहायता से अंगारक वायु से अंगार शोषण करते हुए वृक्ष को बढ़ाते हैं।[2/4]

अब समझ सकता हूं, रोशनी ही जीवन का मूल है। सूर्य की किरण शरीर में लेकर ही वृक्ष बढ़ता रहता है। वृक्ष के शरीर में सूर्य किरण आबद्ध रहती है। लकड़ी

सुलगाने के बाद जो रोशनी और उत्ताप मिलता है, वह सूर्य का तेज है। वृक्ष और फसल रोशनी पकड़ने का फंदा है। जीव-जंतु वृक्ष खाकर प्राणधारण करते हैं। वृक्षों के अंदर सूर्य का जो तेज है वह इस तरह पुनः जंतुओं के शरीर में प्रवेश करता है। आनाज न खाने से हम लोग भी जी नहीं सकते। गौर करने की बात है कि हम लोग भी रोशनी खाकर ही जीते हैं।[3/5]

वृक्ष का सही इतिहास जानने के लिए उसके नजदीक ही जाना पड़ेगा। वह इतिहास अति जटिल तथा बहुधा रहस्यपूर्ण है। उस इतिहास को जानने के लिए वृक्ष और अन्य की सहायता से जन्म से लेकर मृत्यु तक हर घड़ी का क्रियाकलाप लिपिबद्ध करना होगा। लिपि वृक्ष की स्वलिखित तथा हस्ताक्षर की हुई होनी चाहिए। इसमें मनुष्य का कोई दखल नहीं रहेगा। कारण मनुष्य अपनी स्वप्रणोदित भाव से प्रायशः प्रतारित होता है।[4/6]

वन चांडाल वृक्ष के जरिए उम्मीद की स्पंदनशीलता अनायास देखी जा सकती है। इसके छोटे पत्ते अपने आप नृत्य करते हैं। लोगों में विश्वास है कि हाथ से टुसकी मारने से ही नृत्य शुरू होता है। वृक्ष में संगीतबोध है कि नहीं, कह नहीं सकता हूं, लेकिन वन चांडाल के नृत्य के साथ टुसकी का कोई संपर्क नहीं। तरुस्पंदन की प्रत्युत्तर लिपि पढ़कर जंतु तथा उद्भिदों के स्पंदन, जो एक ही नियमाधीन हैं यह मैं निश्चित कह सकता हूं।[5/7]

हमारे इन सब मूक साथियों, हमारे दरवाजे के बगल में जिनकी लीला चलती है। अपनी गंभीर मर्मकथा भाषाहीन अक्षरों में लिपिबद्ध की और अपने जीवन-चांचल्य तथा मृत्यु-आक्षेप आज हमारी नज़रों में प्रकट किया। जीव और उद्भिदों के बीच जो व्यवधान कायम था, वह दूर हुआ। यह कल्पना में भी नहीं था कि इन सब समाचारों को आज विज्ञान की स्पष्ट घोषणाओं से अनेक के बीच ऐक्य की भावना को प्रमाणित किया।[6/8]

सूर्य किरण से पुष्ट उद्भिद खाकर ही प्राणी जी रहे हैं और बढ़ रहे हैं। इससे पता चलता है कि धरती की सभी गतियों का मूल कारण है सूर्य किरण। आकाश के स्पंदन से ही पृथ्वी स्पंदित होती है और जीवनस्रोत चलता है।... जीवन का चरम उत्कर्ष है मानव। हमेशा के लिए यह बात सही नहीं है। जो शक्ति आदि जीव बिंदु से मनुष्य ने पैदा की है, जिसकी उच्छ्वास से महाशून्य में ये बहुरूपी जगत और तदनुरूप आश्चर्य जीवन उत्पन्न हुआ है, वह महाशक्ति आज भी वैसे ही सक्रिय है। सृष्टि की गति ऊर्द्धवाभिमुखी है और आदि से अंतहीन काल तथा अनंत प्रगति तक फैली हुई है।[7/9]

शिव और रुद्र। रक्षक और संहारकर्ता। अब इसका अर्थ समझ सका। वारिकण ने अपने स्रोत से निकलकर सागर की ओर यात्रा की उसके बाद पुनः स्रोत

में प्रत्यावर्तन मानस नेत्रों द्वारा स्पष्ट देख पाया, इस महाचक्र प्रवाहधारा में सृष्टि और प्रलय परस्पर अगल-बगल देखने को मिले।

सामने जो गगनभेदी पर्वतश्रेणी देख रहा हूं, हिमाणुरूप वारिकण उनके शरीर के अभ्यंतर में प्रवेश कर रहा है। प्रवेश कर प्रबल पराक्रम से उनके शरीर को विदीर्ण कर रहा है। टूटा हुआ शिखर वज्रनिनाद से नीचे गिर रहा है।

सामने गगनभेदी जो पर्वतश्रेणी देख रहा हूं, हिमाणुरूप वारिकण से ही नीचे तुषारशय्या बिछा रखा है। टूटा शिखर इस तुषारशय्या में सो गया। तब कणों ने एक दूसरे को पुकार कर कहा, आओ हम इसकी अस्थि द्वारा पृथ्वी का शरीर, नए ढंग से निर्माण करें।[8/10]

[अनुवाद–प्रो. (डॉ.) विनय कुमार महाता, अवकाशप्राप्त विभागाध्यक्ष,
स्नातकोत्तर बंगाली विभाग तिलकामांझी, भागलपुर विश्वविद्यालय, भागलपुर]

20. वेदों में पर्यावरणीय संचेतना

राजन कुमार गुप्ता एवं शिव शंकर मिश्र

पर्यावरण शब्द की निष्पत्ति परि+आवरण—इन दो शब्दों के योग से होती है, जिसका अभिप्राय एक ऐसी परिवृत्ति से है जो मानव को चारों ओर से आवृत्त करती हुई उसके जीवन और क्रियाओं को संपूर्णता में प्रभावित करती है। इसमें जलमंडल, स्थलमंडल एवं वायुमंडल के समस्त भौतिक एवं रासायनिक तत्त्व समाहित हैं।

जीवन की संभावना पर्यावरण की परिधि में जल, वायु एवं भोजन की संपूर्ण आपूर्ति के आधार पर ही साकार हो सकती है। समस्त प्राणी स्थलमंडल से भोजन जलमंडल से जल और वायुमंडल से प्राणवायु प्राप्त कर ही जीवनपथ पर अपने आपको संचरणशील एवं गतिशील करने में समर्थ हो पाते हैं।

प्राचीन समग्र वैदिक वाङ्मय अद्यतन वैज्ञानिक ज्ञान एवं उपलब्धियों का सर्वोत्तम कोश रहा है। इसमें वैज्ञानिक साहित्य की संपदा आशातीत समृद्ध रही है। चाहे वह भूगर्भ विज्ञान हो, चाहे प्राणिविज्ञान हो, चाहे भौतिक विज्ञान हो, चाहे चिकित्सा विज्ञान हो या फिर चाहे पर्यावरण विज्ञान हो। यह मानव मनीषा की सर्वोत्कृष्ट उपलब्धियों का अमूल्य अंश है। इसमें प्रकृति के साथ तादात्म्य स्थापित कर सह-अस्तित्व की भावना से आप्लावित हो जीवन यापित करने वाले मंत्रद्रष्टा ऋषियों ने जीवनदायिनी *उषा, पृथ्वी, जल, वायु, सूर्य, वन, ओषधि* प्रभृति विविध प्राकृतिक शक्तियों की अंतर्भावना से अभ्यर्थना की।

वायु, जल, वनस्पतियां, भूमि, आकाश, सूर्य आदि सभी पर्यावरण के संघटक तत्त्व हैं। वेद में इन सब तत्त्वों को **'देव'** नाम से संबोधित किया गया है, जिसका आशय दिव्यगुण समन्वय से है। अर्थात् ये सभी तत्त्व अपने दिव्यगुणों के प्रकाशन से पर्यावरण को शुद्ध एवं जीवनानुकूल बनाते हैं। *अथर्ववेद* में जल, वायु और ओषधियों को पर्यावरण के संघटक तत्त्वों के रूप में परिभाषित किया गया है। ये संसार को *जीवन शक्ति देकर उसे प्रभावित करनेवाले हैं अतएव इन्हें छंद या*

आच्छादक कहा गया है। ये संसार की समस्त गतिविधियों के प्रवर्तक हैं इनके बिना जीवन असंभव है। इनके नाम और रूप अनेक हैं इसीलिए इन्हें *'पुरुरूपम्'* नाम से संकेतित किया गया है–

त्रीणिच्छन्दासि कवयो वि येंतिरे, पुरुरूप दर्शतं विश्वचक्षणम्।
आपो वाता ओषधयस्तान्येकंस्मिन् भुवन आर्पितानि।।[1]

(*अथर्ववेद*–18.1.17)

उक्त मंत्र से यह चिह्नित होता है कि वायु और जल की तरह औषधियां भी पर्यावरण के घटक तत्त्वों में अंतर्निहित हैं।

जीवेम शरदः शतम् का उद्घोष करने वाले वेद शतायु होने के लिए स्वच्छ जल, विशुद्ध अन्न, पवित्र प्राणवायु एवं अकलुषित भूमि को महत्त्वपूर्ण कारक के रूप में व्याख्यायित करते हैं। एक अनुमान के आधार पर इस सम-विषम समन्वित भूग्रह में संभवतः डेढ़ करोड़ वर्ष पूर्व मानवीय सृष्टि का सूत्रपात हुआ। मानव की जीवनयात्रा झर-झर की ध्वनि से झंकृत करने वाले झरनों, परम पवित्र पानीयपथ धारा प्रवाहित करने वाली कल-कल करती नदियों, वृक्ष-तरु-गुल्मलता प्रभृति वनस्पतियों के संस्पर्श से सुगंधित, मंद-मंद आंदोल्यमान धीर समीर के कोनल स्पर्शों, परमस्वच्छंद गगन, संचरणशील पक्षिकुल के सुश्रवणीय चित्ताकर्षक कलरव, कूंजन एवं चहचहाहट की कर्णप्रिय ध्वनियों के साथ प्रारंभ हुई। निश्चित रूप से पर्यावरण का यह तत्कालीन स्वरूप नितांत चित्ताकर्षक आह्लादकारी रहा होगा, परंतु आज औद्योगिक क्रांति के फलस्वरूप बढ़ती नगरीय व्यवस्था ने समाज की समस्त इकाइयों में, चाहे वे आर्थिक हों, सामाजिक हों, राजनीतिक हों, धार्मिक हों या फिर सांस्कृतिक हों सर्वत्र महत्त्वपूर्ण परिवर्तन हुए हैं। जनसंख्या की असंभावित वृद्धि के परिणामस्वरूप ऊर्जा का अधिकतम उपयोग लोगों की सुख-सुविधाओं एवं आवश्यकताओं की संपूर्ति हेतु किया जाने लगा। उपभोग के इस निरंतर बढ़ते क्रम में लोगों ने प्राकृतिक गैस, कोयला, जीवाश्म ईंधन आदि का प्रचुर मात्रा में प्रयोग किया जिससे उत्पन्न कार्बन-डाई-आक्साइड की मात्रा वायुमंडल में आशातीत एवं अवरोधरहित निरंतर बढ़ रही है। औद्योगिक प्रगति से उत्पन्न प्रदूषण की समस्या इस हद तक विकृत हो गई है कि कई स्थानों पर तेजाबी वर्षा (Acid Rain) हो रही है, जिसका दुष्प्रभाव जीव जंतुओं, भूमि, वनस्पतियों पर स्पष्ट देखा जा सकता है। कल-कारखानों से निकले अपद्रव्य–धुआं, गैस, कूड़ा-कचरा–वाहन-विस्तार, वन विनाश, जनसंख्या विस्फोट आदि प्रदूषण के महत्त्वपूर्ण घटक हैं। इनसे पर्यावरण की कलुषता इस सीमा तक बढ़ गई है कि संप्रति स्वच्छ जल, स्वच्छ वायु, खाद्यान्न एवं निवास योग्य भूमि भी दुर्लभ हो गई है। आज पर्यावरण की समस्या राष्ट्रीय समस्या ही नहीं, अपितु एक वैश्विक समस्या है। यह लगातार सुरसा के मुंह की भांति विकराल से विकरालतम

होती जा रही है। इसके समाधान में वैदिक चिंतन अवलोकनीय है।

वैदिक वाङ्मय में पर्यावरण प्रदूषण एवं पर्यावरण संरक्षण पर प्रकाश डालते हुए भूमि प्रदूषण, जल-प्रदूषण, वायु-प्रदूषण एवं यांत्रिक उपकरणजन्य विविध प्रदूषणों तथा इनके शोधन के उपायों का निर्देश विभिन्न वैदिक ऋचाओं में प्रतिबिंबित किया गया है।

शरीरांतः संचारी वायुः प्राणः इस वचन से इंगित होता है कि वायु प्राणशक्ति है। जीवन का आधार है। इसके बिना जीवन की संचरणशीलता एवं गतिशीलता सर्वथा असंभव है। अतएव जीवन के सम्यक् संचालन हेतु वायु प्रदूषण के प्रशमन की नितांत आवश्यकता है। *ये पर्वताः सोमपृष्ठा आपः उत्तानशीवंरीः। वातः पर्जन्य आदग्निस्ते क्रव्यादमशीशमन्।*[2] (*अथर्ववेद*–3.21.10) इस अथर्ववेदीय मंत्र में पर्वत, जल, वायु, वर्षा और अग्नि को पर्यावरण शुद्ध करने वाले तत्त्वों के रूप में परिगणित किया गया है। ये प्रदूषण को नष्ट करते हैं और पर्यावरण को शुद्ध करते हैं। इसी प्रकार *ऋग्वेद* के एक प्रसंग में इस प्रकार कहा गया है–

द्वाविमौ वातौ वात आ सिंधोरा परावतः।
दक्षं ते अन्य आ वातु परान्यो वातु यद् खः।
आ वात वाहि भेषज वि वात वाहि यद् खः।
त्वं हि विश्वभेषजो देवाना इत ईयसे।। (*ऋग्वेद*)

इस मंत्र का आशय यह है कि श्वास-निःश्वास रूप दो वायु चलती है। एक बाहर से समुद्र तक तथा दूसरी समुद्र से बाहर के वायुमंडल तक। हे मनुष्य! यह प्रथम वायु तुम्हें बल प्राप्त कराए और दूसरी वायु शारीरिक दोषों को अपने साथ बाहर ले आए। हे शुद्ध वायु! तुम अपने साथ ओषधि को लाओ। हे वायु! शरीर में जो मल है, उसे तुम बाहर निकालो। तुम सब रोगों की दवा हो। तुम देवों के दूत बनकर विचरते हो। इसी आशय की अभिव्यक्ति एक अन्य मंत्र से भी होती है–

आ वात वाहि भेषजं वि वात वाहि यद् रपः।
त्वं हि विश्वभेषज दूवानां इत ईथंसे।। (*अथर्ववेद*–4.13.3)

वायु में दो गुण हैं। प्राणवायु के द्वारा मनुष्य में जीवनशक्ति का संचार करना और अपान वायु के द्वारा सभी दोषों को शरीर से बाहर करना, इसलिए वायु को विश्वभेषज कहा गया है, क्योंकि यह सभी रोगों और दोषों को नष्ट करता है।

ऋग्वेद के एक अन्यत्र प्रसंग में उक्त तथ्य की परिपुष्टि *अभि श्रव ऋज्यन्तो वहेयुर्नू चिन्नु वायोरमृतं वि दस्येत्* (*ऋग्वेद*–6.37.3) इस मंत्र में संदर्भित की गई है–वायु में अमृततत्त्व है, जीवनतत्त्व है, जिसको यहां ऑक्सीजन के रूप में संबोधित किया गया है। जो यह संदेश देता है कि हम ऐसा कोई कार्य न करें जिससे वायु

में अमृततत्त्व अर्थात् ऑक्सीजन की कमी हो।

यददो वात ते गृहे अमृतस्य निधिर्हितः।
ततो नो देहि जीवसे। (*ऋग्वेद*–10.186.3)

इस मंत्र के माध्यम से भी *ऋग्वेद* यह घोषित करता है कि हे वायु! तुम्हारे पास अमृत का खजाना है, तुम ही जीवन शक्ति के दाता हो, तुम संसार के जनक, भाई, मित्र और सभी रोगों की ओषधि हो। *ऋग्वेद* के एक और मंत्र में भी ओषधि देकर आरोग्यता प्रदान करने तथा दीर्घायु होने की कामना से वायु की अभ्यर्थना की गई है।

वात आ वातु भेषजं शंभु मयोभु नो हृदे।
प्रण आयूंषि तारिषत्। (*ऋग्वेद*–10.18.1)

यह सर्वविदित है कि कार्बन-डाई-आक्साइड की निरंतर बढ़ती मात्रा पर्यावरण की कलुषता में महत्त्वपूर्ण हेतु है जो जीवन के लिए उत्पन्न विनाशक है। यह वृक्षों एवं वनस्पतियों की उदारता है कि वे शिव की भांति कार्बन-डाई-आक्साइड रूपी विष को स्वयं पीकर मानव जाति के कल्याण के लिए ऑक्सीजन रूपी अमृत का वमन करते हैं। इसीलिए वेदों का यह निर्देश है कि वायु प्रदूषण से बचने के लिए वनों में वनस्पतियों का संवर्धन करें–*वनस्पतिं वन आस्थापयध्वमं* (ऋग्वेद–10.101.11)।

पुनः *ऋग्वेद* के एक महत्त्वपूर्ण प्रसंग में निम्न मंत्र द्वारा

पूर्वीरस्य निष्पिधो मर्त्येषु पुरू वसूनि पृथिवी बिभर्ति।
इन्द्राय द्याव ओषधीरुतापो रयिं रक्षन्ति जीरयो वनानि। (*ऋग्वेद*–3.51.5)

पृथ्वी के अंदर विद्यमान समस्त खनिजों (रत्न, मणि, पेट्रोल, कोयला, तेल) की सुरक्षा के लिए वृक्षों एवं वनस्पतियों को उत्तरदायी घोषित किया गया है। ये वृक्ष और वनस्पतियां एक लंबी प्रक्रिया के द्वारा इन पदार्थों के जनक माने जाते हैं।

यदि व्यक्ति अपने क्षुद्र स्वार्थों में अंधा होकर कार्बन-डाई-आक्साइड का अवशोषण करने वाले वृक्षों एवं वनों पर इसी क्रम में कुल्हाड़ी बरसाता रहा तो वातावरण में कार्बन-डाई-आक्साइड इस मात्रा तक बढ़ जाएगी कि समस्त धन-धान्य, वन-वनस्पतियां स्वयमेव नष्ट हो जाएंगी। जो समस्त मानवता के लिए एक अभिशाप सिद्ध होगी। ग्रीन हाउस प्रभाव भी कार्बन-डाई-आक्साइड की बढ़ती मात्रा का परिणाम है। जो भूगर्भ से उत्सर्जित होने वाली तापीय ऊर्जा को वायुमंडल से बाहर जाने से रोकती है। परिणामतः पृथ्वी के औसत तापमान में लगातार वृद्धि हो रही है जो निश्चित रूप से विनाशकारी है। अतः वृक्षों, वनस्पतियों के कर्तन का परित्याग कर सृजन की शुरुआत करनी चाहिए। इस संदर्भ में मंत्रद्रष्टा ऋषि के यजुर्वेदोय निम्न कथन विचारणीय हैं–

द्यां मा लेखीरन्तरिक्षं मा हिंसी : पृथ्वीव्या संभव अयहिँ त्वा
स्वाधितिस्तेतिजानः प्रणिनाय महते सौभाग्य।
अतस्त्वं देव वनस्पते शतवल्शो वि रोह सहस्रवल्शा वि वयूँरुहेम।। (*यजुर्वेद*–5.43)

अर्थात् हे वनस्पति! इस तेज कुल्हाड़े ने महान सौभाग्य के लिए तुम्हें काटा है। तुम्हारा उपयोग हम सहस्रांकुर के रूप में करेंगे। यहां सहस्रांकुर का आशय एक के बदले हजार से है। कहने का अभिप्राय यह है कि यदि अत्यंत आवश्यक कार्य हेतु वनस्पतियों एवं वृक्षों को काटना भी पड़े तो उन्हें ऐसी विशिष्ट विधि से काटा जाए कि उनमें सैकड़ों अंकुर फूटने के अवसर हों। जिससे वायु प्रदूषण के समापन हेतु उनका हजारों गुना उपयोग हो सके। इस वैदिक कथन से यह भी संकेतित होता है कि हजार वृक्ष लगाने के बाद ही एक वृक्ष को काटना चाहिए। एक अन्यत्र प्रसंग में वैदिक ऋषि सहस्रपत्तों वाली वनस्पतियों से अभ्यर्थना करता है कि पृथ्वी पर जितनी भी सहस्रपत्तों वाली ओषधियां हैं, वे सब हमें प्रदूषण जन्य मृत्यु से बचाएं-

यावतीः कियतीश्चेमा पृथिव्यामध्योषधीः।
ता मा सहस्रपर्ण्यो मृत्योर्मुन्पन्त्वहसः।। (*अथर्ववेद*–6.10.6)

वेदों में तथा संस्कृत साहित्य के विभिन्न ग्रंथों में वृक्षों एवं वनस्पतियों के पूजन की उदात्त परंपरा रही है। हमारी संस्कृति में पीपल की पूजा, वट की पूजा, नीम की पूजा, केले की पूजा, तुलसी की पूजा का प्रायः प्रयोग देखा जाता है। इन सभी वृक्षों के नीचे मलमूत्र विसर्जन का निषेध किया गया है। इसके पीछे एक मात्र वैज्ञानिकता यह है कि ये अमृततत्त्व ऑक्सीजन के सर्वाधिक उत्सर्जक हैं। इन्हीं की कृपा से पर्यावरण पवित्र एवं जीवनानुकूल होता है। अतः दीर्घायु एवं चिरायु होने के लिए इन वृक्षों की पूजा एवं अर्चना की जाती है जो शुद्ध वैज्ञानिक विधि है। इसका उल्लेख *ऋग्वेद, यजुर्वेद* तथा *तैत्तरीय संहिता* में इस प्रकार है–

अश्वत्थ वो निषदनं पर्णे वा वसतिस्कृता अर्थात् तुम पीपल के नीचे बैठो और पलाश के पेड़ों के बीच बस्ती बसाओ। उपर्युक्त भावना की पुष्टि यजुर्वेद के सोलहवें अध्याय की अलग-अलग ऋचाओं में *वनानां पतये नमः, वृक्षाणां पत नमः, आख्यानां पतये नमः* इस प्रकार वृक्षों को सम्मान देकर प्रदर्शित की गई है। आज फसलों में आवश्यकता से अधिक रासायनिक खादों के निक्षेपण से अन्न की गुणवत्ता में वृहद्स्तर पर ह्रास हुआ है, जो स्वास्थ्य के लिए कदापि अनुकूल नहीं है। जिसका परिणाम विविध असाध्य रोगों के रूप में दृष्टिगत है। शायद मंत्रद्रष्टा ऋषि ने इसी अन्न की गुणवत्ता को बरकरार रखने के लिए हजारों वर्ष पूर्व *यजुर्वेद* में इस मंत्र की उद्घोषणा की–

अन्नपतेऽन्नस्य नो देह्यि अनमीवस्य शुष्मिणः। (*यजुर्वेद*–11.83)

अर्थात् हमारा अन्न दूषित एवं रोगोत्पादक न होकर शक्तिदायक एवं पुष्टिदायक हो।

जल जीवन का एक महत्वपूर्ण घटक है। इसके बिना जीवन अकल्पनीय है। शायद इसीलिए जल को जीवन अमृत, भेषज, रोगनाशक तथा आयुवर्द्धक आदि संबोधनों से संबोधित किया जाता है। यह मनुष्य को जीवनशक्ति प्रदान करता है, लेकिन खेद के साथ कहना पड़ रहा है कि आज वस्त्र, कागज, चीनी, धातु, रसायन, ओषधि प्रभृति औद्योगिक कल-कारखानों से निःसृत अपद्रव्य नदियों के पवित्र जल को लगातार दूषित एवं अपेय बना रहा है। इसी प्रकार शहरी मल भी बिना किसी संशोधन के नदियों में प्रवाहित किया जाता है जो जलप्रदूषण की एक गंभीर समस्या है। जल की महत्ता वैदिक वाङ्मय के निम्न मंत्रों में इस प्रकार प्रदर्शित की गई है–

अप्सवन्तरमृतप्स् भेषजमपामुत प्रशासन (*ऋग्वेद*–13.19) अर्थात् शुद्ध जल में अमृततत्त्व होता है और उसमें ओषधि का निवास होता है। इसी प्रकार *शन्नो देवीरभीष्टय आपोभवंतुपीतये शं योरशिस्रवंतु नः* मंत्र द्वारा शुद्ध जलों का पान करके एवं उसके चारों ओर डुबकी लगाकर हम अभीष्ट स्वास्थ्य प्राप्त कर सकते हैं। *ऋग्वेद* के एक अन्य मंत्र भी, शुद्ध जल में स्नान और उसका पान शरीर के मलों को निष्कासित करता है, इस तथ्य को प्रतिपादित करता है–

इदमाप प्रवहत यत्किञ्च दुरितं मयि (ऋग्वेद–10.0.04)

जल में पाए जाने वाले विशिष्ट तत्त्वों की जानकारी *ऋग्वेद* एवं *अथर्ववेद* के कई मंत्रों से प्राप्त होती है–

अप्सु मे सोमो अब्रवीदन्तर्विश्वानि भेषजा।
अग्निं च विश्वशंभु मापश्च विश्वभेषजीः।। (*ऋग्वेद*–1.23.20)
आपः पृणीत भेषु वरुथं तन्वे मम।
ज्योक् च सूर्या दृरो।। (*ऋग्वेद*–1.23.21)
आपो अद्यान्व चारिष रसेन समगस्महि। (*ऋग्वेद*–1.23.23)
आपो विश्वस्य भेषजीर तास्त्वा
मुञ्चन्तु क्षेत्रियात् (*अथर्ववेद*–3.7.5)
आपो ह मह्यं तद देवीर्ददन् हृदद्योत भेषजम्। (*अथर्ववेद*–6.24.1)
आपस्तत् सर्वं निष्करन् भिषजां सुभिषक्तमाः। (*अथर्ववेद*–6.24.2)

अर्थात् जल संपूर्ण रोगों का निदान है। यह प्राणशक्ति प्रदान करता है। यह शक्तिवर्द्धक और रोगनाशक है। इसमें सोम आदि जीवनदायक रस मिलाकर सेवन करने से मनुष्य चिरायु होता है।

जल के शोधन करने की कुछ विशेष प्रक्रिया का संकेत वेदों में अवगत होता है। नदियों आदि के जल को प्रदूषण रहित करने के विशिष्ट उपायों में यज्ञ को एक

महत्त्वपूर्ण घटक के रूप में दर्शाया गया है, इसकी सुगंधित वायु जल के विषतत्त्व का विनाश करती है।

अपो देवी रुप ह्वये यत्र गावः विबन्ति नः सिन्धुभ्यः कर्त्वं सिन्धुम्यः कर्त्व हविः।

(*ऋग्वेद*–1.2.23.18)

यजुर्वेद के एक अन्य मंत्र में भी जलशोधन की विधि इस तरह दिग्दर्शित की गई है–

सवितुस्त्वा प्रसवऽउत्पुनाम्यच्छिद्रेण पवित्रेण सूर्य्यस्य रस्मिभिः। (*यजुर्वेद*–1.31)

आशय यह है कि नैसर्गिक विधि से सूर्यताप को जल में पहुंचाना जलशोधन का एक उपाय है। कुश नामक घास भी जलशोधन का एक महत्त्वपूर्ण कारक है। संभवतः इसीलिए हमारे भारतीय कर्मकांडों में जल को कुश के साथ, हाथ में लेकर संकल्प लेने की परंपरा है। यह विस्मय एवं आश्चर्य की बात है कि आज से सैकड़ों वर्ष पूर्व जब कल-कारखानों एवं उद्योग-धंधों का विस्तार प्रायः नहीं था और प्रदूषण भी प्रायः न के बराबर था, बावजूद इसके उस समय की भारतीय मनीषा ने भावी प्रदूषण की आशंका में मनुष्य को इस प्रकार की चेतावनी दी है *जो पद्मपुराण* में द्रष्टव्य है–

मूत्रं वाडथपुरीषं वा गंगातीरे करोतियः।
न दृष्टा निस्कृतिस्तस्प कल्पकोटिशतैरपि।
श्लेष्माणं वापि निस्कीवं दूषितात्वश्रु वाभलम्।
उच्छिसंट कफकं चैव गंगागर्भे च यस्त्यजेत्।
स याति नरकं धोरं ब्रह्महत्यां च विंदति।।

(*पद्मपुराण*, क्रियायोग–10.10)

अर्थात् गंगा जल में थूकना, मलमूत्र परित्याग करना, कूड़ा-करकट डालना, गंदा जल प्रवाहित करना महापाप है। ऐसा करने वाले व्यक्ति को ब्रह्महत्या का पाप लगता है और वह नरक में जाता है। उक्त पौराणिक वचन जल प्रदूषण को रोकने के लिए मनुष्य को एक अग्रिम चेतावनी व सुझाव के रूप में समझना चाहिए।

वेद समग्र ज्ञान की अमूल्य निधि है। इसमें समस्त ज्ञान बीजरूप में निहित है। इसमें किसी क्षेत्रविशेष के पर्यावरण प्रदूषण की शांति की अभ्यर्थना नहीं, अपितु संपूर्ण विश्व के पर्यावरण को सुगंधित बनाने की भावना का प्रसारण है। पृथ्वी, जल, अंतरिक्ष आदि पर्यावरण के घटक तत्त्वों में शांति की कल्पना का अभिप्राय पर्यावरण को जीवनोपयोगी बनाने का संकेत प्रदान करता है–

द्यौः शान्तिरन्तरिक्ष शान्ति...।

संदर्भ

1. *अथर्ववेद*–18/01/17
2. *अथर्ववेद*–03/21/10
3. *ऋग्वेद*
4. *अथर्ववेद*–04/13/03
5. *ऋग्वेद*–06/37/03
6. *ऋग्वेद*–10/186/03
7. *ऋग्वेद*–10/186
8. *ऋग्वेद*–10/101/11
9. द्रष्टव्य *अखंड ज्योति,* मासिक पत्रिका अक्टूबर 1996 पृष्ठ 17
10. अश्वत्थः सर्ववृक्षाणां, *श्रीमद्‌भगवत् गीता*
11. *मत्स्यपुराण*
12. *महाभारत,* अनुशासनपर्व 30
13. *अग्निपुराण*
14. *ब्रह्मवैवर्तपुराण*
15. *ऋग्वेद*–03/51/03
16. *यजुर्वेद*–05/43
17. *अथर्ववेद*–06/10/06
18. *यजुर्वेद*–11/83
19. *ऋग्वेद*–1/23/19
20. *ऋग्वेद*–10/00/04
21. *ऋग्वेद*–10/00/04
22. *ऋग्वेद*–01/23/20
23. *ऋग्वेद*–01/23/21
24. *ऋग्वेद*–01/23/23
25. *अथर्ववेद*–03/07/05
26. *अथर्ववेद*–06/24/01
27. *अथर्ववेद*–06/24/02
28. *ऋग्वेद*–1/2/23/18
29. *मनुस्मृति*–03/76
30. *श्रीमद्‌भगवत् गीता*
31. *यजुर्वेद*–01/31
32. *पद्‌मपुराण,* क्रियायोग 8-08/09/10
33. *शुक्ल यजुर्वेद*

21. दर्शन और पर्यावरण—एक नवचिंतन

विजय कुमार सिन्हा एवं अशोक कुमार सिन्हा

दर्शन और पर्यावरण पर विचार करने के पूर्व इन पदों का अर्थ स्पष्टीकरण और पारस्परिक अंतरसंबंधों के बारे में सुनिश्चित होना वांछनीय प्रतीत होता है। सभ्यता के आरंभ से ही मानव का जिज्ञासु मन अपने आस-पास के जगत् तथा अपने आपको समझने का प्रयास करता रहा है। इस प्रयास ने ही मानव-सभ्यता की नींव रखी है। सभ्यता ही नहीं, संस्कृति, विज्ञान और दर्शन भी इसी प्रयास का परिणाम है। मानव और पशु में यही अंतर है कि मानव अपने इर्द-गिर्द घटने वाली हरेक घटना का कारण जानने की इच्छा रखता है। जगत् क्या? हमारे जीवन का अर्थ क्या है ? सत्य क्या है? इस प्रकार के अनंत प्रश्न मानव मन को उद्वेलित करता रहा है और जब तक इन प्रश्नों का समुचित कारण वह नहीं जान लेता, उसकी व्याकुलता समाप्त नहीं होनेवाली। इस प्रकार के प्रश्न पशुओं के लिए अर्थहीन हैं। वस्तुतः ऐसे प्रश्न ही मानव जीवन को अर्थवत्ता प्रदान करता है और इन्हीं के उत्तर की ख़ोज मानव को दार्शनिक बनाती है। दार्शनिक के विषय में प्लेटो का यह कथन उपयुक्त ही लगता है कि *दार्शनिक वे हैं जो सत्य के अवलोकन के लिए उत्सुक रहते हैं*। दर्शन का अंग्रेजी रूपांतरण 'फिलॉसफी' है। 'फिलॉसफी' फिलॉस और सोफिया इन दो शब्दों का युग्म है जो ग्रीक पद हैं और जिसका अर्थ प्रेम और ज्ञान है। अर्थात् हम कह सकते हैं कि 'फिलॉसफी' ज्ञान के प्रति प्रेम है। पाश्चात्य दर्शन का प्रथम दार्शनिक थेलिस माना जाता है। किंतु पाइथोगोरस ने पहली बार अपने को अति विनम्रतापूर्वक दार्शनिक यानी ज्ञान का प्रेमी कहा था। 'फिलॉसफी' शब्द का प्रचलन इसी समय शुरू हुआ और जो आज तक चलता आ रहा है। ध्यातव्य है कि दार्शनिक अपने को ज्ञानी नहीं कहता, हां, इतना अवश्य है कि ज्ञान के प्रति प्रेम उसे अच्छा लगता है।

आज के वैज्ञानिक युग में दर्शन की उपयोगिता संदेह के घेरे में आ गई है।

यदि ऐसा होता तो 'ब्रिटिश एसोसिएशन फॉर द एडर्वासमेंट ऑफ साइंस' की एक बैठक में यह प्रस्ताव पारित नहीं किया जाता कि विज्ञान को दस वर्षों के लिए अवकाश ले लेना चाहिए। हमारा भौतिक जगत् का ज्ञान आत्म ज्ञान से आगे बढ़ गया है और प्रकृति पर हमारा नियंत्रण भी आत्म-नियंत्रण की शक्ति से परे हो गया है। विज्ञान को हमारी सामाजिक, आर्थिक, नैतिक, दार्शनिक तथा धार्मिक समस्याओं पर ध्यान देने की आवश्यकता आज महसूस की जा रही है।[1] विज्ञान जिस लक्ष्य को लेकर चलता है जब तक वह लक्ष्य ही उचित स्थान पर अवस्थित नहीं होता, तब तक कोई सीधा रास्ता अपनाकर उसे प्राप्त कर लेना, विज्ञान के लिए संभव नहीं होगा। विज्ञान को जिस चीज की जरूरत है वह है विचार दर्शन, वैज्ञानिक विधियों का विश्लेषण और वैज्ञानिक उद्देश्यों तथा परिणामों का सामंजस्य। बिना इसके कोई भी विज्ञान छिछला ही बना रहेगा।[2] इसका सीधा मतलब यही है कि मानव के लिए विज्ञान से महत्त्वपूर्ण दर्शन है।

आज हम पर्यावरण क्रांति के दौर से गुजर रहे हैं। पर्यावरण के प्रति मनुष्य आज अति सजग होकर अनुक्रिया व्यक्त कर रहा है क्योंकि वह पर्यावरण का ही एक अंश है। मनुष्य का कोई स्वतंत्र अस्तित्व नहीं। वायु, जल, भूमि, वनस्पति, पेड़-पौधे, पशु, मानव सभी मिलकर एक पर्यावरण का निर्माण करते हैं। मनुष्य इसी पर्यावरण में जीता और मरता है। प्रकृति में इन तत्त्वों की मात्रा और रचना कुछ इस तरह व्यवस्थित है ताकि पृथ्वी पर संतुलनमय जीवन चलता रहे। इस संतुलन के भंग होने से ही पर्यावरण संकट एक ज्वलंत विषय बन गया है जिसके प्रति विश्व में व्यापक चेतना जागृत हुई है। इस चेतना के फलस्वरूप एक नवीन शाखा अस्तित्व में आई जिसे पर्यावरण विज्ञान (Environment Science) की संज्ञा दी गई। पर्यावरण अंग्रेजी शब्द 'एनवायरनमेंट' (Environment) का हिंदी रूपांतरण है जो दो शब्दों 'एनवायरन' (Environ) तथा 'मेंट' (Ment) से मिलकर बना है, जिसका अर्थ है चारों ओर का घेरा (Encircle) अथवा परिधि। अर्थात् जो चारों ओर से घेरे हुए है, वही पर्यावरण है। इस प्रकार पर्यावरण से हमारा तात्पर्य उस बाह्य आवरण से है जो चारों ओर से आवृत किए हुए है। विश्वकोष में इसे निम्न प्रकार से परिभाषित किया गया है— *पर्यावरण के अंतर्गत उन सभी दशाओं, संगठन एवं प्रभावों को सम्मिलित किया जाता है जो किसी जीव या प्रजाति के उद्भव, विकास एवं मृत्यु को प्रभावित करती है।* पर्यावरण से ही संबंध रखने वाला एक पद है पारिस्थितिकी, जिसका प्रयोग आजकल बहुत हो रहा है। पारिस्थितिकी पर्यावरण अध्ययन का एक विज्ञान है। पारिस्थितिकी का अंग्रेजी समानार्थक 'इकोलॉजी' शब्द ग्रीक भाषा के 'आइकोस' जिसका अर्थ घर अथवा आवास तथा 'लोगोस' जिसका अर्थ अध्ययन, शब्दों से मिलकर व्युत्पन्न हुआ है। इस प्रकार पारिस्थितिकी का अर्थ है 'स्टडी ऑफ

होम ऑर हैबिट' अथवा घर या आवास का अध्ययन। इस प्रकार पारिस्थितिकी किसी भी जीवधारी का उसके पर्यावरण के संबंध में अध्ययन है। पारिस्थितिकी वनस्पति, पशु, मानव तथा उनके पर्यावरण के संबंधों का अंतिम परिणाम है।

समकालीन युग में पर्यावरण और पारिस्थितिकी विषयक चिंतन ने सर्वग्राही रूप धारण कर लिया है। दर्शन भी पर्यावरण के प्रभाव से मुक्त नहीं रह पाता। कोई भी दर्शन सामाजिक परिवेश और उपस्थित पर्यावरण से प्रभावित होता है। दर्शन में शाश्वतता का अन्वेषण, मेरी दृष्टि में अब अपनी प्रासंगिकता खो बैठा है। दार्शनिक चिंतन में सापेक्षता है जो काल और परिवेश से महत्त्वपूर्ण रूप से प्रभावित होता है। अतः पर्यावरण में परिवर्तन से दर्शन भी प्रभावित होता है और उपस्थित पारिस्थितिकी में अपनी वैचारिक दिशा को समायोजित कर, अपनी सार्थक अनुक्रिया व्यक्त करता है। दर्शन, अब मात्र सैद्धांतिक, अमूर्त और अव्यावहारिक चिंतन का विषय नहीं रह गया है वरन् जीवन एवं जगत् से जुड़ी व्यावहारिक समस्याओं का भी अध्ययन करता है। जब किसी विषय का दार्शनिक अध्ययन करते हैं तो उसके सर्वांगीण पक्ष का अध्ययन करते हैं। दार्शनिक चिंतन पूर्वाग्रहरहित होकर समस्या का सम्यक् मूल्यांकन करते हुए इसके बौद्धिक समाधान के अन्वेषण की ओर प्रयास करता है। पर्यावरण दर्शन में सर्वप्रथम इसके घटकों का विश्लेषण करना होगा तथा उनके पारस्परिक संबंधों की व्याख्या करनी होगी। दार्शनिक दृष्टिकोण अपनाते हुए हमें प्रकृति और मनुष्य के बीच पारस्परिक संबंधों का विश्लेषण करना होगा। हमें इस प्रश्न पर विचार करना होगा कि प्राचीन काल में पर्यावरण संकट क्यों नहीं था, आज वे कौन-सी नई परिस्थितियां आ गई हैं जिनके कारण हमारे अस्तित्व के लिए ही भयावह संकट उत्पन्न हो गया। यह सर्वविदित है कि प्राचीनकाल में हमने प्रकृति के साथ सामंजस्य स्थापित किया था। प्राच्य और पाश्चात्य दोनों ही संस्कृतियों में प्रकृति के अंधाधुंध शोषण का कभी समर्थन नहीं किया गया। दार्शनिकों ने भी अध्यात्मवाद, एकतत्त्ववाद के अंतर्गत प्रकृति तथा अन्य जैविक सत्ताओं के साथ सामंजस्यपूर्ण सुसंगत संबंध की स्थापना की थी।

हमारी प्रथम प्राथमिकता हमारा अस्तित्व है। यदि हमारा अस्तित्व ही नहीं रहेगा तो सारी चीजें स्वतः समाप्त हो जाएंगी। हमारे अस्तित्व के लिए श्वास लेने के लिए ऑक्सीजनयुक्त हवा चाहिए, पीने के लिए पानी चाहिए जो हमें ऑक्सीजन युक्त हवा-पानी व ऐसा भोजन दे जिसका पाचन हम आसानी से कर सकें। हमारा अस्तित्व खतरे में पड़ सकता है यदि ये चीजें न हों या प्रदूषित हों।[3] यह मानव और प्रकृति दोनों के अस्तित्व के लिए प्रश्नचिह्न है। यहीं से जीवन-जगत् अस्तित्व, मूल्य, आदर्श जैसे दार्शनिक विषयों पर चिंतन के लिए बाध्य हो जाते हैं। यह एक वैश्विक समस्या है, जिससे प्रत्येक राष्ट्र किसी-न-किसी रूप में प्रभावित है। एक विचारक

ने तो यहां तक कह डाला है कि 'आजकल प्रकृति के साथ समाज की अंतःक्रिया इतनी व्यापक है कि उससे सारी मानव जाति को प्रभावित करने वाला प्रश्न उत्पन्न हो गया है।' यह एक पर्यावरणीय प्रश्न है। पर्यावरण का सैद्धांतिक आधार 'सामाजिक न्याय' है। इसके समर्थक यह तर्क देते हैं कि धरती किसी की निजी संपत्ति नहीं। यह हमारे पूर्वजों से उत्तराधिकार में नहीं मिली बल्कि यह हमारे पास भावी पीढ़ियों की धरोहर है। अतः हम वर्तमान प्राकृतिक संसाधनों को सुरक्षित रखने के दायित्व से बंधे हैं। वर्तमान पीढ़ी को यह अधिकार नहीं कि वह अपने उपयोग के लिए इसके सारे संसाधनों को निचोड़ कर भावी पीढ़ी के जीवन को खतरे में डाल दे। अतः पर्यावरण की रक्षा के लिए सजग होना हमारा परम कर्त्तव्य है। पारिस्थितिकी विज्ञान ने यह सिद्ध कर दिया है कि आर्थिक विकास की अंधी दौड़ में हमारे पर्यावरण को कितनी क्षति पहुंची है। खनिज पदार्थों की खोज में अंधाधुंध खनन (Mining) के कारण इतने अम्ल बहाए हैं, जिन्होंने निर्मल जल स्रोतों को विषाक्त कर दिया है। दूर-दूर तक फैले हुए कारखानों की चिमनियों और दिन-रात धुआं उगलते वाहनों ने इतना वायु प्रदूषण पैदा किया है जिससे अपार क्षति हुई। उद्योगों से पैदा होनेवाले रासायनिक कूड़े-कचरे (Chemical waste) और आणविक शक्ति के प्रयोग से उत्पन्न रेडियोधर्मी रिसाव (Radioactive Leakage) के कारण धरती रहने योग्य नहीं बची।[4] सारांश में पर्यावरण से संबंधित अनेक समस्याएं मानव जाति के समक्ष उपस्थित हैं— जैसे पृथ्वी के तापमान में वृद्धि की प्रवृत्ति, भूमि के उत्पादन क्षमता के ह्रास, असमय बाढ़, क्लोरो-फ्लोरो कार्बन (C.F.C.) से ओजोन परत का क्षय, भूकंप, तेजाबी वर्षा, वन-जैव संपदा का विलुप्त होने का संकट। इन गंभीर पर्यावरणीय चुनौतियों से उपयुक्त ढंग से सामना किया जाना कैसे संभव होगा। इन समस्याओं की जड़ में वैज्ञानिक विकास और तकनीकी प्रगति है जिसने मानवीय आगम के नए द्वार खोल दिए हैं। सूर्य और चंद्रमा पर पहुंचने का मानव ने सपना देखा था जो वैज्ञानिक तकनीकी के नित्य नए आयामों के अन्वेषण से यथार्थ में बदलने लगा है। मनुष्य स्वर्ग को धरती पर लाने की इच्छा रखता है ताकि इनके बीच जो दूरी है उसे कम-से-कम किया जा सके। हमें यह गर्व होने लगा है कि प्रकृति पर हमारा पूर्ण अधिकार हो गया है। एक विचारक का इस प्रसंग में यह कहना उचित ही प्रतीत होता है कि हम शब्दशः पर्वतों को हरा सकते हैं, नदियों का मार्ग बदल सकते हैं, नए सागरों का निर्माण कर सकते हैं और विशाल रेगिस्तानों को मरूउद्यानों में परिणत कर सकते हैं, हम प्राकृतिक जगत् में मौलिक परिवर्तन कर सकते हैं। हमारे उत्पादक व आर्थिक, वैज्ञानिक और तकनीकी कार्यकलाप अंतरिक्ष तक विस्तृत हो गए हैं।[5] तकनीकी प्रगति या विकास से प्रभावित परिवर्तनों के सम्मोहन में प्राकृतिक जगत् पर स्वामित्व स्थापन का हमारा प्रयास अविवेकपूर्ण अनधिकार के

अतिरिक्त और कुछ नहीं। प्राकृतिक जगत् पर व्यक्तियों द्वारा किए जा रहे अंतहीन अतिक्रमण का परिणाम हानिकारक ही होगा। पारिस्थितिकी अनुसंधान से यह ज्ञात हो चुका है कि जैवमंडल पर मनुष्य का निरंतर एकपक्षीय अनियंत्रित प्रभाव हमारी सभ्यता को मरूद्यानों के स्थानों पर रेगिस्तानों में स्थापित कर देगा और पृथ्वी पर सारे जीवन के विनाश का खतरा पैदा कर देगा।[6] इसी संबंध में एंजेल्स का यह आग्रह महत्त्वपूर्ण प्रतीत होता है कि प्रकृति पर मानवीय विजयों के कारण हमें आत्म प्रशंसा में विभोर नहीं होना चाहिए क्योंकि वह ऐसी विजय का हमसे प्रतिशोध लेती है।[7] इस बिंदु पर प्रकृति से संबंधित आधुनिक पाश्चात्य अवधारणा पर दृष्टिपात किया जा सकता है, जो प्राकृतिक संसाधनों का भरपूर शोषण (Exploitation) की वकालत करता है। प्राकृतिक संसाधनों का जितना शोषण होगा उतना ही विकास की गति में तीव्रता आएगी। आधुनिक युग में ऐसा हुआ है और अभी भी हो रहा है। एंजेल्स का संकेत इसी ओर है कि प्रकृति पर विजय पाने की बात करके मनुष्य को प्रसन्न नहीं होना चाहिए, क्योंकि प्रकृति प्रतिशोध लेती है। प्रकृति का प्रतिशोध पर्यावरण संकट के रूप में प्रकट होता है। वैज्ञानिक आविष्कारों, बड़े-बड़े बांधों और प्राकृतिक संपदाओं के कारण जो पारिस्थितिकीय परिवर्तन विगत दो दशकों से विश्व में हुआ है उसके कारण मानव और अन्य जीव-जंतुओं के अस्तित्व का संकट उत्पन्न हो गया है। इस प्रकार हम देख सकते हैं कि मानव यह मानकर चल रहा है कि जितना अधिक प्राकृतिक संसाधनों का शोषण होगा उतना ही तीव्र विकास होगा जबकि प्रकृति प्रतिशोध स्वरूप इस विकास को विनाश में बदल देती है।[8]

विकास से विनाश का दृश्य प्रकृति के प्रति मानव के गलत व्यवहार के कारण हुआ है। आज मानव की आकांक्षाओं में निरंतर वृद्धि देखने को मिल रही है जबकि इन आकांक्षाओं की पूर्ति के लिए संसाधन अति सीमित हैं। असीमित आकांक्षा और सीमित संसाधन के बीच जब द्वंद्व होगा तो इसका परिणाम मानव के लिए कभी भी हितकर नहीं होगा। मानव विकास के लिए प्रकृति के प्रति उपयुक्त दृष्टिकोण अपनाना होगा। इस तथ्य को आधुनिक विचारकों तथा प्राचीन भारतीय मनीषियों ने स्वीकार किया है। प्रकृति के प्रति सही दृष्टिकोण है मानव द्वारा प्रकृति से याचना करना, प्रकृति से तादात्म्य रखना, ईश्वर, प्रकृति और मनुष्य में तादात्म्य ढूंढ़ना। भारतीय दर्शन में मानव का प्रकृति के साथ तादात्म्य रखने का न केवल भावबोध पाया जाता है बल्कि इस संबंध में बृहत् दर्शन है। मानव प्रकृति की एक चैतन्य रचना है, जिसकी आधारशिला क्षिति, जल, पावक, गगन और समीर है। यही भारतीय दर्शन का सारतत्त्व है। इसलिए इन पांच तत्त्वों का मानव एवं जीव-जगत् के अनुकूल होना स्वास्थ्य और अस्तित्व के लिए आवश्यक है।[9] भारतीय आदर्श भी यह रहा है कि प्रकृति या पृथ्वी से उतना ही लिया जाए जितना कि उसे लौटाया जा सके। परंतु

उपभोगवादी प्रवृत्ति से प्रभावित मानव समाज वस्तुओं के अतिभोग की ओर उन्मुख है। आज का मानव वैभवपूर्ण जीवन जीने के लिए लाभ अर्जन चाहता है और किसी भी प्रकार के अनैतिक साधनों का प्रयोग करने से हिचकता नहीं। यह मानवीय मूल्यों के विनाश के कारण ही शायद संभव हुआ है। हम कह सकते हैं कि मानव की विकास यात्रा पर्यावरण के साथ चलने और उसके उपयोग का इतिहास है। निरंतर विकास मानव की प्रवृत्ति है और पर्यावरण जीवन का स्रोत है। अपने आज तक के विकास यात्रा में मानव ने पर्यावरण का सतत उपयोग किया है और विकास का पर्यावरण पर प्रभाव पड़ा है। जब तक यह प्रभाव सीमित होता है, पारिस्थितिकी तंत्र अधिक प्रभावित नहीं होता, परंतु जब यह प्रभाव अधिक सघन और विस्तृत होने लगता है तो पर्यावरण में विकृतियां उत्पन्न होने लगती हैं और उसका दुष्प्रभाव संपूर्ण मानव जीवन पर पड़ता है। विकास की ओर बढ़ते कदम और पर्यावरण के बीच संतुलन का नहीं होना एक गंभीर चुनौती है। विकास के कारण पारिस्थितिकीय प्रभाव और पर्यावरणीय विकृतियों ने हमें यह सोचने पर बाध्य कर दिया है कि क्या विकास को रोक दिया जाए? यदि नहीं तो विकास की सही दिशा क्या हो जिससे पर्यावरण और पारिस्थितिकी तंत्र पर विपरीत प्रभाव नहीं पड़े? इस बात से इनकार नहीं किया जा सकता कि विकास का प्रभाव पर्यावरण पर पड़ता है; परंतु इसका यह अर्थ नहीं कि विकास को रोक दिया जाए। विकास को सही मानवोपयोगी दिशा देने की आवश्यकता है एवं पर्यावरण पर उसके कुप्रभाव नहीं पड़ने देने की ओर प्रयास किए जाने की आवश्यकता है।

यदि दर्शन मानव जीवन और जगत् के विषय में बौद्धिक, नैतिक या मूल्यात्मक विवेचन प्रस्तुत करता है तो बीसवीं शताब्दी के इस अंतिम चरण में मानव जीवन जिस संकट से गुजर रहा है, उस पर विचार करना दर्शन का लक्ष्य हो गया है। यह संकट जैसे—पर्यावरण प्रदूषण, जनसंख्या विस्फोट, नाभिक युद्ध और शक्ति-क्षरण गंभीर रूप धारण करते जा रहे हैं। ऐसी स्थिति में दर्शन के क्षेत्र के अंतर्गत मानव हित का अध्ययन प्रमुख हो गया है। आज के पहले भी दर्शन में विकासवाद का अध्ययन हुआ है, परंतु वर्तमान में जिन समस्याओं का अध्ययन दर्शन में अनिवार्य हो गया है, वह है औद्योगिक विकास से उत्पन्न पर्यावरण में होनेवाले प्रदूषण की समस्याएं। इन समस्याओं से संपूर्ण विश्व में मानव सुरक्षा खतरे में है। वर्तमान तो मानव के लिए संकटमय है ही, भविष्य भी असुरक्षित दिखाई देता है। विश्व के मानववादी इस चिंता में हैं कि विकास की क्या दिशा हो, जिससे मानव जीवन सुरक्षित रह सके।

दार्शनिकों ने विकास की सही दिशा ढूंढ़ निकाली है, वह है 'जीवन धारण करने योग्य विकास' इसी को सुस्थिर विकास, संपोष्य विकास, अनुरक्षणवादी विकास

(Sustainable devlopment) भी कहते हैं। विचारकों का मानना है कि ऐसा विकास पारिस्थितिकी को दृष्टि में रखकर किया जा सकता है। यह ऐसा विकास होगा जो मानव जीवन की उत्तमता को, पर्यावरण को बिना क्षति पहुंचाए, बनाए रखता है। यह विकास पर्यावरण के साथ सामंजस्य स्थापित करके होगा या ऐसे तकनीकी का विकास करके होगा जिससे पर्यावरणीय क्षति को रोका जा सके। इस जीवनदायी विकास में पारिस्थितिकी (Ecology) के साथ-साथ मानव जीवन के विभिन्न आयामों को भी ध्यान में रखा जाएगा। जीवन के सामाजिक, सांस्कृतिक, राजनीतिक, आर्थिक एवं मनोवैज्ञानिक पक्षों को भी ध्यान में रखना होगा। सारांश में पारिस्थितिकी के दर्शन का मूल बिंदु मानव हित के लिए ऐसा विकास, जिससे पारिस्थितिकी की रक्षा हो, क्योंकि पारिस्थितिकी और पर्यावरण के विनाश से मानव या जीव जगत् की रक्षा संभव नहीं। मानव-हित और विकास के परिप्रेक्ष्य में पारिस्थितिकीय दर्शन की परिभाषा कुछ इस प्रकार दी जा सकती है—'पारिस्थितिकीय दर्शन, दर्शन की वह शाखा है जो मानव जीवन और उससे संबंधित विभिन्न क्षेत्रों में होनेवाले विकास का मानव-हित के परिप्रेक्ष्य में अध्ययन करती है। दर्शन की यह शाखा इसका अध्ययन करती है कि जो चारों ओर विकास हो रहा है, क्या उससे प्राकृतिक धरोहर का क्षरण हो रहा है? या सामाजिक, राजनीतक और आर्थिक विकास क्या मानव हित की दृष्टि से उचित है ? यदि नहीं है तो विकास की क्या दिशा हो, जिससे मानव जीवन या जीव जगत् का विनाश न हो? विकास ऐसा हो जो संपोष्य, सुस्थिर या रक्षणकारी हो। दूसरे शब्दों में पारिस्थितिकीय दर्शन और कुछ नहीं संपोष्य विकास का अध्ययन है।'

विकास पर्यावरण से जुड़ा हुआ है। विकास तभी संभव होगा जब पर्यावरण को बिना कोई क्षति पहुंचाए निर्माण करें। यदि निर्माण के कारण प्रकृति में अव्यवस्था उत्पन्न होती है तो उसे विकास नहीं विनाश कहा जाएगा। आज पाश्चात्य देशों में जो विकास की स्थिति देखी जा रही है, वह एक संक्रामक रोग की स्थिति है। आज के विश्व में एक ओर तो विकास का अति निम्नस्तर देखने को मिलता है तो दूसरी ओर विकास सभी मर्यादाओं का अतिक्रमण करता हुआ दिखाई देता है। मनुष्य के लिए भोजन आवश्यक है, परंतु आवश्यकता से अधिक भोजन खा लेने की संभावना से इनकार नहीं किया जा सकता। *कोकोपौक* घोषणा के अनुसार, 'अधिक से अधिक वस्तुओं का उत्पादन और उपभोग करने से हमें सहायता नहीं मिलती, यदि उसके परिणामस्वरूप हमें नींद की गोलियां और मानसिक अस्पतालों पर अधिक निर्भर होना पड़े।' आज अधिक विकसित देश ही पर्यावरण पर भारी दवाब डाल रहे हैं और न केवल अपने के लिए, दूसरों के लिए भी नई समस्याएं खड़ी कर रहे हैं। पर्यावरण को क्षति पहुंचाने के लिए विकसित देश को ही अधिक उत्तरदायी

माना जा सकता है, क्योंकि इन्होंने लापरवाही के साथ प्राकृतिक साधनों को समाप्त करने की ओर प्रवृत्ति दिखाई है। इस प्रवृत्ति के कारण ही विभिन्न राष्ट्रों में असमान संबंधों में दृढ़ता आई है। इसलिए आवश्यकता एक ऐसे न्यायपूर्ण वितरण की है जिसमें मनुष्य द्वारा न तो प्रकृति का शोषण है और न प्रकृति द्वारा मनुष्य का शोषण है। इसलिए जो कम विकसित हैं उनके विकास की ओर अधिक ध्यान देने की आवश्यकता है।

निष्कर्षतः हम कह सकते हैं कि हमें अपनी आवश्यकताओं पर दूसरों की आवश्यकताओं के आलोक में विचार करने की आवश्यकता है। हमें यह ध्यान रखना होगा कि प्रकृति ने जो संसाधन हमें दिए हैं, उनके दुरुपयोग का अति हानिकारक परिणाम होगा। आवश्यकताएं जब सीमित होंगी तो समस्याओं की जटिलता नहीं होगी और न होगा प्रकृति का स्वेच्छाचारी दुरुपयोग। इस दिशा में विज्ञान की अपेक्षा दर्शन ज्यादा सहायक सिद्ध होगा।

संदर्भ

1. जी.टी.डब्ल्यू. वौटिक, *दर्शनशास्त्र का परिचय,* पृ. 8
2. बिल ड्यूरेंट, *दर्शन की कहानी,* पृ. 126
3. *विश्व शांति और अहिंसा,* पृ. 10
4. अनु. जगदीश चंद्र पांडेय, *समाज और पर्यावरण,* प्रगति प्रकाशन, मास्को, 1986, पृ. 05
5. उपर्युक्त, पृ. 05
6. उपर्युक्त, पृ. 06
7. *खादी ग्रामोद्योग,* 1955, पृ. 55
8. उपर्युक्त, पृ. 55
9. उपर्युक्त, पृ. 55

22. भगवान बुद्ध और पर्यावरण प्रदूषण

वीरेंद्र पांडे

पर्यावरण असंतुलन के कारण आज का जीवन जीना अत्यंत कष्टप्रद तथा भयावह हो गया है। वातावरण इतना प्रदूषित हो गया है कि लोग सोचने पर मजबूर हो गए हैं कि यदि प्रदूषण इसी तरह से बढ़ता गया तो क्या हम जी सकेंगे? क्या हमारी आनेवाली नस्लें सुरक्षित रह सकेंगी? यह सब सोचकर इससे निजात पाने के लिए कई वैज्ञानिक शोध कर रहे हैं ताकि जीवन जीने में सरल तथा सुगम हो। इसके साथ ही पर्यावरण असंतुलन के कारण प्रकृति में जो विकृति आई या आ रही है वह ठीक हो तथा अपना कार्य कुशलतापूर्वक संपन्न कर सके। 'पर्यावरण' शब्द 'परि' उपसर्ग पूर्वक 'वृ' आवरणे तथा ल्युट प्रत्यय के योग से निष्पन्न है जिसका अर्थ परिस्थिति, परिवेश या वातावरण होता है, अर्थात् जो वस्तु या पदार्थ पृथ्वी के सभी जीवों और जंतुओं को चारों ओर से संचालित करता हो, उसे पर्यावरण कहते हैं। या यूं कहें कि मनुष्य एवं अन्य जीव-जंतुओं चाहे वह वातजीवी हो, तृणजीवी हो, जलजीवी या वृक्षजीवी हो, इन सबों को जो वस्तु पदार्थ परिवृत करता है, उसे ही पर्यावरण कहते हैं। पर्यावरणविदों की अवधारणा है कि परिस्थिति या पर्यावरण की परिशुद्धता के होने पर ही इस चराचर जगत् का कल्याण एवं अभ्युदय संभव है, अन्यथा समस्त प्राणियों का विध्वंसन संभव है।

मनुष्य या यों कहें पृथ्वी के सारे प्राणी और पर्यावरण एक-दूसरे के ऊपर आश्रित हैं, इनमें अन्योन्याश्रय संबंध है। वे संरक्षक एवं विध्वंसक दोनों हैं यदि दोनों आपस में मैत्रीपूर्ण एवं सहयोगात्मक रवैया अपनाते हैं तो दोनों के विकास और संवर्द्धन की अप्रतिम संभावना प्रबल है। किंतु यदि दोनों के बीच ऐसा सुमनस्कता नहीं है, सपत्नभाव विद्यमान है तो दोनों एक-दूसरे से प्रभावित होते हैं। भगवान बुद्ध के अनुसार दोनों अंतःसंबद्ध हैं। मानव अपने विचारों एवं अपने किए गए कर्मों के

चिंतन के अनुरूप ही कार्य करता है, परिणामस्वरूप सद्वृत्तियां और दुश्वृत्तियों का जन्म होता है। सद्वृत्तियों के प्रादुर्भाव से सौमनस्य का जन्म होता है और सुमनस्कता का प्रादुर्भाव होता है। ठीक इसके विपरीत बुरे व्यसनों के कारण दुर्मनस्कता तथा दुर्भावना जन्म लेती है।

भगवान बुद्ध के अनुसार यदि मनुष्य की शारीरिक, वाचिक एवं मानसिक क्रियाएं विप्रसन्न होती हैं तो वह सुखात्मक एवं सौमनस्यपूर्ण जीवनयापन कर सकता है और यदि उसकी शारीरिक, वाचिक एवं मानसिक क्रियाएं अनैतिक हैं तो मानव-समाज में प्रत्यूहों, विघ्नों-तनावों का वातावरण अनुस्यूत हो जाता है और इससे पर्यावरण भी प्रभावित हुए बगैर नहीं रहता।

भगवान बुद्ध के समय पर्यावरण अर्थात् प्राकृतिक पर्यावरण की कोई समस्या नहीं थी। इसका कारण था कि उस समय के लोगों में पर्यावरण प्रदूषित करने की कलुषित प्रवृत्ति नहीं थी। वन, बाग, बगीचे लगाना लोग पुण्य का कार्य समझते थे। इसका प्रमाण हमें पालि के कई निकायों में मिलता है। जैसे-अंबलहिका, अंबपाली के आम्रवन, श्रावस्ती के जैतवन इत्यादि। इन्हीं सब कारणों से बुद्ध हमेशा प्रकृति के सुरम्य मनोहर एवं रमणीय स्थलों में ही अपना निवास रखते थे। यहां तक कि उनका महापरिनिर्वाण भी कुशीनारा के दो पुष्पित शाल वृक्षों के बीच ही हुआ। परंतु आज पवित्र गंगा, यमुना आदि विशिष्ट नदियां बड़े-बड़े नालाओं के दुर्गंधपूर्ण जल से प्रदूषित हो गई हैं। आज पर्वतों के ऊपर उगे पेड़-पौधों का कटाव बृहत् रूप से जारी है। इससे पर्यावरण सर्वथा प्रदूषित हो गया है। अतः इसका निराकरण अपरिहार्य हो गया है।

भगवान बुद्ध दूरद्रष्टा थे इसीलिए उन्होंने प्रदूषण की समस्या के निदान के लिए अनेक वैनयिक नियमों का प्रज्ञापन कर भिक्षुओं को हरित तृणों, घास तथा जीवनदायी जल को थूक, खर-पतवार, मल-मूत्र से प्रदूषित करने से वर्जित किया था।[1] भगवान बुद्ध के समय प्रदूषण के ये सामान्य उपादान थे। भगवान ने भिक्षुओं को यह अनुज्ञा दी थी कि कूड़ों-कचरों को यत्र-तत्र न फेंककर एक सुनिश्चित स्थान में छोड़ना चाहिए[2] *चुल्लवग* के *पस्सावच्च-मालावच्छरोपनदारुमंडादि कथा* में भगवान बुद्ध ने आराम में यत्र-तत्र मल-मूत्र के उत्सर्जन का निषेध किया है।[3] यहां-वहां मल-मूत्र के त्यागने से विहार प्रदूषित होता था जिससे आश्रम में दुर्गंधपूर्ण वातावरण बनने का भय रहता था। यह जानकर भगवान ने किसी निश्चित स्थान पर ही मलोत्सर्जन की अनुज्ञा प्रदान की थी।[4] कूड़ेदान तथा उससे दुर्गंध न फैले इसलिए उसे ढांपने का भी विधान बनाया गया था।[5]

समंतपासादिका में एक स्थान पर महार्धवृक्ष को काटने मात्र पर पाराजिक नामक अपराध से आपन्न होने का नियम था ऐसा चिह्नित है। वृक्षों का काटना,

वनस्पतियों को नष्ट करना इत्यादि से भगवान का अभीष्ट नहीं था। उनका मानना था कि वनों तथा वनवृक्षों से पर्यावरण शुद्ध तथा पर्यवदात रहता है। जिससे समाज को वन प्रभूत संपदाएं भी मिलती हैं तथा वन्यप्राणी सुखी रहते हैं। भगवान बुद्ध हमेशा वृक्षारोपण की प्रशंसा करते हुए कहते थे कि उद्यानों में, वनों में वृक्ष लगानेवाले, नदियों पर पुलों का निर्माण करनेवाले, यात्रियों के लिए धर्मशाला, कुआं तथा तालाब बनानेवाले, प्यासे को पानी पिलानेवाले का पुण्य हमेशा बढ़ता है–

आराम रोपा वन रोपा ये जना सेतुकारका।
पपं च उपादानं च ये ददांति उपस्सयं।
तेसं दिवा च रत्तो च सदा पुञ्जं पवढति।।[6]

भगवान बुद्ध हमेशा तालाब के मेड़ को काटने से मना करते थे। उनका मानना था कि सस्यादि का भरण-पोषण तालाब या नदी के जल से ही होता है *तलाकमरियादं मा छिंदी*[7] जल ही जीवन है इसे ध्यान में रखकर ही शायद भगवान बुद्ध ने इस वाक्य को कहा होगा। जल की शुद्धता हमेशा बनी रहे इसलिए उन्होंने उद्यानों, तड़ागों तथा कूपों के जल परिशुद्ध रखने की अनुज्ञा हमेशा दिया करते थे। घास पशुओं का आहार है। अतः इसके बचाव के लिए भी बुद्ध ने कई वैनयिक नियमों का प्रज्ञापन किया था। *दीर्घनिकाय* के कुटदतं सूत्र में यह वर्णित है कि कूटदंत जो यज्ञ का आयोजन करता था उसके यज्ञ मंडप के निर्माण के लिए कई वृक्ष काटे जाते थे किंतु भगवान बुद्ध के यज्ञों में वृक्षों की कटाई नहीं होती थी।

न रूक्खा छिज्जिंसु भूपत्थाय, न दब्भा लूयिंसु वरिहिसत्थाय।[8]

ध्वनि प्रदूषण :– आज प्रत्येक प्राणी ध्वनिप्रदूषण से संत्रस्त है। इससे निजात पाने के लिए कई महत्वपूर्ण कदम उठाए जा रहे हैं। परंतु यह दिनो-दिन सुरसा के मुंह की तरह विकराल रूप से फैलता ही जा रहा है। यह अति गंभीर पर्यावरणीय समस्या है। इसके कारण श्रवणरंध्र विदीर्ण हो रहा है। जिससे व्यक्ति बहरापन का शिकार हो रहा है। मानसिक तनाव, चिड़चिड़ापन तथा मानसिक परेशानी इसी के कारण होती है। भगवान बुद्ध उच्चाशय के प्रतिमान थे तथा कोलाहल के विरुद्ध थे।[9] भगवान के भिक्षुसंघ की परिषद् जहां होती थी, वहां कोई कोलाहल या निर्घोष नहीं होता था। उनकी परिषद् पूर्णतः शांत होती थी। जीवक के साथ भगवान बुद्ध के दर्शन के लिए जाते हुए अजातशत्रु को महा-आश्चर्य हुआ कि साढ़े बारह सौ भिक्षुओं के बृहत् संघ के एक साथ रहने पर भी किसी वस्तु के गिरने की ध्वनि तक नहीं हो रही थी। *कथं हि नाम ताव महतों भिक्खु संघस्स अड्ढतेलसतानं नेव खिपितसद्दोभविस्सति न उक्कासितासद्धो न निग्धोसो ति।*[10] इसे देखकर अजातशत्रु के मुख से यह उद्‌गार निकला–मेरा राजकुमार भी एवंविध शांति से समन्वित हो

जिस शांति से भिक्षुसंघ है।[11] एक बार भगवान बुद्ध भिक्षुओं के एक संघ को कोलाहलपूर्ण वातावरण उत्पन्न करने पर विहार छोड़ने की आज्ञा तक दे डाली थी।[12] भगवान बुद्ध ने भिक्षुओं को एकांत एवं अभिरम्य वनप्रांत में रहकर ध्यान करने की अनुज्ञा प्रदान की थी। जनाकीर्ण प्रदेश या भूमिभाग को भगवान ध्यान के लिए अनुपयुक्त एवं बाधाकारी मानते थे।

भगवान बुद्ध वचन व्यापार की मधुरता तथा लक्षण्ता के पक्षधर थे। उचित समय पर बोलना, सत्य भाषित होना, बोली में नम्रता, उपयोगी तथा लाभप्रद बोली ही उन्हें प्रिय था। यही कारण था कि आष्टांगिक मार्ग तथा दस शिक्षा पदों में भी इसको उचित स्थान मिला है। भारतीय संतों ने भी सुभाषित को ही श्रेष्ठ वचन कहा है। भगवान बुद्ध ने कहा है कि साधक को वही वचन बोलना चाहिए जिसे बोलने के पश्चात् पश्चात्ताप न करना पड़े तथा उससे दूसरों को कोई कष्ट न हो, इसे ही सुभाषित कहते हैं।[13] व्यक्ति को हमेशा प्रिय तथा सत्य वचन बोलना चाहिए जो सुनने में मधुर लगे तथा जो प्रसन्नतादायक हो। जो अपनी वाणी से दूसरों के दोष नहीं निकालता वही प्रिय वक्ता कहलाता है। सत्यभाषण ही सर्वोत्तम है।

इस प्रकार भगवान बुद्ध मधुर एवं शांत वाणी के समर्थक एवं प्रशंसक थे। परंतु आज ध्वनिविस्तारक यंत्रों के द्वारा तथा विविध यानों की कर्कश ध्वनि विस्फोटक के कारण समस्त पर्यावरण पर्याकुल है। यदि इस ध्वनि प्रदूषण का शीघ्रातिशीघ्र निराकरण नहीं किया गया तो मानव समाज विनाश की ओर अग्रसर हो जाएगा।

वायु प्रदूषण :– वायु ही जीवन है, इसकी सार्थकता किसी को बताने की आवश्यकता नहीं है। फिर भी वायु प्रदूषित हो रही है, इससे नई-नई बीमारियां फैल रही हैं। लोग यह देखकर भी कोई सार्थक उपाय खोजने में सक्षम नहीं हैं, परंतु भगवान बुद्ध इसके प्रति सदा सजग व सचेष्ट थे। वायु के बिना जीवन का श्वास तंत्र टूट सकता है। यही हमारे प्राणों की रक्षा करती है। श्वास-प्रश्वास तथा निःश्वास की गति संचालक वायु ही है। साथ ही स्वच्छ वायु सभी को प्रिय लगता है, वहीं दुर्गंधपूर्ण वायु हमारे मन को खिन्नता प्रदान करता है। भगवान बुद्ध खुली एवं स्वच्छ वायु के संवाहक थे। यही कारण है कि जब वे अपने घर से ज्ञान की खोज करने के लिए निकले और जब उन्होंने उरूवेला की निरंजना नदी को देखा तो उनका मन उल्लसित हो गया तथा वे मन ही मन विचार करने लगे कि तपस्या के लिए यही उपयुक्त स्थान है। (*नज्जा नेरंजाय तीरे समागतो सिद्धत्थे विप्पसन्नो जातो*) भगवान बुद्ध इस भूमि भाग की प्रशंसा करते हुए कहते हैं कि यह भू-भाग अति रमणीय एवं प्रसन्नता का उद्भावक है। नदी का यह तट समुज्ज्वल और मनोरम है, इसकी धारा स्वच्छ एवं कलकलाती चंचलता के साथ प्रवाहित है। साथ ही प्रदेश ग्रामों से आवृत्त है। यह भूमि भाग उनके लिए मनोरम है जो अपने चित्त को समाहित और

एकाग्रचित करना चाहते हैं।[14] *रमणीया वत भो भूमिभागो, समंता च गोचरगामो कुलपुतस्स पधानत्थिकस्स पधानायाय ति।* जैसा कि विदित है कि भगवान ने छह वर्षों तक निरंतर तपस्या करने के उपरांत ही बुद्धत्व की प्राप्ति की थी। जिस स्थान पर उन्होंने तपस्या की वहां एक वटवृक्ष था जो आज बोधिवृक्ष के नाम से विख्यात हुआ तथा उस स्थान को बोधगया के नाम से जाना जाता है।

भगवान बुद्ध का निवास हमेशा जंगलों एवं उद्यानों के बीच ही हुआ करता था। इससे यह उद्भावित होता है कि उन्हें प्रकृति से कितना प्रेम था। वे सदा एकांत, शांत और प्रकृति सौंदर्य से अनुप्राणित प्रदेश में ही रहना पसंद करते थे। वे भोजनोपरांत ध्यान एवं समाधि भावना के लिए सुरम्य-अरण्य प्रदेश में ही जाते थे। राजगीर के गिज्झकूट पर्वत पर उन्होंने अनेक धर्मदेशना दी है, इससे यह ज्ञात होता है कि सुरम्य पर्वतों का दृश्य उन्हें अत्यधिक प्रभावित करता था। *थेरगाथा* में तो अनेक भिक्षुओं को सुंदर एवं रमणीय स्थलों की प्रशंसा करते हुए देखा गया है। सुंदर वातावरण व मौसम की बात वे सहज ही व्यक्त करते हैं। कालुदायी नामक भिक्षु प्रफुल्ल एवं पुष्पाभरणों से समलंकृत वृक्षों की शोभा का वर्णन करता हुआ कहता है कि अंगारों के समान पुष्पों से अलंकृत ये वृक्ष अत्यंत मनोरम लगते हैं। इन वृक्षों ने फलों की पर्येषेणा में पत्रों का परित्याग कर दिया है। ये वृक्ष दीपशिखा के समान चमत्कृत है–

अंगारिनो दानि दुमा विप्पहाय।
फलेसिनो छदनं विप्पहाय ।।
ते अच्चिमंतो व प्रभासयनि।
समयो महावीर भागी रसानं।।
दुमानि फुल्लानि मनोरमानि। (*थेरगाथा,* पृ. 1139)

इसी प्रकार तालपुटथेर अपने मन का उद्गार इस प्रकार व्यक्त करता है–वर्षा काल में मेघ बरसेगा और नवीन जलधारा से मेरा चीवर वन में अभ्ययंजित होगा तथा मैं ऋषियों के मार्ग पर पुरस्सृत होऊंगा। कब मैं मयूरों के मधुर ध्वनि से कूंजित एवं गुंजित वन में उनके मधुर शब्दों को सुनकर गिरिगह्वर से उठकर निर्वाण की प्राप्ति के लिए चिंतन करूंगा।[15] इस प्रकार के उदाहरण थेरगाथा के अलावा भी अन्य पालि निकायों में अनेक स्थानों पर मिलते हैं।

इससे यह परिलक्षित होता है कि भगवान और उनके अनुयायियों को प्रकृति का सुंदर पर्यावरण अतीव अभिरम्य प्रतीत होता था और वे यह कोशिश करते थे कि प्राकृतिक पर्यावरण को किसी प्रकार की हानि न हो। साथ ही, इन संदर्भों से यह प्रमाणित होता है कि भगवान बुद्ध पर्यावरण के प्रति कितने सहज और सजग थे।

बौद्ध वाङ्मय में यत्र-तत्र उपदिष्ट वचनों से पृथ्वी, जल, वायु, ध्वनि आदि

पर्यावरण संबंधी तत्त्वों की परिशुद्धता के लिए प्रयासरत थे। धार्मिक चेतना के बिना पर्यावरण का संवर्द्धन और संरक्षण असंभव है। अतः धार्मिक चेतना के लिए बौद्ध धर्म के तत्त्वों एवं सिद्धांतों का अवलोकन सर्वथा उपयोगी एवं कल्याणकारी है।

पर्यावरण प्रदूषण के कारकों में जनसंख्यों की अभिवृद्धि, नगरीय एवं उद्योगीकरण के साथ उपभोक्तावाद का विशेष योगदान रहा है। भगवान बुद्ध द्वारा उपदिष्ट शिक्षा में इन प्रदूषण कारक तत्त्वों के निराकरण के सुंदर मार्ग प्रशस्त करता है। *कामेसुमिच्छाचारा वेरमणी* के सिद्धांत से जनसंख्या की बढ़ती दर को रोका जा सकता है। इसके साथ ही भगवान बुद्ध की जीवनचर्यायों से नगरीकरण एवं उद्योगीकरण की समस्या का निदान संभव है। साधु जीवन से हम उपभोक्तावाद को नियंत्रित कर सकते हैं जिससे उपभोक्तावादी विषम संस्कृति अपनी हो सकती है और प्राकृतिक, सामाजिक पर्यावरण विप्रसन्न और प्रासंगिक हो सकता है। इसी से भवतु सब्ब मंगलम की परिकल्पना संभव होगी।

संदर्भ एवं टिप्पणियां

1. *संयुक्त निकाय (सं.नि.)*, पृ. 55, वो.भा.प्र., वाराणसी
2. *सारत्थ दीपनी टीका (सा.दी.टी.)* भाग-2, पृ. 112, सं.सं.वि.वि., वाराणसी
3. *दीर्घनिकाय* (दी.नि.) पृ. 154 (कूटदंत सुत्त)
4. *चुल्लवग्ग (चु.व.)* पृ. 231

   अनुजानामि भिक्खने एकमंतं वच्चं कातुं ति।
   वच्चकुपो अपारूपो, दुग्गनधो होति अनुजानामि भिक्खवे अविधानं।।

5. *समंत पासादिका*—महाधक्खंधे छिन्नमत्त पाराजिकं
6. *सं.नि.* I, पृ. 55, वो.भा.प्र., वाराणसी
7. *सा.दी.टी.,* भाग-2, पृ. 112
8. *दी.नि.,* I, पृ. 154
9. *दी.नि.,* पृ. 25
10. *दी.नि.,* I, पृ. 55
11. *दी.नि.,* पृ. 55-56

    इमिना में उपसमेन उदयभछों कुमारो होतु त्ति।
    येनेतरहि भिक्खुसंघो समन्नागतो ति।।

12. *मज्झिम निकाय (म.नि.)* I, पृ. 55
13. *सं.नि.,* I, पृ. 304

तभेव वाच भासेय्य भायत्तानं न तापये।
परे च न विहिंसेय्य, सावेवाचासुभासिता।।
प्रियवांच च भोसेय्य सावे वाचा पटिनंदिता।
यं अनादाय पापानिपरेसंभासते पिंय।।
सच्चं वे अमतावाचा एस धम्मो सनन्तनो।
सच्चे अत्थे च धम्मे च आहुसन्तो पतिद्विता।।

14. *म.नि.,* I, पृ. 216 (*ना.स*)
15. *थेरगाथा,* पृ. 523.

कदानु मं पावुसकालमेघो नवेन तोयेन स चीवरं वने।
इसिययातम्हि पथेवजंतं ओवस्सतंनुकदा भविस्सति।।
कदामयुरस्स सिखंडिनों वनें,
दिजस्स सुत्वा गिरिगब्भरे रूतं।
पच्चुद्वहित्वा अमतस्स पत्तिया,
सचिंतये तं नु कदा भविस्सति।